You Like to Think You Are Free.

*Those Who Want to Control You
Know That Very Well*

The purpose of media sexploitation is simple:
to arouse and manipulate your basic sexual
drives below the level of your consciousness
—and for purposes that are not your own.

The goal may appear simple, but the psychological expertise and media technology
employed are incredibly sophisticated and
subtle—tricky enough to bypass your every
natural defense.

This extraordinary book exposes all the ways
in which newspapers, magazines, television,
movies, and popular music mind-rape the
public. After reading it, you will look, listen,
and perceive in an entirely new way.

Media Sexploitation

SIGNET and MENTOR Books of Interest

If you wish to order these titles,

please see the coupon in the

back of this book.

Media
Sexploitation

by Wilson Bryan Key

Introduction by
Richard D. Zakia

A SIGNET BOOK
NEW AMERICAN LIBRARY
TIMES MIRROR

Para Iris . . .

Till the sun grows colder,
The stars grow older,
And all the windmills are
defeated.

In Gratitude

I wish to express my appreciation to those kind friends who supported and helped with the research that made this book possible. These include the hundreds of students in my classes over the past six years, the thousands of interested and patient people in lecture audiences across the nation, and the many who have written, called, or spoken to me about their reactions to my research into American media.

Though the publication of *Subliminal Seduction* plunged my wife and me into a veritable caldron of often painful controversy, we have been steadily encouraged with the realization we are not alone in our anxious concern over what appears to be happening to the people of North America. Ruthless avaricious self-interest, indifference toward human suffering, repressed blindness toward realities, and endless sensory indulgences are the modern four horsemen of the Apocalypse. It is at least comforting to know they are so widely recognized.

Many, many students contributed to the manuscript research, far too many to ever individually thank. A handful, however, worked closely over many months on areas critical to the book's factual structure. These included James Johnston, R. Lee Palser, and Peter Stemp—who also contributed heavily to my earlier book—and Carol Applegate, Darlene Bourdon, Rosemary Broemling, Grace Ciappa, Peter Clare, Steven Collins, Mark Hammon, Ron Ludlow, and Dan Peterson.

I was also grateful for the exchange of information on *The Exorcist* with feature writer Joe Campbell of *The Delaware*

State News & Daily Eagle. John W. T. Judson, Canadian solicitor and good friend, helped hold the Philistines at bay until the manuscript could be completed.

Special and affectionate appreciation should be expressed for both their friendship and their encouragement to a very long list of colleagues which included Marshall, Corrine, and Eric McLuhan, Orrin and Evelyn Klapp, Jean Veevers, and Douglas Cousineau. Dr. Murray Hoover's humanistic orientation toward the complex world of addictive behavior was much more important than he will ever realize. Artists Henk Vervoets and York Wilson helped importantly by sharing their unique perceptions of reality. Ian Connerty, Canadian political scientist, supplied pragmatic insights into the complex politics of the communication industry.

And, finally, once again Jean Stone should receive a medal for valor in return for her patience with my overly creative grammar and original spelling.

This author was fortunate to know and honored to work with people such as these.

W. B. K.
Costa Mesa, California

> *The perverse are hard*
> *to be corrected, and the number*
> *of fools is infinite.*
>
> *Ecclesiastes 2:16*

MaMa Media: An Introduction

Marshall McLuhan started his introduction to Professor Key's earlier book, *Subliminal Seduction*, with a joke: A customer in an antique shop asked "What's new?" It has taken me a full year and a careful reading of this new book to appreciate the depth and seriousness of what I had initially perceived (and forgotten) as a cute little joke. What's new is old and has a lot of meaning if we expend the time and effort to perceive that what is new is what is old. Advertising is old, but its technology is new. The theories of human behavior upon which effective advertising is based are old, but the techniques used are new. The audience, in one way or another, is forever new: new because of age, or new because of innocence.

This is what Professor Key's book on *Media Sexploitation* is all about. It is a comprehensive and integrated work, which demonstrates how theories of human behavior are surreptitiously being used by some advertisers to manipulate, control, and direct our buying behavior. Where his earlier book dealt primarily with visual deceit, this book continues not only with more examples of visual deceit, but also extensions into auditory and olfactory deception techniques.

In his chapter on *The Exorcist*, Key reveals the remarkable way both audio and visual technologies were integrated and mutually reinforced to produce the film's frightening effect. Brief flashes of light on the screen projected consciously imperceptible death-mask apparitions. Strange and frightening sounds, in what might be called an audio collage, wove in and out of scenes to heighten the sensation of fear.

A variety of similar techniques are also discussed, which attest to the overwhelming ability of media to manipulate man—to produce uncontrollable fear and deep visceral responses. In his chapter on odors, you will gain new insights regarding Mr. Clean and the sperm whale. You may be shocked when you read about the drug culture and rock music.

Modern technology has provided new ways to manipulate sight, sound, and smell in multisensory approaches to human deception, which are designed to bypass our conscious defenses and enter our subconscious.

Professor Key's concern is not so much that we are exploited, as that we do not *know* that we are exploited. He has no quarrel with mutually agreed-upon seduction, but is violently opposed to deceitful seduction—and so against sexploitation.

Even when we are given overwhelming knowledge of this sexploitation, as Key has provided, we are somewhat reluctant to believe it. Even if we get to the point of believability, we feel helpless in combatting it. But combat it we must, because unless we do, it can become a malignant, psychologically terminal disease.

So what's new? Better yet, what's old? One thing that's old is sayings like "Don't let them pull the wool over your eyes." It's so old and so familiar that we have put it in the dead-storage compartment of our memory, where it has gathered dust and rust. We have heard it enough, we know what it means, we have in a way labelled it, so now we can forget about it.

So what's new? Well, perhaps we should recycle the old saying, "Don't let them pull the wool over your eyes" and revitalize it to distill its truth for 1976 and the years beyond. Old sayings, like works of art, persisted throughout the history of mankind because their message, sometimes hidden, transcends time and place.

Key's reference to ads based on the classical sculpture *The Three Graces* is a case in point. Since we have advanced from an agricultural to a highly technical society, let us accept the fact that there are not as many wool merchants around. There are, however, many merchants around merchandizing products which are not much different from one another.

Ads are designed for emotional, not intellectual impact; in educational terms, for *affective* rather than *cognitive* appeal. Ad men do not rely on thinking, but rather feeling.

Also, read about how advertising people rely on demographic and psychographic studies of the population to design advertising to our individual images of ourselves. The demographic information tells them about such things as our age, sex, finances, and the like. The psychographic data tells them about our fantasies and intimate personal habits. Such data provide a personal profile that the advertising conglomerate uses so that *their* ad fits *our* profile. When this happens, they have got us and can manipulate our buying behavior. We've been had!

So Buyer Beware! Beware first of advertising designed to project you into a Dizzyworld of Fantasy. This is the message of *Media Sexploitation*. So what's new? "Don't let them pull the ads over your eyes." Beware also that they don't pull the ads over your ears, nose, or any other sensory input.

Regarding Theory

The theories Dr. Key uses to support his analysis of ads are not new. What is new—is his perceptual insight that has strongly related psychological theories to the practices of advertising. Freud's psychoanalytical theories, such as the oral, anal, and Oedipal stages of human development, provide the rationale behind the themes of many ads. Freud believed that children grow through a series of dynamically differentiated stages during the first five years of life. Frustration and anxiety accompany each new step in the child's development. Throughout his book, Key speculates on how certain ads and media are psychographically tuned to play on a person's fixations experienced during his personality development as a child.

The importance of cueing-in information retrieval can be easily demonstrated by having people look at a picture or an ad for a few minutes and then asking them to tell you what they saw. Initially, they will tell you quite a bit, and then less and less. When they get to the point of "I can't remember anything else," provide some verbal cues like "remember the vase next to the books? Tell me about its shape." You will find that verbal cues trigger information that had been stored in memory, in such a way that it was not readily retrievable. Dr. Ralph Norman Haber has written extensively on information retrieval and picture memory.

According to Key, there is no way to defend ourselves from subliminal stimuli, since they circumvent our normal defense mechanisms—mechanisms outlined by Freud as repression, projection, reaction formation, fixation, and regression. These are ways that help us deny, falsify, or distort reality, so—some theorists suggest—we can avoid anxiety and survive conflicts with socialization demands.

Much of what Freud said about art is relevant to advertising. Freud saw in art an opportunity to use fantasy for the fulfillment of wishes that are thwarted and frustrated in ordinary life, either by external obstacles or internal moral inhibitions. In the following 1913 quote from Freud, try substituting the word 'ad' for 'art':

> ... Art is a conventionally accepted reality in which, thanks to artistic illusion, symbols and substitutes are able to provoke real emotions. Thus art constitutes a region half-way between a reality which frustrates wishes and the wishfulfilling world of the imagination—a region in which, as it were, primitive man's strivings for omnipotence are still in full force.

Regarding Research

Roughly speaking, there are two broad categories of research: experimental and descriptive. Experimental research consists of a tightly controlled situation, usually occurring in a laboratory, with statistical design, randomized groupings, etc. Professor Key's work is not experimental, but rather descriptive, as was Freud's. It occurs in the so-called "real world" and consists of careful gathering of data through observations, surveys, interviews, and so forth. Both methods can be valid or invalid depending upon how rigorously they are conducted. Both hope to extend our field of knowledge by testing existing theories and hypothesizing new ones.

One interesting thing about Dr. Key's research is that it is based firmly on actual observable situations in media and advertising that are not experimentally contrived. He uses multidisciplinary theories to relate these observations to theory. Our beneficent ad and media men are spending billions of dollars each year to provide Dr. Key with interesting research stimuli he can use to test the validity of existing theories of human behavior. More researchers should take advantage of this resource. Marketing researchers have, but their studies on the effect of advertising and media are highly secret and made for quite a different reason.

Key's studies are highly innovative, as were Vance Packard's back in the early sixties. It is heuristic research, which helps us discover and learn and encourages further investigations. Testable hypotheses based on his work should find their way into the galaxy of social scientists who are doing experimental research in the universities. This could provide converging independent data, useful in supporting or questioning his position.

Theories in Key's thinking are only tools which provide a structure for inquiry. They need only be useful to justify their existence. Some may consider his research too speculative and not supportable. Time will have to decide this. In the meantime, while the scientific community studies human behavior in laboratory situations, Key studies it in the world of media and advertising, gathering evidence on how human behavior theory is being used by some to manipulate our buying, regardless of the cost to the human psyche.

Regarding Technique

One of the major techniques used to teasingly hide or disguise information—that of embedding—is not new. A few years ago, I visited the New York Metropolitan Museum to see a special display of fine old tapestries from France. They were, of course, beautiful, breathtaking, colorful, and highly tactile. Some were unbelievably large, covering huge walls. A few were unbelievable because of the peculiar shapes and sizes of phallic symbols embedded in the foliage. Perhaps the crew of artisans were at odds with the nobility who commissioned the work and decided to make a nonverbal statement—to broadcast their grievances to the world.

A recent exhibit at Xerox Square, prepared by Lillian Silver, entitled "Curious Deceptions in Art and Play" further demonstrated how far back this technique reaches. Hidden portrait-type pictures were a favorite of eighteenth-century artists, who would use the technique for satirical comment on current events. Likenesses of royalty, politicians, and military men would be hidden by the artists in foliage, flowers, urns, architecture, and landscapes. Two centuries later, this phenomenon was discovered and experimented with by the Danish psychologist Edgar Rubin, who was studying the role of figure-ground relationships in visual perceptions. His famous reversible figure-ground profiles and vase, first published in 1915, have been used over and over to illustrate countless psychology and other textbooks. Highly illustrated information on this can be found in my *Perception and Photography* (Prentice-Hall, 1975), which presents a Gestalt approach to how we process visual information by simplifying it.

Embedding of figure-ground is used extensively in preparing some advertising copy. What you see when you look at an ad is called figure and it is always against some ground. Black letters on this page, for example, are figure. You do not attend to the white shapes around the letters that serve as ground. Old sayings such as "Be sure to read between the lines" and "What is not said is more important than what is said" have a common origin with embedded information. The art of embedding involves the application of skills, technology, and understanding of human perception and behavior to arrange information, so that what is obvious is seen as figure. This serves as a decoy for the real message, which can be hidden within the ground (foliage, flowers, landscapes, reflections in bottles, ice cubes, symbols, and so forth). Although it is not consciously obvious, it may very well be obvious to our subconscious and recorded there. If the medium is the message, as McLuhan suggests, then perhaps the medium is ground. Ground is message, figure is decoy—so Buyer Beware!

Contemporary artists who have used ground to deliver their messages include such notables as Salvador Dali, in the

"Slave Market with Apparition of the Invisible Bust of Voltaire" and Maurits Escher, who began using figure-ground designs as early as 1921. These works were discussed in *Scientific American* articles by Fred Attneave and Marianne L. Teuber.

Another interesting technique used to embed is the use of anamorphic images—what you see yourself as when you look into a funny mirror at an amusement park or into a shiny coffee pot at home. The image is highly distorted, often grotesque, consciously distinguishable at times, but at other times not. Again, the technique is not new. As early as 1533, Hans Holbein painted *The Ambassadors*, two dignitaries with elbows resting on a mantelpiece and an eerie, slanted anamorphic painting of a consciously unrecognizable (except when viewed from a certain angle) human skull, seemingly floating in the air—perhaps a subconscious death message.

Surprisingly few people, including artists, are familiar with anamorphic art—except, of course, those in advertising. Photointerpreters and optical engineers are very familiar with anamorphic problems, but from a different point of view. Anamorphic images are sometimes planned, sometimes accidental. Professor Key refers to an article written by Gay Talese, in which a young boy reveals a true account of his twenty-year obsession with a nude photograph. My curiosity aroused, I located the article in the August 1975 issue of *Esquire*. When I looked at the photograph, it puzzled me why such a benign-looking picture should have such holding power on a man. A careful study will reveal a mysterious and awesome shadow alongside the nude woman—an anamorphic projection of her own shadow, which would look quite normal if it had fallen on a flat surface. It is rather eerie and compelling, as is the anamorphic skull from which she turns her face. The picture is much more than a nude lying on the sand, and there is much more that can be said about it. For more information about anamorphic art, try the January 1975 issue of *Scientific American*.

Regarding Believability

When you finish reading *Media Sexploitation*, you should become a believer in the potential power of media and advertising to influence, control, and direct our behavior. You should also become a thinker and look at media and advertising in a more critical fashion. *Stop, Look, Listen, and Question.* Talk back to the ads that you see and hear, question their intent, analyze the techniques being used to persuade you. Consider your personal needs and possible shortcomings and decide whether or not the ads are not, in fact, exploiting your weaknesses, fears, and anxieties. Not all advertising exploits, but the ads that do constitute advertising malpractice.

The purpose of advertising is to persuade, to sell products. For some advertising agencies, this may mean selling regardless of the human consequences. Advertising is very big business and, at times, under the archaic illusion that what is good for advertising is good for the country. Advertising is part of a much larger conglomerate, which includes Marketing and Media. All are interdependent, but are dependent upon the consumer for survival. And there, dear friends, is where our collective strength lies.

Richard D. Zakia
Director/Instructional Development
Rochester Institute of Technology

Contents

Prologue

> *People who want a sane, static,
> measurable world take the first
> aspect of an event or person and
> stick to it, with an almost
> self-protective obstinacy, or by a
> natural limitation of their
> imaginations. They do not
> indulge in either deepening or
> magnifying.*

ANAÏS NIN
D. H. Lawrence: An Unprofessional Study

> *Can democracy survive
> the mass media?*

ROBERT CIRINO
Don't Blame the People

The Commercial Appropriation of the Unconscious

> *. . . one of the chief sources of cultural paranoia is the ever-widening rift between the beliefs of a people and their actual behavior, and the tacit assumption among these same people that this practice—this contradiction between idealism and practice—is a normal state of affairs.*
>
> LIONEL RUBINOFF
> *The Pornography of Power*

The Subliminal Sell

This book probes the individual and social effects of mass communication media, their use of subliminal techniques, and what these media are doing to American society.

The American culture was founded upon the basic concept of *free will*—the belief that all individuals can in their own interest consciously determine for themselves their moral values, political and economic interests, and social environment. Indeed, free will is the foundation of all Western democratic and republican philosophical thought. Therefore, it is especially difficult for Americans to believe this treasured concept of free will has been subverted and appropriated in the interest of an efficient merchandising-consumer oriented economic system.

It may also be difficult to believe that a secret technology has existed and been in widespread use for years which modifies behavior invisibly, channels basic value systems, and manages human motives in the interest of special power structures. This all reads much too much like the past half century of science fiction.

In spite of the evidence presented in this book, most Americans will still find it difficult to believe that their trusted, high-credibility information sources long ago betrayed them into the hands of profit-hungry marketing executives who have quietly researched, developed, and exhaustively applied a subliminal technology of communication that now appears to be driving larger and larger segments of the population into pathological behaviors.

"Subliminal," of course, is merely another word for the unconscious, subconscious, deep mind, third brain—there are a dozen labels which have attempted to describe the portion of the human brain which retains information and operates without our conscious awareness. Today, subliminal stimuli assaults the psyches of everyone in North America throughout each day of their lives—from infancy into old age. The effects of this bombardment are cumulative.

Subliminal stimuli in art often involve humor. Many theories of humor, in fact, involve the invisible functions of the unconscious. To some extent, we all enjoy being tricked—being made victims of our own illusions and fantasies. America's popular literature is rich in archetypal fables about the con artist or magician who deceives someone by manipulating their greed and selfishness. We become angry only when we discover the deceiver has taken advantage of us individually instead of the other guy. And, of course, we are usually unwilling to concede we have been tricked, or unwilling to consciously admit to our greed and selfishness which made us vulnerable.

2

Jantzen Looks for You?

To briefly illustrate subliminal stimuli, study the rather innocuous advertisement for Jantzen swimsuits that appeared in the Canadian edition of the April 1972 *Reader's Digest* (see Figure 1).

The ad portrays two suntanned models posed crotch-deep in boiling surf, wearing red and blue swimsuits designed on a Union Jack motif, still a stirring patriotic symbol for many Canadians. The fabric designs also incorporate portions of the red maple leaf, now the national emblem of Canada.

The ad's headline reads, "Jantzen looks for you." The question of at *what* or *where* Jantzen looks for you is not explained. But as the ad copy affirms, "the All-Canadian statement at better stores everywhere." What could be more reasonable than urging readers to buy a swimsuit and "capture a piece of beach where you can watch the sun go by?" *His* and *hers* making "a joint statement in patriotic red, white, and blue." Who could be so unfeeling as to question the motives of a company so deeply concerned with good health, patriotism and togetherness?

Before reading further, I urge the reader to relax and study the Jantzen ad. How does it make you feel?

There appear to be several details in the photograph which do not make sense. First, the female model's trunks do not fit. Notice the wrinkles and sagging front. Considering the high cost of commercial art, the least the art director might have done was find a correctly sized suit for the female model.

But look again. The female model's trunks also have a zipper fly—a highly functional device in men's clothing, but not really necessary in women's.

On the other hand, the male model's trunks fit quite snugly. And in addition, his suit design matches the female's brassiere. In short, she is wearing his and he is wearing hers.

The art director has utilized a subliminal sex-role reversal strategy. This dissonant idea of men wearing women's clothes, highly taboo in our culture, will not be perceived consciously. But it will be instantly perceived at the unconscious level.

For reasons we will probe later, the unconscious portion of

3

the brain is highly sensitive to dissonant elements of a picture, event, or scene which do not add up logically or which violate cultural taboos. This sensitivity is easily demonstrated in hypnosis. Unconscious perceptual sensitivity appears most acute when the stimuli involves a cultural taboo in subject areas of reproductive behavior (sex) and death.

Another somewhat disconcerting question involves the female hand, gently resting upon the female model's hip. With the wrist at that angle, there is no way it can belong to the female model—unless her arm is six feet long. The hand, resting on this erogenous zone, suggests subliminally the possibility of a *ménage à trois* relationship—two women and a man. There is a third model standing beside the two models.

Feeling Is Also Believing

Shortly after encountering the Jantzen advertisement, I was having lunch with a young woman sociology professor and several other faculty friends. The group was vaguely familiar with my field of research, but none had seen or discussed the Jantzen ad.

After she had studied the ad for a minute or so, I asked the young woman how it made her feel.

"It makes me feel cool, I think," she replied.

"Cold?" I asked.

"No. Cool, fresh, refreshing, pleasant."

"Where does it make you feel cool?" I probed. "Where on your body?"

"On my thighs," she replied thoughtfully.

"Where on your thighs?"

"Up high, near my—" She broke into a laugh.

Her response to the ad was the kind of response you become familiar with after dealing with subliminal stimuli for several years. People often respond with quite specific feelings without conscious knowledge of what is guiding their response.

Looking at the ad, you might easily justify the "cool" feeling in the upper thighs as a projection into the cool surf in which the two—or three—models are standing. But there was something included in the Jantzen advertisement the professor had not consciously perceived. She was quite surprised when it was pointed out.

If you hold the ad upside down (see Figure 2), a face appears in the surf. The face is reminiscent of the old Farmer's Almanac drawing of the weatherman, cheeks distended, his puckered mouth blowing the cold north winds down across the nation. The old weatherman in the surf is—perhaps we should look the other way—blowing on a delicate portion of the model's anatomy.

This is a *subliminal embed*, or at least one form of embedding used to invade the reader's unconscious. There are many such techniques in use today and they do many things to people—things besides simply selling products.

The Still Undiscovered Brain

Subliminal stimuli's subtle effects upon human behavior are most difficult to specify in simple cause-and-effect terminology. At least the symptoms of what "subs" do to people, can be demonstrated with mechanical devices that register the operation of unconscious processes inside the brain and body—the electroencephalograph (EEG) galvanic skin response measurements (GSR); retinascopes, which measure the compulsive expansion and contraction of the eye's retina; the Mackworth camera, which tracks the lightning-fast movements of the eye's fovea across any visual scene; the polygraph or so-called lie detector; and a score of similar devices. The inked graphs produced by these machines tell us, indeed, that something is going on. But the precise nature of the complex process remains largely unknown. One neurophysiologist friend delights in reminding his more abstract-theory-oriented colleagues that we do not really understand how a human is able to lift and lower his finger. The interrelated factors involved in even this simplest of all gestures are awesomely complicated.

Some students of the brain believe we may never know how the processes work. In the meantime, we can deal with what goes on inside the brain only through the help of various theories. And, there is no completely validated theory of language or behavior. For example, I have no idea whether Sigmund Freud, Alfred Adler, Carl Jung, or for that matter,

J. B. Watson were right or wrong about human behavior. Perhaps they were all producers only of elaborate, self-flattering illusions. On the other hand, perhaps all hit truth right on the mark. These great theorists and the many others who followed them, however, gave us a way of viewing human behavior that over the past half century has often proven *useful*.

One relatively simple, though useful, theory involves a hypothetical model of the brain as containing two major systems or levels of operation that respond to perceptual (sensory) inputs. For the moment, limit your consideration to these two systems—*conscious*, or cognitive, and *unconscious*.

Though they are highly integrated at some unknown level, each system has the capability of operating independently of the other. Instead of the simplistic five senses of Aristotle— sight, hearing, taste, touch, and smell—which are still anachronistically taught in many universities today, there are at least thirty-seven known, differentiated sensory inputs into the brain.

These so far definable thirty-seven senses appear to operate simultaneously and constantly, with a dominant bias shifting from one sense to another. An enormous quantity of perceived information is thus fed into, we believe, the brain's outer layer or cerebral cortex. In the cortex small quantities of data are somehow edited into consciousness. Another portion is directed into unconscious storage. And, much irrelevant data is probably dumped.

There is no simple, single dividing line in the brain between the conscious and unconscious systems. The threshold between the two constantly shifts and fluctuates. Perceptual defenses are believed to involve a rerouting process whereby threatening or taboo percepts are shunted into the unconscious. Though repression is generally considered the major perceptual defense, others include isolation, regression, fantasy formation, sublimation, denial, projection, and introjection.

What is vaguely called consciousness is a very limited state of awareness, considering all that is available. The *unconscious*, on the other hand, includes a vast memory storage system which includes repressed data that we would find difficult to cope with at the conscious level.

6

"Subliminal" Means Unconscious

Under the term *subliminal stimuli*, my primary concern here is with only that group of consciously unperceived words and picture symbols purposely designed into media with the motive of soliciting, manipulating, modifying, or managing human behavior. Most of what we perceive, we have no conscious awareness of having perceived. Subliminal stimuli probably account for much of the vaguely defined entities often explained as "culture" or "aesthetics."

One of the enigmatic aspects of subliminal perception phenomena recently involved a most excellent and comprehensive study published in England by Dr. N. F. Dixon. His book views perception from the perspective of an experimental, behaviorist psychologist, and details exhaustive laboratory research on subliminal phenomena.

But Dr. Dixon's most carefully researched book never once suggests the author's awareness of what is going on around him in the real world with great intensity through television, magazines, motion pictures, newspapers, radio, and billboards. The paradox is eloquent testimony to the power of human perceptual defenses—those techniques we can use to hide or disguise from ourselves what is going on around us. Strangely, these unconscious defenses appear exceptionally powerful among the so-called "trained observers": scientists, physicians, engineers, and other specialists.

Most of the available published research on subliminal phenomena in North America since the mid-fifties has been conducted by eight scholars—G. S. Klein and R. R. Holt at New York University, L. Luborsky and H. Shevrin at the Menninger Foundation, C. Fischer at Mt. Sinai Hospital, E. R. Hilgard at Stanford University, N. F. Dixon in London, and G. J. W. Smith, who has worked both in the United States and in Sweden. Though interesting and often revealing, none of their studies—and I believe most would agree—even scratched the surface.

SEX in Politics

The word SEX is frequently hidden in political propaganda, advertisements, and television and motion-picture frames. The simple three-letter symbol, usually invisible to consciousness, appears instantly perceivable at the unconscious level.

In a recent U.S. congressional election campaign in Virginia's 10th District, SEX "embeds" were discovered in the campaign literature of all candidates except one who could not afford to hire an advertising agency. In Figure 3, one example of embedded campaign literature is shown. If you relax under a good light, the very lightly etched letters are easily apparent. Check the marked inset detail. There are in addition dozens of SEX embeds in this photograph of the candidate.

This election was fascinating. When a charge was made against the use of subliminal devices in campaign literature, the press around the Washington area generally rallied to the support of the candidates who had used the advertising agencies. Everyone was aghast at the audacious charge one newspaper referred to as a "sex hoax" campaign gimmick. Though many Virginia journalists privately admitted they could clearly perceive the embeds, they still claimed in print the whole idea of subliminal perception being used in an election campaign far too bizarre to be plausible. Yet these embedding techniques have been used in every political campaign of any magnitude in the United States and Canada for at least twenty-five years—if not much, much longer. SEX embeds can even be designed into campaign buttons.

A formal complaint was initiated by one candidate with the Virginia Election Commission, charging the use of subliminal techniques in the candidates' literature. The commission refused to accept the complaint, even though SEX embeds are quite easy for most people to perceive if they merely look for them. The Virginia election proved quite clearly that most Americans—at least at this point in their history—do not want to deal with the issue of subliminal manipulation. The press was also understandably reluctant to get into the issue, of course, because most newspapers, like other media in America, are careful not to compromise the ad agencies.

A Subliminal Trigger

My research has encountered three specific techniques by which the word SEX is embedded, for unconscious perception, in print media. SEX is often painted on a photoengraving plate with asphaltum and the plate briefly immersed in acid. The word, usually in a mosaic (an interwoven series of SEXes), is lightly etched on the plate's surface. The etching technique is often utilized in photographs that must be published with little apparent retouching. Many magazines and newspapers use the technique on news pictures which help sell the publication.

A second frequently applied technique involves airbrushing SEX into a drawing or a photograph very lightly or painting it into hair, creases in clothing, facial lines, or rough background surfaces.

A third is to write numerous SEXes (mosaic) on a transparent overlay for a photograph or drawing. The overlay is photographed alone at high speed, say 1/2,000 of a second, and the overlay is double-exposed over an art layout at, say, 1/100 of a second. By varying speed and light, the SEX mosaics can be superimposed into any photograph at any intensity level desired.

In reviewing several thousand magazine covers, advertisements, news photographs, etc., eight embedded words have been discovered. Admittedly, this eight-word vocabulary of taboo words, such as SEX (by far, the most frequently utilized), CUNT, and FUCK, is not the most articulate form of verbal communication ever developed. Nevertheless, the technique does affect behavior. A surprisingly large amount of subliminal death symbolism is also utilized—skulls hidden in ice cubes, clouds, etc., the word DEATH or DETH often hidden in backgrounds.

During the evolutionary development of humans, subliminal perceptions were certainly involved with survival and adjustment. Creative innovators such as artists, poets, writers, and composers have utilized man's subliminal potentialities for many centuries. In at least one Rembrandt painting, for example, a hidden SEX appears. The seventeenth century Dutch word for SEX was SEKS, SEKSUAL, SEXES. The simplified SEX would have, in the popular idiom, meant pretty much what it means today—sans Freud, Masters & Johnson, Kinsey, etc.

The use of subliminal techniques in print communication media has been going on in the United States at least since the World War I period. Norman Rockwell's first cover on *The Saturday Evening Post* during 1917 incorporated embedded SEXes. Furthermore, up to now, no one outside the trade even suspected what was going on. Whenever an embedded word or picture accidentally became consciously visible, the readers would pass it off as a joke, an accident, or a product of their imaginations.

Human perception of reality, at least in our society, depends heavily upon what our peers admit they perceive. And who would ever openly admit to perceiving such nonsense? What is "real," therefore, is often the product of consensus rather than of an individual's critical, autonomous perceptual evaluation. This may turn out to be man's most vulnerable Achilles' heel.

SEX Can Also Be Crunchy

Ritz crackers, which are baked and distributed under licensing agreements with Nabisco in a dozen nations, offer purchasers much more than merely a crunchy eating experience.

Take half a dozen crackers out of the box and line them up on the table, face upward. Now relax, and let your eyes linger on each cracker—one at a time. Do not strain to see the surface, however. Usually in about ten seconds, you will perceive the message. Embedded on both sides of each cracker is a mosaic of SEXes (see Figure 4).

The number and precise location of each SEX embed appear to depend upon the temperature and time during which each cracker was baked. The SEXes are apparently embedded in the molds pressing out the dough. When baked, the SEX patterns vary slightly from cracker to cracker.

There is probably nothing uniquely evil about using embedded SEX mosaics on soda crackers. In all fairness, embedding really makes the damned things taste better. Visual stimuli, it should be clear by now, are an aspect of taste or flavor sensation. No single sense can be isolated in any perceptual situation. Multisensory media response is not a new concept in communication theory, nor is *synesthesia*, stimulating one sensory response via another sense in a crossover effect.

The idea of SEX-embedded Ritz crackers, however, does produce a rather uncomfortable situation when you consider the multitude of men and women all of us have known who seriously argued the quality of crackers, a preferred beer or cigarette brand, an automobile, etc.

SEX embeds, which at first appear to be crude jokes, have quite profound behavioral implications. The effects upon society of intense, long-term bombardment of subliminal stimuli have been completely ignored by social and behavioral scientists. This is strange, especially as a large body of philosophical and experimental evidence demonstrates that subliminal devices have powerful effects upon human memory. The memory can be theoretically modeled with at least two (many would be more likely) levels—one servicing the conscious or cognitive mechanisms, the other servicing the subliminal or unconscious.

Hypnosis has frequently been a productive technique of investigating subliminal phenomena and the level of awareness variously described as the unconscious. Narco-synthesis—sodium amytal and other drugs—has also been utilized with varying degrees of success. A wide range of studies, from those done with hypnosis to work such as that of Canadian neurosurgeon Dr. Wilder Penfield, indicates that the unconscious memory is prodigious. Hypnotic regressions have retrieved minute data on events consciously forgotten—events, say, from early childhood. Hypnotic experiments clearly suggest that at this unconscious level, each individual has an eidetic (photographic) memory potential.

Emotionally loaded or taboo words like SEX, perceived subliminally appear to firmly fix themselves and their related content in this unconscious memory system.

The retentive capacity of such a drive and emotion-related subliminal perception is astounding. Such embedded stimuli can be retained in the unconscious memory for very extended periods—possibly throughout life.

The relationship between subliminal stimuli and posthypnotic suggestions was recognized as early as 1917 by Dr. Otto

11

Poetzle, a Viennese physician. The Poetzle, or Alarm Clock, Effect demonstrates the power of a "sub" to evoke behavioral response when certain conscious relationships occur, long after the initial percept of the subembedded stimuli. For example, a subembedded ad for a specific gin brand might never be consciously recalled. But several weeks after having perceived the ad, the reader might opt for that particular brand without ever consciously realizing the basis for his decision.

Further, when the sub is consciously perceived, a conscious memory fix appears to be established—quite possibly for a lifetime.

Memory Fixing

When this author and his students began collecting examples of media (advertising, etc.) containing subembeds, each example was carefully recorded in card files. After several months, however, it was discovered that once the subembedded ad was consciously perceived, the example was never forgotten. Our collection of subliminally embedded media on slides now numbers well over a thousand. The original researchers, while reviewing material collected as long as five years ago, immediately recall the subembeds and precise circumstances that led to their original discovery. Many of these examples required weeks of analysis before their subliminal embeds were discovered. The Jantzen ad (Fig. 1) required several weeks of study before all the subliminal details emerged. But once subs are consciously apparent, they appear to become a permanent part of the conscious memory system.

Though data is still limited to seventeen verifiable cases, a startling long-term subliminal stimuli effect upon conscious memory was uncovered. During the mid-1930s, *Life* magazine published a black-and-white photograph of a then popular young movie starlette. The photo depicted the young woman posed in a strapless evening gown. A subliminal embed had been airbrushed into skin wrinkles and shadows under her armpit in the portrait. By blocking off the area of her bent arm, and turning the picture on its side, a picture of a female genital area and two shapely legs appeared. The hidden detail was publicly discussed at the time—probably leaked by the *Life* publicity offices. Officially, *Life* rationalized the embed as a product of the readers' dirty minds.

This author has encountered seventeen individuals in various places throughout North America who clearly remembered the picture. Most could identify the year it was published and the name of the actress. The conscious recall of one page out of *Life*—a seemingly innocuous page at that—after some thirty-five years is remarkable to say the least.

The significance of subliminal stimuli in human behavior has been exhaustively tested in eight different experimental contexts. Subliminals have been demonstrated to affect dreams, memory, adaptation levels, conscious perception, verbal behavior, emotional responses, drive-related behavior, and perceptual thresholds.

This unconscious provides *attitudinal frames* or *basic perspectives* or a *cultural bias* through which our consciously perceived data is evaluated. If you wish to modify behavior, for example, you must somehow penetrate and manipulate this unconscious structure—such is the work of psychoanalysis, advertising, literature, art, and music. Advertising's significance, for example, has very little to do with conscious perception. The last thing most manufacturers would want a consumer to do is evaluate their products consciously and objectively.

In individual terms, however, the technology sells—programs into the brain—much, much more such as ideas, concepts, fantasies, the basic attitudinal frames for both human personality and relationships. American media, utilizing subliminal techniques, has evolved into a massive behavior modification system. It is curious that psychologist B.F. Skinner never realized that his behavior conditioning system of stimulus-response-reward was a working reality of American life in the mass communication media. However, the system that he thought theoretically capable of producing a utopian millennium for mankind has some manipulative twists to it he never anticipated. The magnitude and creative ingenuity of this behavior modification system—which has been going on around us for years—was completely missed by Skinner and by so many others who neglected to look critically into the "real" world.

13

Adaptation-Level Value Systems

In terms of behavior modification, perhaps the most significant of the demonstrable effects of subliminal stimuli involves adaptation-level theory, which can be briefly illustrated by taking two polarized verbal values such as *light* and *heavy* on, say, a nine-point scale. A pictorial stimuli is then shown any group and they are asked to evaluate the weight of the object shown—say, a loaf of bread. The "adaptation level" or "anchor point" would be the position on the scale a particular group (occupational, demographic, psychographic, etc.) would tend to select as their most common evaluation. For example, watchmakers likely have a somewhat different perceptual agreement on weight (anchor point) in relation to *heavy* and *light* than would a heavy construction crane operator.

In a long series of experiments, the ability of subliminal stimuli to change anchor points was established in relation to sound, weight, electric shocks, and visual size. Most of these experiments utilized tachistoscopic displays—a high-speed still projector (1/3,000 per second) that flashes invisibly over, say, a motion picture being projected. No evidence suggests significant differences between tachistoscopically induced subliminal stimuli and that induced via other visual or auditory illusions or embedding techniques. The high speed subliminal tachistoscope and several other subliminal induction devices were patented in 1962 and 1966 by Dr. Hal Becker of the Tulane Medical School.

It is not at all improbable that under intensive, repetitive, and long-term subliminal bombardment, entire value systems could be rearranged. Moving from adaptation-level anchor points for *loud* vs. *soft, heavy* vs. *light, weak shock* vs. *heavy shock*, and *large* vs. *small* to anchor points for *good* vs. *bad, moral* vs. *immoral, beautiful* vs. *ugly*, and *sane* vs. *insane* is an unsettling though quite reasonable extension of easily demonstrated laboratory technology. Marshall McLuhan commented that, "1984 happened about 1930, only we just never noticed."

In the Ritz cracker example, the hidden SEX would be unconsciously perceived, thus adding emotional significance to the cracker's value. It could also connect this symbolic value to an individual's unconscious sex drive—one of the strongest of human drive systems. The sexualization of persons, drinks, food, money, and other objects should be very carefully studied as it would ultimately change human behavior on a vast scale.

Since American media, through the use of subliminial embedding, has sexualized virtually everything that is advertised or presented in media, the sexualization of food is perhaps the ultimate triumph. According to the U.S. National Council on Health, roughly sixty percent of U.S. citizens are presently overweight.

As students of subliminal phenomena began to grasp the wide extent of the phenomena in American life, they have often asked if there is anything within the culture that does *not* ultimately relate to SEX. Even death and violence are heavily associate with SEX.

Consider the values consciously ascribed to human relationships, which are often evaluated in terms of sex and death, often involving various forms of self destruction. The problem is easily apparent—and frightening—especially as our perceptual defenses hide much of the phenomenon's significance from conscious awareness.

Economist John Kenneth Galbraith, among others, has pointed out that large corporations cannot afford to compete with one another. Their survival is predicated upon cooperation and market segmentation. In a truly competitive system *someone* stands to lose. If General Motors, for example, were to lose, Ford would also. American big business has finally learned that everybody has to protect everybody else's investment. This is even more ominous when you consider that by 1980, seventy percent of the productive capacity in the non-Communist world will be controlled by 200 corporations. These giant corporations, with their huge yearly media expenditures, are literally in control of American culture and its value systems. In 1974, U.S. ad expenditures totaled $26.7 billion, in 1975 $28.3 billion, and 1976 volume might top $31 billion. Most of this advertising utilized subliminal techniques. These are not merely a few advertisements, but a mind-bending media saturation of the society.

15

The Gay Playboy's Penthouse

> *Since man lies to himself even more than to others, the psychologists should draw conclusions from what people really mean, rather than from what they say or do.*
>
> FRIEDRICH NIETZSCHE
> *Thus Spoke Zarathustra*

Nobody Is Doing It

American media publishes and broadcasts endlessly about sexual permissiveness. The sad reality, however, seems to be that this hypersexuality is at best only a fantasy, merely another flimflam illusion of merchandising technology.

Current data available on American family life—an academic euphemism for sex life—portray the United States as a sexual wasteland. W. H. Masters and Virginia Johnson estimated conservatively that half of North American families are sexually dysfunctional. Theodore Lidz, head of psychiatry at the Yale Medical School, estimated that sexual dysfunction afflicts up to 75 percent of American families. In a society interminably preoccupied with sex in everything it touches, no one appears to be getting very much.

Psychologist Rollo May commented recently that when Dr. Alfred Kinsey published his famous study of male sexuality in 1948, about 3 percent of adult males appeared to have some problem with impotence. Current studies, Dr. May explained, reveal that over 30 percent of adult males now may have problems with impotence.

In a survey, several hundred young people were asked who they privately considered the most sexually permissive group in American society—the over-thirties or the under-thirties? Almost unanimously they replied the over-thirties. Older adults were similarly questioned. Unanimously they replied the under-thirties.

Simply put, almost everyone in America appears to believe someone *else* is getting it all. Many attempts to study the sexual behavior of young Americans have resulted in the same general conclusions—only a minority can be described as permissive or promiscuous. Repeated studies in college co-ed dormitories, where young men and women freely mixed, showed that usually less than 5 percent were sexually indulgent. Those who paired off, lived together, or sexually played the field usually left the co-ed dormitories very soon. Many were actually forced to leave. After their initial fantasy expectations diminished, most of these so-called "swinging" dorm residents assumed what could be described as a brother-sister relationship.

Sexuality is threatening to the American young because of the restraints on individual freedom that are ultimately demanded by the sexual partner, and because of the intimacy that is eventually required. Ironically, intimacy is highly threatening to the lonely and alienated—a fearsome prospect today unless safely projected into the fantasy world of media. The young *Playboy*-oriented male attempts to substitute sex or *physical* intimacy for deeper involvements and commitments. His search for meaning and satisfaction in human relationships often involves only images of persons—not persons themselves.

Like most heavily repressed cultures, Americans have strong sexual vulnerabilities. Sexual interpretations are made of virtually all human interrelationship phenomena we do not understand or wish to openly deal with. Almost any subject can be totally dismissed by simply labeling it—Oedipal, oral, perverse, deviant, etc. One problem in talking so much about sex is that talking, like labeling, is an avoidance technique. In past epochs, a father might have taken his son to a local bordello where he could be introduced to the so-called mysteries of life by a skilled (and hopefully patient) prostitute. Today, American fathers are far more likely to purchase a *Playboy* subscription for their sons as an introduction to life's mysteries. They cannot be infected with venereal disease by a magazine, but they will learn little about human sexual realities from masturbating with embedded pictures of nude models.

Americans are drenched in symbolic sexualization from their media virtually from birth. Many young readers, trapped in the infantile *Playboy* syndrome, elevate these pictorial illusions into icons with near religious significance. Much like Konrad Lorenz's ducks, imprinted with a human figure they took for their mother—American men are imprinted with sex object fantasies—the illusion often becoming far more *real* than the real thing. Masters and Johnson discovered that American men and women who achieved orgasm by masturbation from fantasy or pictorial stimuli experienced much more intense and fulfilling climaxes than through actual heterosexual coitus. There is strong reason to suspect that the intensity of American's fantasy-provoked orgasm is unique and a product of media conditioning.

After his thorough training to view women as sex objects, the media-oriented young American male finds it most difficult to relate or interact with women as human beings. If the only real function in a man's or woman's life is to serve as a useful sex object, then a man's and woman's value, usefulness, and significance to each other will be short-lived. The vernacular terms used in America to describe sexual communication, the most beautiful, sensitive, and intimate relationship experienced throughout life, are crude, hard, male-aggressive verbs—"to fuck," "to knock up," "to screw," "to lay," "to make," etc. They are more like those words directed toward conquered and enslaved enemies than toward those with whom loving relationships are shared.

Casualty Rates Increase

Best-selllling author Gay Talese, in a July 1975 *Esquire* article, documented a Chicago man's sixteen-year masturbatory affair with a nude photo portrait from a 1957 photography magazine. The photograph included subliminal techniques.

Interviews with a dozen clinical psychologists and psychiatrists quickly revealed the Chicago man's experience was not at all unique. Many American males appear to obtain more intense gratification from subliminally embedded photographs of women than with the "real" thing. Sometimes the fixation focuses upon a single photograph, often several photographs, which may endure for years, but most often the addiction involves an endless succession of fantasy sex partners collected and discarded from month to month in what was described as an "American's harem." Cheesecake art, considered as harmless entertainment, has addictive potentialities when embedded with subliminal devices. Indeed, *Playboy* and its ilk have changed American sexual mores in far more bizarre ways than their profit-obsessed editors ever guessed.

Male sexuality superiority may be one of the basic mythologies of Western civilization. Consider that virtually any average female is physically capable of at least a dozen orgasms every twenty-four hours. She can repeat this performance three or four times weekly without ill effects. To bury the myth even deeper, each woman is easily capable, phsyiologically and emotionally, of servicing the sexual tensions of at least half a dozen men. So why has the mythology of male sexual superiority been sustained by the economic, political, social, and religious institutions of Western societies? And what of the American woman who depends upon the media for her orientation toward life?

Her life as a sex object is predicated upon her body's ability to compare favorably with that of an immature child. Women are carefully trained by media to view themselves as inadequate. They are taught that other women—through the purchases of clothes, cosmetics, food, vocations, avocations, education, etc.—are more desirable and feminine than themselves. Her need to constantly reverify her sexual adequacy through the purchase of merchandise becomes an overwhelming preoccupation, profitable for the merchandisers, but potentially disastrous for the individual.

A woman's usefulness as a mere fantasy fulfillment of male sexual expectations is necessarily limited. Under these rules, sexual fulfillment rapidly diminishes. Female obsolescence is

19

a very prevalent event in American family life. The moment a woman's body and skin matures, she is headed socially downhill—and sometimes very rapidly. North American statistics show that divorce around the age of forty is a highly predictable event. Usually the male remarries a younger woman, while the aging female is most often headed for loneliness and sexual ostracism through the remaining half of her life.

The Normal Neurosis

North American society has a vested interest in reinforcing an individual's failure to achieve sexual maturity. By exploiting unconscious fears, forcing them to repress sexual taboos, the media guarantees blind repressed seeking for value substitutes through commercial products and consumption. Sexual repression, as reinforced by media, is a most viable marketing technology.

One of the most important findings on both major studies on human sexuality by Masters and Johnson was a reaffirmation that the sexual attitudes that influence and condition us through life are subliminally—not consciously—induced from the environment, most especially from the family and home. This finding would certainly include advertising media as an integrated part of the American family and home environment. For example, it doesn't really make much difference how a parent, school system, or government may attempt to instruct, or avoid instructing, young people about sex. They unconsciously learn from the world around them, and such subliminal "learning" is far more persuasive than any consciously-perceived sermon or brochure.

In other words, those things going on around us that we take for granted and consciously ignore form the basis for most value systems and human interrelationships. The most significant of these subliminal perceptions are derived from high-credibility sources, of which the public communication media are among the most virulent and far-reaching.

Advertising creates a massive subliminal environment where men and women appear most frequently in fantasy relationships designed to enhance or optimize the mass audience's consuming orientation. We have, of course, made the illusionary media world the real or natural world, permitting the actual material environment to become quite pale, insipid, and ordinary by comparison.

Sexually insecure males would probably have great difficulty in admitting that a woman's breasts symbolized maternal security and comfort. Most men would more comfortably express themselves as, "Breasts turn me on, excite me." This statement would appear to their self-image as masculine, virile, and safe.

One of the earlier, ingenious appeals to doubts over sexual identity and to latent maternal conflicts appeared on the April 1967 *Playboy* cover (see Figure 5). The cover model is attractive but, strangely, lacks overt sexual appeal. The background figure appears—at first glance—to be masculine, while the foreground model appears to be a young woman in a masculine costume sitting at the feet of her master, presumably the playboy. It is, of course, this first glance that sold the magazine on the newsstands. Now, let's look more carefully at it with much the same care that must have been used by the photographer for this important illustration.

Several details involving sexuality appear not quite as they should be—the kind of incongruity to which unconscious perception is peculiarly sensitive. The model's face is curious—not one line, shadow, dimple, or wrinkle is shown. The outlines of the face are sharp—on each side and under the chin. The face seems flat and one-dimensional.

The cover was tested with half a dozen individuals in a deep trance level of hypnosis. Each identified the face as a mask. Several mentioned that the eyes appeared detached from the face, as though they were peering through from behind.

The straight, coarse hair is obviously a wig. This was again strange, since *Playboy* cover models, considering the cover's merchandising significance, are most precisely cosmetized and the final photograph is carefully retouched. There is never a hair out of place, and even the most subtle expression or complexion details are finely engineered. The model's masculine cap brim further shadows her eyes. When eyes are in shadow, the artist is often suggesting that the subject has a secret.

An examination of the white shirt shows that the female

breast line is missing. The creases are merely folds—a strange inconsistency in a magazine famed for its exaggerated portrayal of the female bosom. The ubiquitous *Playboy* rabbit logo is embedded in the sleeve with the rabbit's nose just below and to the right of the model's right elbow. One rabbit ear goes up the sleeve while the other appears in the fold diagonally across the shirt front.

The masculine polka-dot necktie, a phallic symbol, is held very gently, caressingly, in the model's right hand. If you look at the wrist and little finger positions, the left hand is pressing with considerable force against the background model's leg. A list of possible emotions being felt by the blond model was given a group of test subjects unfamiliar with subliminal techniques. Over a third of the responses centered around "slight fear" and "apprehension." The remaining responses were scattered widely across a dozen possible reactions.

Behind the Mask and Under the Wig

Who is hiding behind the mask and under the blond wig? There are only two possibilities—a boy or a girl. There would be no apparent reason for a girl to disguise herself as a girl, which leaves open the other possibility of a boy hiding in a girl's costume.

However, if the model is a boy disguised as a girl, it is doubtful he would seek protection by running to his father. American fathers take a dim view of their sons dashing about in women's clothing. This brings into question the background figure, which at first glance appeared to be the trimly masculine figure of the playboy.

Three large men's clothing store chains were checked for horizontally striped men's pants. None were available, nor had the stores' buyers ever heard of horizontally striped men's pants. Even the so-called unisex clothing stores had never stocked, in the memory of their oldest employees, men's slacks with horizontal stripes.

At least up to 1974, men's slacks had never utilized horizontal stripes—women's slacks, yes, but never men's. The problem of the belt buckles was also curiously discrepant on a magazine cover famous for precise symbolic details. Men's belt buckles are usually square, women's usually round. This clue suggested, again, the cover figure's sexuality had been symbolically reversed.

The male in the picture is, therefore, hiding in a girl's costume. The female is standing in the background. Who, then, might be this background female? Small male children often assume this position with their mothers when threatened by their fathers. Many writers on child behavior have commented that children achieve solace and security with their heads near their mother's genital area. Children find their mother's genital odors tranquilizing and pacifying.

The genital area in this cover, however, is carefully guarded by the *Playboy* logo in the belt buckle. Our young frightened playboy is literally surrounded by the logo—one in back on the belt buckle and one in front on the shirt.

Boy children, when frightened, also frequently hold on to their penises—symbolized in the illustration as a phallic necktie.

The detailed analysis of this logo as a symbol of paternal castration fear, with its scissorlike ears, was included in my earlier book *Subliminal Seduction*. This earlier work also probed in greater detail, *Playboy*'s use of symbolic mothers and small infants in their cover designs. Out of roughly thirty *Playboy* covers analyzed, over 70 percent had some symbolic maternal representation included. The mother was always in some form of close relationship with a symbolic, often a nursing, infant.

On the cover we've just been discussing, the colors black and white reflect a clear-cut male and female gender differentiation. Only the golden belt buckles, the blond hair, and the flesh-colored skin are unnaturally colored. All these human details (hair and skin) turned out to be fake. The hands, incidentally, appeared to be male. A short fingernail appears on the right forefinger holding the tie. The long fingernails on the left hand, however, had been retouched. A careful examination of the finger outlines reveals they are quite irregular—obviously another retouch job.

The *Playboy* reader's unresolved Oedipal conflicts have simply been put to the service of circulation-building and advertising-selling. What the reader sees subliminally, but certainly not at the conscious level, is what he gets. But we will never know for certain whether this is really what he *wants*.

Role Consistency

American men unconsciously place rigid restrictions upon touching each other. When it happens, it must be made to appear an accident. Virtually any male American can be made intensely uncomfortable if touched or patted during a conversation. In Tanzania and other African cultures, it is a common practice for men to hold hands while talking. In Latin or Arabic cultures, close physical proximity between men is still considered quite normal—even socially desirable. But it is amusing to simply move close, without any actual physical contact, to an American at a cocktail party. Perceiving the threat of physical contact, most American men will move away. They can literally be steered all over a room by simply edging closer to them during a conversation. Usually, they soon crack under the strain and make some excuse to terminate the conversation and leave for less threatening companionship.

It is certainly not my intention here to laugh at any individual's weaknesses, sensitivities, or fears, but to examine deeply those things that surround us each moment of each day and unquestionably condition and manipulate us.

The Silver Queen

The January 1973 edition of *Oui* magazine, published by the Playboy organization, displayed a beautiful blond model dressed in a silver brassiere and miniskirt. Considering the blatant pornography regularly published in the so-called men's magazines, there was nothing remarkable on the surface about this *Oui* cover (see Figure 6).

However, several researchers studying the cover became quite uncomfortable, though they could not at first clearly articulate their feelings. Before reading further, you should study this *Oui* cover and attempt to assess your own feelings. What appears to be going on in the illustration?

A recent study by *The New York Times* disclosed that cover designs could affect newsstand sales of a publication as much as 35 percent. *Playboy*, for example, sells about 75 percent of its over 6 million copies monthly on newsstands and about 25 percent by subscription. As *Oui* had been on the market for only four months at the time of the Silver Queen issue, virtually 100 percent of its circulation—claimed by the magazine in excess of a million copies—was newsstand-originated. The cover is by far the most important page in this publication. And the subliminal cover story should tell us something highly significant about the motives of the young readers being editorially engineered to purchase the publication.

The Silver Queen cover portrait was compared with male and female physiology text descriptions in a medical school library. Five specific anatomical details supported the hypothesis that their blond model was actually a man in drag.

The model's wrists, shoulders, neck, fingernails, and breasts are strongly and clearly male. In addition, the blond hair is a wig. Some curious changes were airbrushed into the photograph, suggesting that the artists and editors knew precisely what they were doing. Male navels, for example, appear to be horizontal and the female appear vertical due to a layer of fatty tissue women usually carry just below their navel. Microscopic examination of the photoengraving revealed the navel had been carefully airbrushed into a vertical appearance.

Nearly fifty male college students who had purchased at least one copy of *Oui* were then interviewed. The questionnaire began, "Would you like to date the blond model on this cover? Where would you take her? What would you order for dinner? What would you talk about? Would you dance with her? Would you park on the way home? Would she invite you up to her apartment?" etc., etc., etc. Had these interviewed students even suspected what was going on, the interviewers would have been in serious trouble.

Where a Man's a . . . (?)

All the questions, nevertheless, were answered in detail by each respondent as they fantasized themselves on an exciting date with the silver blond. Surprisingly, not one of the young men even suspected there might be something queer, if you will pardon the expression, about the *Oui* cover. These young men appeared so entranced by the high-credibility image of *Oui* that they repressed their perceptual ability to differentiate sexual gender.

It does not appear reasonable to assume that so important a page in a prestigious national men's magazine would be used as simply a crude joke, ridiculing its readers' masculinity. If the joke were discovered, the magazine would obviously be in trouble. Nor did it appear reasonable that the magazine was trying to build circulation among male homosexuals, who are estimated at roughly 3 percent of the American adult male population. Besides, few advertisers would want their products identified with homosexuality, at least not at the conscious level. The transvestite cover was clearly designed to appeal to the *latent* homosexuality presumably inherent in all males at the unconscious level. In several other world cultures, homosexuality is not considered a taboo subject, but latent homosexuality has a substantial potentiality for subliminal manipulation in American culture, which consciously demands a strict adherence to clear-cut heterosexual divisions.

Note, however, that the face of the model is not animated or enticing. "She" actually appears to be waiting somewhat ill at ease, looking into the middle distance. The miniskirt appears to be a cage of wire netting over the genital area, and the hands rest on it uncomfortably, as if "she" would prefer to be rid of it. The anxiety of repressed homosexual feelings is effectively dramatized.

Of course, the *Oui* silver queen was not the only example of media utilizing repressed sexual identity reversals as a marketing technique. *Playboy* has utilized the approach many times over the years, but only infrequently on covers and as a subliminal trigger in ads and illustrations. Latent homosexuality has become a frequently utilized subliminal management device in advertising.

One intriguing aftermath of the experiment was a small survey conducted among fifteen female college students. They were asked a series of simple questions about what kind of personality they thought the cover model would have. Very quickly, about half of the young women consciously identified the model's *male* sexuality.

"Playboy" Meets "Playgirl"

In February 1973 Douglas Lambert—a Los Angeles pub-sisher—launched a new marketing concept for advertisers with *Playgirl*. The first press run included an ambitious 600,-000 copies. By mid-1974 the publication was selling in excess of 2 million copies monthly—one of the most successful of the crotch publications. The magazine was widely publicized as aimed at the "new American woman." By November 1974 *Playgirl* bragged of being the fifth largest women's magazine in America.

So, faced with this overwhelming success in both circulation and advertising sales, we asked the simple question, "What kind of girls read *Playgirl*?"

It is widely known in the trade that out of the 25 to 30 million readers of *Playboy* magazine, about 20 percent are women—but usually the wives or girl friends of the male *Playboy* purchasers. By themselves, very few women purchase *Playboy* or any of the other men's magazines.

After interviewing proprietors in roughly forty magazine retail stores throughout the Midwest, only three could recall ever selling a copy of *Playgirl* to a girl or woman. Boys and men were apparently purchasing the magazine with ferocious intensity, but the very few women purchasers anyone could recall appeared to have purchased out of casual curiosity.

Many stores knew their regular male purchasers; none could recall a regular female purchaser of *Playgirl*. The phenomenon was unprecedented in American publishing. A major national magazine was—with heavy fanfares—announcing itself as a women's magazine, but was apparently purchased only by men.

Playgirl's unique contribution was the nude male photographs and centerfolds. In every issue featured photographs were nude, young American males romping gleefully through some form of healthful outdoor activity with their exposed genitalia flapping impressively in the wind. And, these male genitalia *were* impressive. Dr. R. L. Dickinson's *Atlas of Human Sex Anatomy*, a standard work used in medical schools, reports the normal range of flaccid penis length varies between roughly 3 3/8 and 4 1/8 inches, with the general average in roughly the 3 3/4-inch range. In research conducted by Masters and Johnson, full erection usually doubled the organ's length over its flaccid state size. There appeared some variation, however, as larger flaccid organs increase somewhat less in the erect state.

Genitals portrayed in *Playgirl* were, at the time of the study, pictured only in flaccid state. The models used by the publication, however, must have been carefully screened. In examining several issues, the flaccid exposed penises consistently appeared to exceed six inches in length. It was not difficult to imagine the modeling agencies listing on their male clients' application forms "flacid penis size," much as they list the sizes of female models' mammary glands.

When you consider the detailed scientific statistics that have been compiled on male penis size for whites (and blacks, though it may surprise you that there is no difference), *Playgirl* must maintain a rigorous recruiting effort to find male models with abnormally long, flaccid penis dimensions. They appear to be using models who represent about 3 to 5 percent of the male adult population. Assuming male models are statistically representative of the total male population, this means that out of every one hundred models interviewed, ninety-five to ninety-eight must be rejected for undersized endowments.

Kinsey Perceived Something Else

According to *Playgirl*'s promotional logic, women—at least the "new women"—find these photographs appealing and presumably a source of sexual stimulation. But Dr. Kinsey and his associates at Indiana University made some interesting discoveries in their famous 1953 study, *Sexual Behavior in the Human Female*. The late Dr. Kinsey wrote, "Photographs of female nudes and magazines exhibiting nude or near-nude females are produced primarily for the consumption of males. There are, however, photographs and magazines portraying nude and near-nude males, but these are also produced for the consumption of males. There are almost no male or female nudes . . . produced for the consumption of females.

"The failure," Dr. Kinsey continued, "of nearly all females to find erotic arousal in such portrayals is so well known to the distributors of nude photographs and nude magazines that

28

they have considered that it would not be financially profitable to produce such material for a primarily female audience."

The centerfold in the June 1974 issue of *Playgirl* displayed the former pro-football player Lou Zivkovich in the buff. The issue sold well over 2 million copies. Most of the crotch publications have roughly 3.5 readers per copy, so the total readership of this issue would be roughly 7 million, most of whom *Playgirl* claims are women. America's leading advertisers at first appeared shy about the "new woman" concept, but have lately been surging forward to climb upon the sexgame bandwagon.

Viva, published by famed *Penthouse* publisher Robert Guccione, launched a counterattack in September 1973 to the *Playgirl* invasion. Guccione described his magazine, *Viva,* as "edited by men who truly love women . . . for women who truly love men." Like *Playgirl,* the most notable quality of *Viva* is its displays of male genitalia.

By mid-1974 *Viva* had reached a most respectable 700,000 circulation which provided their advertisers with a pool of roughly 2.5 million readers. Even though his circulation was smaller, Guccione appeared to have outdone *Playgirl* in seeking out male models with large flaccid penises. Guccione explained how this made advertisers approach *Viva* with caution. "They're pretty uptight about its pictures of nude men," he admitted almost compassionately. Apparently referring to the jealousy that *Viva* must elicit from less well hung males whose girl friends are regular *Viva* readers, Guccione played the game all the way through. "Guys," he said, "naturally like their women to believe that they're well built," as though this were something guys could keep secret from gals.

In a survey of magazine store proprietors, similar to that done on *Playgirl,* investigators were unable to find any dealer who recalled ever selling a copy of *Viva* to a female. Copies of both *Playgirl* and *Viva* were shown to a sample of young women on a midwestern university campus. Interviewers were female students, carefully selected and trained to present the two magazines during the interviews as women's publications. They were specifically trained to display enthusiasm toward the magazines during all interviews and to solicit as much female support for the publications as was possible. They were even offered small rewards for each verifiable supporter of the publication's concept they could produce. In other words, a favorable bias toward the magazine was built into both the questionnaire and the interviewers.

In over a hundred interviews with female university students, the female interviewers could persuade less than 5 percent into a positive attitude toward the two publications. A few respondents, roughly 10 percent, appeared extremely annoyed at the "sexist," "degrading," "insulting" portrayal of women as "malleable," "inert," pieces of "disposable furniture," in the pictorial art of both publications.

Male Fantasies Differ From Female Fantasies

Most female respondents, roughly 85 percent, saw the publications as some kind of a joke. They appeared more indifferent than anything else. In answer to whether they would purchase the magazines, over 95 percent said most emphatically no. Of those who said they might purchase one issue, none would commit to two or more. In answer to the final question, "What kind of girl reads *Playgirl*?" most respondents said they did not know or could not be certain. Roughly 15 percent replied with answers such as "a weirdo," "a prostitute," "a pervert," "a freak," etc. The magazine's image projection was so strangely negative to the female respondents that even those who thought they might purchase a copy commented in negative terms.

In one of the Kinsey researchers' case studies, the showing of nude male figures to 4,191 men disclosed that 54 percent were erotically aroused by photographs, drawings, and paintings of nude males. By comparison, from a sample of 5,678 females, only 12 percent were aroused as a result of viewing male or female nudes.

In a further Kinsey study of 617 females who had observed photographs of male genitalia, 21 percent reported definite and/or frequent erotic response and 27 percent some response; 52 percent reported they had never been aroused by viewing male genitals. This final study was done with sexually mature women.

It would be a serious mistake to view *Playgirl* and *Viva* as publications designed for homosexuals. Again, the appeal is to latent homosexuality, which, to some degree, involves every male.

There appears to be a latent, deeply repressed, homosexual potentiality in all males, some more than others, of course. The Kinsey data can be considered conservative, since male respondents had to admit openly their arousal by photographs, drawings, and paintings of nude males.

While *Playboy* occasionally dabbled in the playground of sexual role anxieties, *Playgirl* and *Viva* must be given credit for having turned Kinsey's interesting little observation into multimillion-dollar publishing empires. Virtually every issue of *Playgirl* and *Viva* carried at least one article strongly rationalizing male homosexuality.

The Rationalization of Homosexuality

A review of specific *Playgirl* content is even more revealing. In the February-March 1973 issue, television's *Hee Haw* stars, the Hager brothers, appeared in the centerfold. One Hager stands behind a guitar which coyly hides his genitals. The other brother sat beside him, his genitals also hidden from the camera. The Hager brothers appeared to be hairless, probably the result of airbrushing the photograph. Their postures were clearly effeminate. Their jewelry also appeared quite inappropriate for males, and their smiles hardly reinforced any concept of masculinity. This was the magazine's more restrained first issue. By June, genitalia were in full display.

In the first issue an article titled "Don't Get Driven into Marriage" contains curious comments. The author, Miriam Gilbert (feminine first name, masculine second) emphasized, "There's no reason for you to be ashamed of being single," and that "Being single won't make you worry-free, but at least your problems won't be doubled and possibly tripled [a reference to pregnancy?]." Homosexuality, of course, offers a simple solution to all these vexing problems. Another statement by the author, "Marriage can tie you into knots," has similar implications. At the very least, married intimacy was presented as more trouble than it's worth; an escape into sex-object status is shown as the way out. This is a far cry from the primary theme of every other women's publication in

North America. Dr. Kinsey's study of the American male revealed, perhaps curiously in this context, that half the men who remained unmarried by the age of thirty-five were overtly homosexual.

In two other articles in this issue titled, "What a Woman Looks for in a Man (and What She Settled For)" and "How to Make a Play for a Playgirl," an appeal to male readers as well as clear rationalizations for male homosexuality are evident. Once again, females were portrayed as dumb and their expectations of what a man should be appeared absurd and ridiculous. The female is portrayed as a starry-eyed, romantic, naïve fool. The article even advised the woman, "The cardinal rule, the backbone of the chase is: Be an idiot!"

Why Can't a Woman Be More Like a Man?

The underlying statement in all these articles advised male readers to avoid troublesome, silly females and richly enjoy the companionship of men. Fun is liberally poked at the "normal" male who is still vulnerable to females.

A justification for male homosexuality appeared in an interview with Jacqueline Susann in the October 1973 issue. "Where is the law that says men must marry women if they don't want to? Where is it written?" Susann asked. She also expressed her position loud and clear in behalf of homosexuality: "I'm all for it! I think it's highly civilized," citing ancient Greece, where it is alleged to have been "women for babies, men for love." Virtually any practicing homosexual will confirm with proselytizing enthusiasm the myth that Greece was the gayest of all countries. (Modern Greek men have been known to take a very dim view of such nonsense.)

Playgirl's cartoons invariably demean women, emphasizing their disloyalty, their undependability as sex objects (citing irregularities caused by menstruation and birth control pills), stupidity, selfishness, dominating tendencies; and superstitiousness. Ads in *Playgirl* and *Viva* are also predominantly aimed at men. The ads that do appear to involve female products are displayed as gifts for dumb women who respond to bribes purchased by men.

Playgirl also printed a color portrait of a young woman

posed with sunglasses, dressed in a sleeveless blouse and simple skirt (see Figure 7). The caption reads simply, "What kind of girl reads *Playgirl?*" Though attractive, she did not appear as sexually provocative as other females portrayed in the magazine. Her dress was quite commonplace, hardly an appropriate, exotic, sexually provocative costume for the erotic fantasies of a young American male. The reader, however, cannot see what she is thinking as her eyes remain obscured behind the sunglasses, suggesting she may have had a secret. As your eye drifts casually across the photographic surface, focus for thirty seconds upon the model's genital area. Embedded lightly on the model's blue skirt is a very large, erect penis (see Figure 8).

What kind of girl, indeed, reads *Playgirl?*

And—After Long-term Conditioning?

Playing around with the very insecure sexual identities of North American young males may have serious consequences. Someone should look carefully into the possible media imprinting, reinforcement, and legitimatization of homosexual perspectives. Even though libido-imprinting involves every male in the world to one degree or another, a search of scientific literature revealed the subject had rarely been researched. Since magazines like *Playgirl* and *Viva* are widely used as stimuli for early masturbatory practices by young men, it might be useful to consider the possible long-term effects of an alienation toward women subliminally induced and reinforced by these and similar media.

At this moment, the possible imprinting effects of homosexual influences through masturbatory stimuli can only be speculated upon. Much like the specific cause-and-effect link between smoking and lung cancer, they may be difficult to isolate concretely and demonstrate to everyone's total satisfaction, especially because the culture has a vested interest in not perceiving such a relationship.

This does not mean, however, the relationship does not exist. It simply means that we do not as yet have sensitive enough instruments capable of isolating the precise number of homosexual stimuli that will produce a full-fledged queen.

Much of North American so-called social science—often antisocial and quite unscientific in its methods and illusions—is devoted to proving that things do not exist. Quite often these things proven not to exist have been subjects the society has a vested interest in avoiding.

Masters and Johnson, after their extensive research into *Human Sexual Inadequacy*, blamed the lack of strong, positive self-images as the basic cause of sexual dysfunction in both men and women. Writers such as Abraham Maslow, Sigmund Freud, Karl Menninger, Orrin Klapp, and dozens of others have dealt in great depth with the lifelong significance to every individual of self-image concepts. All agree in one measure or another that a fundamental aspect of self-image is sexual gender identity—how individuals perceive themselves both alone and in comparison with others. Models, such as parental figures—or perhaps more importantly today in North America, communication media-induced models—form the base from which self-image is developed, especially with the young. The process of self-image construction, however, appears to be a dynamic process which continues throughout life.

In his book *The Collective Search for Identity*, sociologist Orrin Klapp referred to the American's problem of "identity despair," which has led some into suicide and other such self-destructive acts. Identity despair, however, is more likely to lead most people into what Thoreau called "quiet desperation," to which media offers heavy product consumption as an answer. Consumption as part of a search for psychological fulfillment is as lacking in hope as are brand-loyal cigarette smokers just after their diagnosis as lung-cancer victims.

After three years of matching male genitalia against *Playgirl* magazine, *Viva* finally decided to give up the game and go straight. Beginning with its March 1976 issue, *Viva* editor Kathy Keeton announced publicly what most people in the business had known for years, as well as most women—"Women get turned on by personality, not physique. *Viva* will no longer use male frontal nudity in its pages."

At *Playgirl*, however, the profitable reader manipulation continues. When queried on the *Viva* editorial policy change, editor Marin Scott reported "*Playgirl* will add more pages to its centerfold, featuring full-color foldouts of naked men. Women," she added, "want to see more male nudes. They love it."

What kind of girl reads *Playgirl*, indeed?

3

The
Fashion Massage

> *The best way to get someone*
> *to be what one wants them*
> *to be is not to tell them what*
> *to be, but to tell them what*
> *they are.*

R. D. LAING
Politics of the Family

Planned Psychological Obsolescence

The new synthetic fabrics simply do not wear out fast enough: it often requires months, even years, of continuous wear before synthetics even begin to show deterioration. With the growth of synthetic fabrics, it became almost a matter of survival for the textile industry to intensify fashion's significance.

The primary function of fashion is simply to sell clothing. The secondary function is to make obsolete all older, out-of-fashion clothing. Both the men's and the women's fashion industries are efficient—and highly profitable—systems of planned obsolescence for the multi-billion-dollar textile industry.

In 1968 you might have been one of millions of Americans to purchase a new tailored suit. Many new fabrics, including Italian silk, were popular. Linings that year were cheerfully designed and expensive—often made of silk satin. You could still obtain superb handcraftmanship if you could afford it.

Many men even foolishly let themselves be talked into taking an extra pair of pants with their suits.

By 1970 even the most expensive 1968 suit was obsolete, most not yet beginning to show wear. Any man would have been quite uncomfortable wearing the two-year-old suit even on a quick trip to the corner store. In just two years lapels had inched out about a half inch per year, the pants had slowly become more tightly fitted around the seat and legs—at the rate of about a half inch per year—and those obnoxious bell-bottomed flares were also inching out at about the same rate.

While these carefully programmed suit-design changes were being engineered, closets full of white shirts were also being obsoleted throughout America by the changeover to colored shirts. By 1971 a white shirt worn to a business conference would have made an executive feel like Calvin Coolidge at a Yippie convention. One Salvation Army officer even discouraged his contributors from donating white shirts during used-clothing drives: they were difficult even to give away to the poor. Meanwhile, across America, neckties became wider—a half inch per year—and belts also became wider, a quarter inch per year.

Any readers doubting the success of planned sartorial obsolescence can simply check their own closets for clothes, ties, shirts, belts, and whatever else they cannot bring themselves to throw out, even if they do not wear them anymore. If the cost of this waste was totaled each year for North America alone, it would easily finance a gourmet's diet for every starving famine victim on the earth's surface. And so far, we have only considered men's fashions.

The textile industry has been manipulating women along these same lines for many decades—often much more ruthlessly.

A Positive Self-Image Is Vital

Consider the American woman's self-image in relation to her bodily endowments—biologically derived proportions over which most individuals have little power to change or modify. Young women with small breasts, for example, are quite likely to perceive themselves as deficient in personal value.

American media establish and sustain the cultural models of desirable human configurations, Women with heavy legs in America are also programmed almost automatically for a lifelong inferiority complex, as are generally larger, heavier women.

The techniques are perhaps more easily visible when other cultures are compared with North America. For example, many Latin American cultures idealize heavy women with heavy legs. Unfortunately, thin Latin American women who might win beauty prizes in North America are condemned to a lifelong sense of inferiority among their own people.

These phenomena apply more or less in all cultures. North American culture, however, can hammer artificial cultural norms deeply into the population's collective unconscious via media saturation.

Diets and other reducing techniques are a regular staple for every women's page or magazine in America. Every issue of *Cosmopolitan* features an article such as "Get Thin and Stay Thin." *Vogue* features an endless succession of articles such as "Underweight? A Fresh Look at the Problem" (as though a "fresh" look were really necessary). Had any of these fantasy schemes actually worked, the problem would have been solved and forgotten long ago. That, however, would not have sold advertised products.

Advertisers of rich cake mixes, desserts, and other calorie-packed indulgences actually fight to place their colorful, mouth-watering ads, loaded with subliminal triggers, in close proximity to articles on dieting and weight reduction.

Advertisers spend annual fortunes finding out which techniques sell best. The various contradictions and inconsistencies add up to profitable merchandising strategies. Intense guilt feelings, communicated to both men and women about their body structures, produce heavy product consumers who attempt to compensate for their imagined biological deficiencies via the never-ending river of new products. The guaranteed failure of fantasy schemes for remaking the human body also guarantees further inferiority feelings, which often result in further depression, self-rejection, frustration—and, almost inevitably, increased consumption of high-caloried foods, clothing that promises to make one look slimmer, and a veritable potpourri of look-thin merchandise.

38

Women, perhaps even more than men, have been painstakingly programmed to feel inferior unless they are dressed appropriately. Costuming, of course, is essentially a matter of money. If you can afford exclusively designed clothes, you will be one of the best-dressed clothes horses in town. Social ascendancy in America is most often a prerogative of what you are wearing and how much it costs—in terms, however, of other people's abilities to assess that cost. Simply *being* expensive is not enough; the apparel and its design must *appear* expensive.

The Ins and the Outs

Training in fashion dependence must begin young to assure lifelong servitude or dependence upon the industry that rules on what is *in* and what is *out*. Teen-agers and their high level of discretionary income (they can spend it for whatever they want) are primary targerts of subliminal fashion media which include articles, so-called news, motion pictures and TV costuming, etc.

Young people look for models as they always have, but today they search for self-acceptance or identities among their peers rather than from within themselves. Psychopathological casebooks are loaded with evidence that this form of identity-seeking courts disaster.

Several years ago, fashion conditioning was also initiated among the pre-teen market. These young people are extremely vulnerable to the society around them as they grow through chemical and biological changes at puberty. They seek out confirmation when they ask, "How do I look?" or "What am I like?" Of course, friends usually accommodate—if they are interested in remaining friends. All media—newspapers, magazines, television, film, records—flatter our young relentlessly, paying court to their uncertain egos.

Narrow, tight-legged "pegged" trousers of several years ago are "camp," out of it, archaic throwbacks from an out-of-step past. During 1971 it was already almost impossible to purchase trousers with straight legs. For a short while, tailors did a brisk business of cutting off the flare for men who were annoyed at the teen-aged fashions creeping up to dominate the adult world. Within a year, however, most surrendered—the extra tailoring was too expensive and time-consuming. Obedient, though often begrudgingly, men replaced their wardrobes with bell-bottomed pants and wide-lapeled coats.

Most American teen-agers today would not wear out-of-fashion clothing to cut their parents' lawns. But they are consciously unaware they have been carefully trained to fear a loss of image among their peer group. Teen-agers view themselves in a mirror with their bell-bottomed trousers as being in close step with the modern world. They have been trained to view themselves as socially acceptable because they dress appropriately. *I consume, therefore I exist* has become the basic maxim of the American young as they respond predictably to the subliminal value manipulations of the textile industry.

Bell-bottomed trousers are merely a designer's technique of obsoleting tens of millions of dollars in wearing apparel. The intensity and rapidity of these change cycles have been increased during the seventies. Several years from now, as sales volumes begin to decrease in response to the durability of synthetic fabrics, pants designs will move slowly back to narrow bottoms with more loose-fitting legs and seats.

In the Jungles of Manhattan

There is a great deal of technique in fashion design carefully planned to provoke the unconscious. In a highly competitive industry, costume and accessory designers utilize every subliminal trick in the book to move their merchandise.

For example, a most curious parallel appears between the intricate designs on modern jewelry and textiles and man's tribal instinct for the expression of repressed cravings or needs. Among primitive peoples, facial and body painting confer upon the individual great dignity and value as a human being, aid them to cross the frontiers between nature and culture, differentiate the mindless animal from civilized man, and define men and women's social status. Body and facial painting motifs in primitive societies often parallel—in both meaning and psychological significance—the symbolic representations of modern merchandisers in the fashion industry.

One intricate and expensive jeweled costume necklace advertised in *Vogue* utilized a design strikingly similar to that recorded by anthropologist Claude Levi-Strauss nearly fifty years ago in a Stone Age Caduevo Indian village in the Brazilian Amazon River basin (see Figures 9 and 10). The body-painting design motifs of the Caduveos are shown in the inset drawings taken from Dr. Levi-Strauss's book *Tristes Tropiques (Sad Tropics)*.* These designs had been carefully painted on the bodies and faces of Caduveo tribal royalty with fine bamboo spatulas dipped in *genipapo* juice, producing a color that turns blue-black after oxidation. The two-opposed spiral designs were often used on the face and neck.

The Caduveo designs appear very consistent in style, technique, and inspiration. Recorded in drawings by two anthropologists—Boggiani and Levi-Strauss—who visited the tribes forty years apart, the tribal designs remained unchanged. The chain design on the left was recorded by Guido Boggiani in 1895, and the design on the right by Levi-Strauss in 1935 (see Figure 11).

The primitive Caduveo appear to repress the meanings of these designs. Though they had names (labels) for each design, they could not clearly explain the meanings. At the time, Levi-Strauss thought they were being secretive, though he wrote that the designs appeared motivated by some form of eroticism.

Another anthropologists, Jesuit missionary Father Sanchez-Labrador, detected the presence of the demon in these chain designs. Much like their modern North American counterparts, Caduveo women openly and systematically exploited the erotic effects of makeup. Caduveo women of high birth even plucked out their facial hairs.

Specific design meanings remained ambiguous and obscure within the tribes. Reminiscent of modern Americans, the Caduevos did not wish to talk about meanings. Necklace and wrist decorations in the form of tattooed linked chains were

---

* From *Tristes Tropiques* by Claude Levi-Strauss. Copyright © 1955 by Librairie Plon. English translation by John and Doreen Weightman, copyright © 1973 by Jonathan Cape Limited. Reprinted by permission of Atheneum Publishers, New York.

common among high ranking Caduveo women, but chains were also used by women of lower social status.

Body-painting designs in primitive societies are directly—though subliminally—involved with political, social, and economic status. Painted or tattooed on the face, neck, and body of Caduveo noblewomen, the intricate designs symbolized virility and fertility and established the wearer as the property of a man of wealth and power. The interlocking design chain links testified to everyone in the tribe that this woman was chained to a husband of importance, with the implied admonition of "Hands off!"

These designs include symbolic representations related to religious, reproductive, and fertility rites. The *meanings* and *significance* of the ornate, jeweled *Vogue*-advertised necklaces—similar to the primitive vegetable-dyed, body-painting designs—are also subliminal to the North American woman. The Monet jewelry designs were shown to several dozen North American women of affluence who were asked to briefly interpret the design's meaning. Their verbal rationalizations were consistently vague and obscure. Apparently, at least at any conscious level, they simply did not know what the designs meant.

Yet many of these women admired the jewelry, and several expressed a desire to own the pieces.

Conscious Rationalizations

Not unlike the Caduveo women of status, overt meanings of the body decorations were repressed behind conscious rationalizations such as, "It's a good investment"; "It brings out the real me"; "It will go well with such and such new gown"; "It's pretty." The high price of this costume jewelry requires a strong purchase motivation—much stronger than such conscious rationalizations would support. Several investigators have commented upon how extraordinary it is that American women have no conscious idea of the symbolic meanings of even such simple decorative devices as the ribbon pinned snugly around their necks—a symbolic bondage collar whose significance must date back millenniums in human evolution. It is also curious that many men can sense sexual excitement from such symbols without consciously understanding the reasons behind the stimulation.

Modern counterparts to these chain designs can be found in virtually any women's magazine or jewelry store. The bondage suggested by these symbols is far more comfortable, however, then the version symbolized with vegetable dyes on the necks and wrists of Caduveo women. Nevertheless, a heavy chain-linked neckpiece definitely symbolizes female bondage to the male—both sexual and psychological.

The important fact is that the jewelry designs are commercially successful, purchased at substantial expense by enough women to justify mass production, distribution, and advertising. The designs are, therefore, significant symbolic representations in their purchasers' lives. Most designs are said to originate in nature, yet there are so many millions of possible combinations and variations that it is most unlikely the Monet and Caduveo design similarities could be purely random chance. Monet jewelers could easily have adapted their designs from the aboriginal culture. Or reacting to subconscious archetypes, the designers might well have come up with the similar design motifs entirely on their own.

The frequent occurrence of symbolism with similar meanings among peoples who appear unrelated geographically, technically, or culturally is much too frequent to be dismissed as mere coincidence. St. Augustine pondered archetypal religious symbolism during the Fourth Century A.D. Carl Jung's and Claude Levi-Strauss's theories of archetypal symbolism are two more contemporary ways of trying to explain the phenomena. Jung theorized that these symbolic archetypal meanings have been with humans "since the beginning," suggesting a genetically inherited form of symbolic information. Levi-Strauss, on the other hand, theorized that humans have biological-based predisposition to interpret myths and symbols in highly consistent and similar ways.

Whatever the ultimate explanation, archetypal symbols clearly involve—especially in modern technological man—unconscious more than conscious significance.

Color as an Archetype

Archetypal symbols cover an enormous range of sensory phenomena, both visual and auditory. Color also has archetypal characteristics. The entire range of color meaning operates at subliminal levels.

One of the difficulties in color research is that contextual variations in meaning are, for practical purposes, infinite. There is also an infinite range of possible shades for each basic color. All have meanings which are quite difficult, if not impossible, to express consciously. Yet everyone knows that a dark shade of red produces a vastly different feeling when painted on an automobile than when designed into a cigarette package. International research firms, such as Louis Cheskin's Color Research Institute in Chicago, have reaped fortunes out of testing colors on package designs.

If there is a single generalization possible about color, it would attest to the impossibility of generalizing on color meanings. Precisely the same color can change meaning drastically from one application to another. Further, color is a non-verbal medium of communication—not unlike design, music, and touching. Whatever words are used to describe color's effect upon behavior, the words will always be inadequate approximations of actual meaning.

Whatever color may be all about is extremely complex when the neuro-mechanisms of the eye are considered. It is presently an enigma as to how color information passes from the eye to the brain. Successful color testing on packages, for example, has developed nonverbal tests of feeling or emotion in order to probe color meanings. Some experimenters have successfully used electroencephalographs, galvanic skin response measurements, polygraphs, pupil dilation measurements, and retinascopes to access the unconsciously motivated, automatic response of humans to color stimuli.

Reality vs. Dream

One curious aspect of color's archetypal significance can be observed in publications such as *Vogue*. Thumb through any copy and compare *meanings* between black-and-white and colored illustrations. With the high budgets usually available to this important mass merchandiser of fashion, the whole magazine could be published in four-color reproduction if it could sell or communicate more effectively. If a $20,000 advertisement or illustration (the two are often the same in *Vogue*) sells effectively, the advertiser will easily sell more than twenty times the price of the ad.

In *Vogue* the black-and-white illustrations consistently appear to represent what the reader would perceive as her world of reality. Black-and-white fashion series in *Vogue*—most photographed by world-famous photographers of women such as Richard Avedon, William Penn, and Helmut Newton—display their slim, small-breasted models in moody, lonely, contemplative, and usually serious though sensuous poses.

The color illustrations, on the other hand, most often reflect what the reader would perceive as a dream or fantasy world—action or festive situations involving other women or men, and dreams or fantasies involving aspirations. This can be demonstrated on the four pages of a Peck & Peck advertisement in *Vogue* (see Figures 14, 15, 16, and 17).

In Figure 14, the black-and-white model has returned to her room from the beach. She is alone, looking down. The caption above the photo states, "I am on vacation indefinitely. Do not disturb my plans or do anything to upset me." On the opposite page's color layout, Figure 16, the same woman appears in an aspirational dream fantasy. She is part of the beach-resort vacation crowd and is looking at the photographer, her presumed companion. The captions, however, reflect black-and-white reality: "I feel I've spent my whole life alone." "Have you ever met a man you couldn't find?" "I'm in silver water, I'm coming up fast."

The following evening gown illustrations, Figures 15 and 17, carry the model's dream fantasies of solitude a step further. In the black-and-white layout she walks toward her dream on the opposite page, wearing a simple polka-dotted evening gown. In the dream fantasy she attends a gay, intimate terrace sunset party. The captions, however, make reality statements: "I remember it the way it should have been." "Motion. It's the outside of emotion." "How do you photograph a feeling?"

These advertisements were published in the December 1972

issue of *Vogue*, picturing the model—with whom the reader will identify—on a lonely Christmas pilgrimage to the Bahamas. Every fashion design on the four pages subtly incorporates ancient religious symbolism.

A Rose Is a Rose Is a Rose . . .

On the black-and-white illustration (Figure 12) the swimming suit and skirt pattern is strikingly similar to a design discovered in ancient water markings. Religious scholar Harold Bayley described the symbolic design as originating from the Paradise of Brahmin—a high-caste Hindu sect. The Hindu prophet said, "The Almighty has his home in the heart of a white rose." In Christian legends the white rose was often a symbol of Jesus and was also identified with the Greek virgin Sophie.

The red rose in its wild state has five roundish petals. Compare the Peck & Peck pattern with Bayley's drawings of the ancient water marking (Figure 13). It is, of course, possible that the designer copied the design from drawings or from the actual watermark, but this would hardly explain the symbolic design's commercial success among wealthy (high status) American women.

In the illustration (Figure 18) the swimsuit is designed with a fish and dolphin symbolic pattern. In the ancient shield symbol (Figure 19) the shield on which the symbol appeared even resembled the silhouette of a modern swimsuit. These drawings of the rose watermark and the dolphin shield were taken from Harold Bayley's book *The Lost Language of Symbolism* published in 1912.

Both the fish and the dolphin are ancient symbolic representations of Christ the Savior. The fish symbol was frequently used by early Christians in the catacombs, and its popularity was at least partially explained by the word for *fish* in Greek which yielded the initials of the sentence "Jesus Christ, Son of Man, Savior." Even today, the fish is often used as a symbol of Christ.

The fish, as a symbol for the Deity, often took the specific form of a dolphin, which was anciently regarded as a friend of man. The Greeks venerated the dolphin as the savior of the shipwrecked, and later Christians often used the dolphin to symbolize their Christ.

The Peck & Peck bathing suit design pattern utilized both the fish and the dolphin symbolism on a shield formed by the bathing suit which covers the woman's reproductive anatomy from breasts to genital area.

The evening gown displayed in the color illustration, Figure 17, was also based upon ancient Christian symbology. The pattern on the blue evening gown is a series of circular designs that are almost exact reproductions of the legendary Catherine wheel. The teeth on some of the design's wheels are shown turned inward (see Figure 20).

St. Catherine, so the story goes, was a virgin from Alexandria, Egypt, who openly confessed her loyalty to Christian gospel in A.D. 307. She was sentenced to death on toothed wheels—a popular, though painful, form of execution and torture reserved for important heretics and other deviants of the time. Fifty pagan philosophers were sent to pervert and corrupt St. Catherine while she was in prison awaiting execution. Through winning and irresistible eloquence, she converted the philosophers to Christianity. Thereafter, St. Catherine was regarded as the patroness of philosophers and learned scholars.

St. Catherine rejected all offers of marriage and reward. In a vision she visited Heaven and became the spouse of Christ. Christ plighted their troth with a ring in the design of the torture wheel.

The story of St. Catherine might be considered an archetypal Christian version of a much more ancient legend. Catherine (the word is from the Greek *Catharos*, or pure) was also the all-pure, immaculate, and undefiled Bride in the Song of Solomon. The toothed wheel in this earlier legend with which she is identified is the four- or six-rayed solar wheel. Cinderella, from the German legend, was sometimes called La Bella Catarina. Even today, a firework design used in Fourth of July celebrations bears the name Catherine wheel.

The Catherine wheel design appears also on another evening gown on the Peck & Peck advertisement (Figure 17) in the smaller photograph of our tourist dancing in an orange gown. She is surrounded, we might reasonably assume, by pagan philosophers attempting to corrupt her. Another version or adaptation of the Catherine wheel theme appeared in an earlier *Vogue* advertisement for Best & Company, an exclusive Fifth Avenue clothier. The hostess robe and turban are decorated with large toothed wheels—the teeth either covered or turned inward (Figure 21).

Keepers of the Secret

Women's unconscious taboos are massaged just as often as men's. Thumb through any women's magazine and study the ads, illustrations, and copy for symbolism that would stimulate unconscious taboo mechanisms. Observe carefully such details as body contacts; where eyes are looking; fingers, feet, arm, and leg lines and where they point; model relationship dominance and subordinance; and, of course, background and embeds.

With this in mind, one illustration was selected from a Sears catalog (Spring and Summer 1971) as typical of the unconscious story line and hidden taboos manipulation (see Figure 22).

Each photograph in a catalog of this kind involves many thousands of dollars in merchandise inventory. The Sears Catalog art department people must know precisely what they are doing. Where women's fashions are concerned, a blunder in an illustration or a passive design that could not motivate sales could easily result in a major disaster. Carefully examine this—at first glance—innocuous fashion photograph. Try to find out how it sells the product.

These models, appear to have been photographed separately and their pictures pasted upon the background in interlocking poses. The composite layout was then rephotographed. Outlines are sharp and even. The grass around the models' shoes appears retouched.

The foreground brunette in the light blue slacksuit is feigning sleep. She appears relaxed. Though probably listening carefully to what is going on behind her between the other two models, she is—at the moment—detached. Her left arm hangs limply at her side: her right arm and hand effortlessly prop up her chin and head. The forefinger of her right hand is interesting, as it is pointed toward her left breast.

Of the two background models, the one in blue-white appears dominant. Blue and white are much more masculine and dominant colors than the pale green and yellow.

The designs are curious. The blue and white pantsuit blouse carries a design often used on men's ties and shirts—symbolic of tadpolelike, wiggling spermatozoon. The brunette model's right foot is placed firmly upon the ground; her right hand, held in a loose fist, forcefully pressed against her hip.

The brunette model's hair is short and bound in a white ribbon, again masculine and dominant. The most provocative detail in the photograph, however, is the brunette's eye contact line directed at the blonde's right breast. Her gaze is quite intent. Her mouth is open in an expectant expression, suggesting an oral caress.

Her left hand is behind the blonde's back, though as might be logically expected the hand does not appear at the blonde's waist. The missing hand, following the brunette's left shoulder line, would likely be on the blonde's buttocks.

Applied Body Language

There seems little doubt that the brunette is making a rather specific sexual overture to the blonde. The blonde, however, appears passive—at least so far. Her pale green and yellow slack suit is covered with flowers, symbolic of virginity, fertility, passion, freshness, and sexuality. The flower of course, is the plant's reproductive organ.

The blonde's right foot and knee are positioned aggressively between the brunette's legs. Right hands and arms denote symbolically, a course of action. Left hands, as symbols, are usually passive or supportive. The blonde's right hand rests lightly against the inside of her thigh. The hand's thumb and forefinger provide a vaginal symbol halfway between the genital areas of the two models. Tracing a line from the blonde's forefinger upward to the left, the line intersects the blue and white flower in the border design located precisely over the brunette's genital area.

In terms of story line, the two brunette models in blue appear to be *a couple*—the light blue with the passive or feminine role, the blue-white with the dominant, masculine role. The passive partner is pretending sleep, unaware of all the interesting things going on behind her back. The pale green and yellow model appears to be an outsider, a newcomer. Her slack suit really is not compatible with the other two. The blonde, her eyes on a distant horizon, appears to be weighing the possibility of joining the pair.

The Sears fashion artist did not leave his audience dangling, so to speak. To consciously discover what happened to the three-way relationship—which bears a remarkable resemblance to the Dionysian Greek statue *The Three Graces* and the countless adaptations of the idea in European Renaissance art—all the astute Sears catalog reader need do is look at the small photographic inset at the left. All three models have removed their pants and presumably their inhibitions. The blonde had to completely take off her one-piece slack suit. She is now wearing a short flowered dress.

The light blue brunette has reassumed her role as lady of the house. She proudly, if not arrogantly, displays her body to the others, her right arm inactive and the thumb and forefinger in the vaginal symbol with the knuckle and forefinger pointing toward the blue and white model's genital area. Blue-white, on the other hand, appears to be still on the make, her right hand on the blonde's shoulder, her eyes now peering down at the blonde's left breast.

Blue-white's left hand now appears behind light blue. Her attention is divided between the other two women. The blonde, however, is still the outsider. But she now appears more relaxed and at ease. Her arms are relaxed at her sides, though her right thumb and forefinger still symbolize her vagina.

The Best in the Business

Remember, this single illustration is not the work of amateurs. Sears is widely known to employ some of the best technicians in the business. Their catalog art department can obtain, from year to year, the most direct and simple feedback verification available in modern mass communication media. Sears could tell you, through a simple computer run, how many of each of the three slack suits pictured in this single illustration were sold. Should these communication techniques not work effectively, it would be rapidly discovered.

The Sears, as well as other retail merchandising catalogs, are loaded with similar salacious implications. As these phenomena are very widely and repetitively used, they simply cannot be dismissed as accidental. Most of the techniques described in this chapter have been used by artists for centuries. None are even remotely what anyone could call *new*. What appears new is our inability to recognize the manipulative objective of these illustrations and designs and the profit-seeking industry they sustain.

Modern consumers seem to believe they are deciding purchase preferences all on their own, much like the man who smokes the "thinking man's cigarette." The significance of art and design—most of which involves the unconscious—has been almost completely detached from the study of human behavior in American universities' mechanistic-oriented psychology, sociology, and anthropology departments, suggesting that somehow this is a subject our so-called modern civilization simply does not wish to deal with. It is quite possible that societies—much like individuals—collectively repress information, concepts, and ideas which would produce high anxiety levels if dealt with consciously.

4

Children of the Tit Culture

> You want to know, Little Man,
> how you are? You listen on the
> radio to the announcements of
> laxatives, dental creams and
> deodorants. But you fail to hear
> the music of propaganda. You
> fail to perceive the bottomless
> stupidity and the disgusting
> bad taste of things which are
> designed to catch your ear.
> Have you ever paid close
> attention to the jokes which a
> master of ceremonies makes
> about your whole small
> miserable world? Listen to your
> laxative's propaganda and you
> learn who and how you are.

> WILHELM REICH
> *Listen Little Man*

With Lifetime Consequences

Substantial evidence supports the view that America's media-oriented economy has actually changed human life patterns from infancy through old age, at both *conscious* and—more importantly—*unconscious* levels.

During the approximate first two years of a child's life, every infant grows through clearly observable stages. Sigmund Freud proposed only two major stages of psychosexual development during this early period—the *oral*, roughly the first year; and the *anal*, roughly from one to three years. Other theorists such as Jean Piaget and Erik Erikson have described these early stages in much greater detail—Piaget identifying six stages during the first two years of an infant's life. For the moment, Freud's theoretical structure will be useful to consider in relation to media, even though the theory is diffuse in many respects. (The reader is urged to examine a much more detailed synthesis of insights into early growth patterns in Dr. Theodore Lidz's excellent book *The Person*.)

Freud's oral phase roughly divides into two parts. During the first six months of an infant's life, food is of primary importance. The infant's life centers upon the taking of food through sucking. The first and most vital of all human relationships involves receiving nourishment from the mother, upon whom the infant is totally dependent. During this early process, the infant orients for the first time toward feeding, an affectionate need for others, and varied mouth-centered activities. Infant sucking behavior produces erotic (sexual) stimulation and, of course, is highly pleasurable. This is easily apparent as infants tranquilly suck away at their mother's nipple, a nursing bottle, or when there is nothing else handy their thumbs.

During the following six to eight months, the infant's concern with food expands to include socialization, which also centers upon the mother. Tactile or touching experiences appear to reinforce the child's sense of security. Touching—hand, mouth, genital, body, the whole range of tactile experience—is vital social learning during this early oral growth stage. No portion of an individual's life experience will be as thoroughly incorporated into their personality or become so much a basic part of lifelong character as infancy or roughly the first two years of life.

Children eventually mature, but an indelible lifelong cultural imprint has been made upon their individual personalities. Keep in mind that these early sensory experiences that focus upon oral and tactile gratification are fundamental to virtually everyone's personality. The need for such experiences will endure in one form or another, in one degree or another, throughout life.

Most individuals periodically regress throughout their lives to oral dependency when confronted with tensions, anxieties, or fears of rejection—a psychic or symbolic return to the maternal breast. In adults the real nature of these oral sensual stimulations is usually camouflaged while they suck away at cigarettes, cigars, pipes, food, and drinks. Sucking continues as a primary, normal, healthy, and emotionally fulfilling activity for both sexes at all ages.

Nursing and touching practices are largely culture-adaptive. Some cultures, for example, encourage breast-feeding the infant for two years or more. Other cultures, such as that of North America, have virtually eliminated breast-feeding or have shortened the period to only a few weeks.

Unlike their counterparts in most parts of the world, North American women consider breast-feeding undignified, an annoyance, and inferior to mechanical systems of infant feeding. Some cultures encourage extensive handling, touching, or caressing experiences between the infant, brothers, sisters, and parents, as well as other adults. Other cultures, like ours, reduce touching and handling experiences to a minimum.

American mothers are not permitted by their cultural taboos to consciously admit, even to themselves, that they obtain sexual stimulation while nursing their infants. Such distortions of the life process by both conscious and unconscious traditions provide insights into cultural forces invisibly at work in modifying human behavior.

Strong Traditional Taboos

At least two definable reasons appear behind the Anglo-American mother's aversions to touching and nursing her child. This culture has a strong incest taboo and a homosexual fear tradition whose roots go far back into its history.

American mothers stop touching their sons, and fathers stop touching their daughters much earlier in America than in most parts of Asia, Latin America, or Africa. But in *all* cultures, touching between parents and children of the opposite sex eventually stops. The incest taboo appears universal.

One insight into America's strong incest taboo tradition recently turned up in research on legal sanctions. Over the past century, one midwestern state had enacted nineteen laws that attempted to define acceptable and unacceptable marital relationships. These laws prohibited marriages between various specific distant relatives. Even considering the current genetic theories of recessive gene inheritance and its effect upon intra-family marriages—theories far from universally accepted by geneticists—only three of these laws would have been justified. But their very existence betrays their society's high level of underlying incest fear. In many nations and states, not even a trace of such prohibition can be found in legal statutes, implying a much lower level of concern.

Touching fills a healthy need in many cultures for the expression of affection and for reassuring tactile stimulation. In America, very possibly the world's most advanced no-touch culture, touching threatens to invite intimacy. Training children to avoid touching experiences with parents, other adults, or even with other children is a solidly established though usually unnoticed (repressed) norm in North America.

In other cultures where this taboo is not so highly developed, it is a common sight to view children communicating nonverbally through physical contact well up into the late teen or even adult years. But because Americans have been taught to both consciously and unconsciously sexualize *all* forms of touching, the physical caress or desire for body contact from a member of one's own sex becomes a highly threatening gesture, even though in reality there may be no more sexuality involved than in stroking a kitten.

Between people of the same sex, touching also implies homosexuality—possibly the most feared and terrifying betrayal of the inner self possible in America. Should an American child openly display physical touching behavior with other children, most parents either overtly or covertly punish the child for doing something "*dirty*" or "*bad*." The parents' unconscious fears are projected on their children's behavior. Children so conditioned, of course, will condition their children, who in turn when they become parents, will condition . . .

Repressed sexual fear, much like all types of repression, makes humans highly vulnerable to subliminal management and control technology. Through subliminal appeals and reinforcements of these fears, some consumers can be induced into buying almost anything.

Lolita Is Alive, Well, and Living in Media

American culture has strong taboos concerning older men and young women relationships—a major American taboo sometimes called *the dirty-old-man syndrome.* Today. we even hear of his counterpart, *the dirty old woman.* These syndromes are derivative of incest fear—father and mother symbols identified with the young.

The exploitation of sex guilt between parents and children, or adults and children, is frequently apparent—if you look carefully—in marketing products. As one example, the child in the Bell Telephone bill insert is probably about twelve years old (see Figure 23). These messages were mailed with monthly statements to subscribers all over North America in a money-saving (for the phone company) attempt to induce subscribers to use directories instead of calling information.

At the surface level, a twelve-year-old girl appears posed on a phone book. She stands on tiptoe, stretching upward, apparently reaching for something. She might be reaching for a telephone number, but somehow that just doesn't make logical sense.

The insert provoked the anger of a group of women attorneys in Toronto who strongly objected to the use of pedophilia—the utilization of children as sex objects—in advertising. The twelve-year-old is obviously posed in a sexually provocative posture, her dress stretched above her exposed fanny.

Lightly embedded in the child's leg—to be perceived subliminally—are several SEXes. In the top of her white stocking appears an embedded word FUCK lightly shadowed into the stocking folds (see Figure 24). These subliminal stimuli would be most effective in a culture such as North America's where any suggestion of adult-child sexuality is instantly repressed. Though these particular embeds are clearly observable in the photograph, many parents cannot consciously perceive them.

To strengthen the sexuality concept at the subliminal level, Bell's advertising agency included some even more suggestive verbalisms in the ad copy on the insert's backside. The headline advises, "The book is yours TO DO WHAT YOU WANT WITH." A reasonable question might be whether the headline refers to the book or the child standing upon it. The printed script includes some other interesting words and phrases. The word "flick" in script transposes subliminally into something more aggressively Anglo-Saxon. "You can make it" certainly evokes a salacious implication, as does "Bend over." "Make red marker slashes" might even suggest a sadomasochistic theme while "the harder it works" is hardly an appropriate description for a telephone book in action— the user may work hard at "it," but never the book itself (see Figure 25.)

The Bell Telephone Company message was not an isolated case. Sexualization of infants and children, though subliminally perceived, strongly appeals to the society's underlying sexual taboos. There is no question that the technique sells products by the millions of dollars' worth and otherwise manages behavior.

Foote, Cone, and Belding, Inc.—America's sixth largest advertising agency—took great pride in their Miss Clairol "Does She or Doesn't She?" campaign. The agency's creative director, Shirley Polykoff, even published a best-selling book in which she romantically describes the trials and tribulations of Madison Avenue. She used the Miss Clairol slogan as her book's title.

Miss Clairol, of course, is a hair dye aimed at a market of teen-aged girls. Aside from teaching teen-agers to dye their hair as a means of attracting males, the "Does She or Doesn't She" slogan has clear sexual implications for young women going through puberty.

To cite only one example of the level of venality into which American media have fallen, a Miss Clairol ad on the inside front cover of the February 1975 *Reader's Digest*, (a publication which used to be a staunch defender of middle-class morality), asks the familiar question. The illustration portrays two models in the role of mother and daughter—the daughter portrayed by a model eight or nine years old. The model portraying the mother holds the child's skirt up with her right hand. The mother's left hand appears to be under the skirt. "The "Does she or doesn't she?" question is answered in the copy head with the statement, "She Still Does!"

Simply put, those taboos held most strongly by any culture intensify that culture's vulnerability to subliminal manipulation. *Pedophilia*—the sexualization of children—is unquestionably the most feared taboo within the American culture. Therefore, it makes a superb subliminal advertising theme.

The Thoroughly Integrated Culture

The American mother is exhaustively trained throughout life to fear that damage to her breast contours may occur from child nursing, resulting in rejection, a loss of sexual attractiveness, and loss of life. The rapid disappearance of infant breast-feeding in America has a great deal to do with the American breast fetish.

Male preoccupation with the large, virgin-contoured mammary glands—denied them in infancy—as reflected by Hollywood, television, and *Playboy* magazine—is also largely the result of media conditioning. Media exploits the American male breast fetish which, in turn, reinforces the female aversion to breast-feeding infants. The highly integrated, mutually reinforcing elements of culture function like a fine watch mechanism.

Americans are frequently astonished to discover that the breast is not a primary erogenous stimulus in many of the world's cultures, including several where female breasts even remain uncovered in public. In the Far East, for example, small feet are every bit as sexually provocative as large breasts are in America. In both cultures the "natural" look of the female body was dropped in favor of highly artificial symbolic representations—the Chinese tightly bound women's feet with bandages while Americans bind women's breasts with uplift brassieres. Somewhere in both cultures there was a payoff. In the Far East bound feet imprisoned the woman and made her into an economic and sexual asset that simply could not run away. In America the uplift brassiere has made fortunes for clothing manufacturers and imprisoned the woman psychologically as a conical-breasted sex object.

A Media Hold-up

The brassiere industry is a multimillion-dollar annual economic event within the American economy, a vital and basic sector to the whole garment and textile industry. Puerto Rico manufactures over three fourths of America's brassieres and is known in the trade as the bra capital of the world. One economist sardonically commented that the famed Operation Bootstrap Economic Development Program was held up by a padded bra.

In America, possibly more so than in any other national culture, the idealized shape and contour of large virgin breasts have developed as a cultural focal point largely through the effects of commercial media—newspapers, magazines, and television providing visual emphasis upon the mythical breasts of the idealized American woman (i.e. Mother).

This cultural ideal is a blatant fiction. Breasts, like the women equipped with them, come in all shapes and sizes which change continually throughout life. Biologically speaking, there is no such thing as a meaningful norm as far as natural breast contours are concerned. In fantasies, however, there is a virtual absolute American standard breast configuration.

In one composite image study assembled by a national marketing organization, dozens of men's publications were reviewed. From advertising and illustrations directed at male readers, the breast pictures were collected and cut out. In isolation from the ad copy, trademarks, etc., they were shown to several dozen women who were requested to describe the woman who belonged to the pictured breasts—age, occupation, height, weight, physical condition, etc.

A substantial majority of the female respondents described the breasts as those of young pregnant or nursing mothers.

The cut-out breasts were then given to several artists, who were requested to synthesize the individual variations in contour, size, nipple, etc., into a composite drawing. There was no question the final composite breasts were the large, full, bulging mammary glands of a young, lactating mother.

A panel of brassiere designers estimated the composite image was a size 38D cup. This large, full bra size was then compared with the annual national bra sales by size of a large North American department store chain. Only 8.9 percent of women wear a size 42 or larger bra; over half, 56.5 percent, wear a size 34 or 36; only 34.7 percent of all North American woman (roughly one third) wear a C cup or larger in any size, and only 13.6 percent wear a D cup or larger.

The media fantasy—a size 38D—represented a very small percentage of North American women—only 1.6 percent wear 38D or 38DD bras. But the heavy use of this fantasy standard by media conveys an unconscious ideal that can only place the vast majority of real women on the defensive. Young women with small breasts, literally most young women in North America, are thus educated to feel themselves inferior misfits. They are thusly transformed into ardent consumers of tit decoration techniques—padded brassieres, foam injections, or even plastic surgery. But no real-life woman could ever match the symbolic maternal perfection of the centerfold *Playboy* magazine and its competitors do not touch breasts, they retouch them.

Retouching Beats Touching

Our *Playboy* reader is often doomed to a lifelong search for someone to mother him—a role no mature woman in her right mind would accept. A woman who fails to qualify as this fantasy ideal—and no woman is ever likely to qualify completely—must resign herself to become merely a sex object for the playboy to manipulate and use. The playboy may wander the earth for a lifetime without ever forming a meaningful relationship with a woman. Of course, as is unconsciously implied in the playboy concept, he may eventually give up his search and opt out with another man.

An even more dismal fate befalls the young woman who

does not conform to the fantasy expectations of acceptable feminine beauty. The big-breasted magazine, newspaper, and television models are not offset by the homosexual or narcissistic image norms communicated by the small-breasted models for the specialized female audiences of *Cosmopolitan*, and *Vogue* magazines. Every large American city has tens of thousands of working women—many highly talented, sensitive, and interesting women—who are unlikely to establish permanent mates because they physically do not fit into the current media-induced fantasy of what an attractive woman should look like.

The cartoon character Linus, in *Peanuts*, symbolizes the American male's search for security, if only in the form of a satin-edged blanket. It is significant that prolonged thumb-sucking is virtually unknown in cultures where infants are breast-fed. Thumb-sucking, later in life, is transposed into a search for oral gratification through symbolic breasts, cigarettes, alcohol, foods, and drugs. The search for comfort, security, and love through oral gratification is another fundamental cultural theme of American commercial media. Merely sit for an evening in front of network television and make notes on how many commercials you view per hour that are involved with mouths or the putting of things into mouths.

Literally everyone has some oral characteristics. Some individuals appear more orally centered in their behavior than others, but oral characteristics tend to surface when any individual experiences intense anxiety or insecurity, often when consciously-perceived stimuli trigger memory traces repressed within the unconscious during early childhood or infancy.

The oral character is often consistent, however, in his techniques of passively seeking to obtain needed fulfillment from others. Oral personalities are likely to fear abandonment. Unless there is someone to feed and care for them, they generally lack self-confidence. Some of the more aggressive oral types doubt they can fulfill their needs without controlling and managing other people. They may drive themselves mercilessly while exploiting others in their never-fulfilled search for security.

If indulged excessively as children, "oral" adults can develop an unshakable optimism that interferes with their ability to care for themselves, assuming others will somehow look out for them. Those who were orally deprived and frustrated as infants tend to deep-rooted pessimism and are easily hostile or resentful when their needs are not met. They tend to easily give up when frustrated. Many famous literary figures and orators have been dominantly oral in their personalities, openly displaying (for example) love for both words and food. The interrelated oral problems of love, food, insecurity, and dependency are also visible in the histories of many psychosomatic diseases such as ulcers and asthma.

Both media information content and advertising—pushing food, drinks, security, insurance, affection, maternal dominance, and upset stomachs—testify eloquently to widespread unconscious oral preoccupations.

The Crest Cavity

The Crest advertisement from the September 10, 1971, issue of *Life* is another illustration of an advertiser's appropriation of a nation's collective unconscious in merchandising its products (see Figure 26). This ad is a superb example of a subliminal oral-regression persuasion technique.

The one-toothed baby in white is, of course, a boy—a pink dress would have meant a girl. When dealt with at the conscious level, the overt genital symbolism is obvious and annoying; the mother's phallic forefinger holding down the bottom lip of the child's open, female-genital symbolic mouth, provides the photograph's primary focal point. For most readers, the fovea in the eye's retina saccades from the open mouth and finger up to the father's face (the curve lines retouched into his cheek), then directly left to the mother's eyes, diagonally down from her nose across the baby's face, down to his arm and hand, then a quick jump to the left and you see the Crest toothpaste tube.

Now, let's go back and look at what was perceived on the periphery of the retina's fovea, during the lightning-quick conscious perceptual experience.

On the back of the child's hand appears a series of embedded SEXes (see Figure 27). SEXes are also embedded on the faces of both parents, in their hair, on the mother's hand and fingers, and mosaiced across the child's dress.

Just think about all that Crest has to offer in addition to "No Cavities."

5

The American Clean

> Civilization has progressed
> toward cleanliness, as a result
> of the repression of anality.
>
> SIGMUND FREUD
> *Letters*

The Hard Sell of Clean

Supporting an industry that merchandises a vast array of products dedicated to making us clean, Americans have been exhaustively taught (programmed, if you prefer) to be clean, think clean, and buy only clean. Clean, however, is far from a universally agreed-upon concept. The meanings attributed to the word "clean" vary substantially from culture to culture and from time to time. What is clean in one country may be dirty in another; what was clean twenty years ago may be dirty today or *vice versa*. Clean depends almost entirely upon where you happen to be standing and when. The meaning of words, however, is far more related to the ways people react to them than to what the dictionary says about them—especially words like clean. What someone *says* and what someone *does* about conceptual words often provides distinctly different definitions of meaning.

The concepts of clean and dirty in American media are based primarily upon what we have been educated (programmed) to believe exist—germs, bacteria, dirt, as well as other microscopic or submicroscopic threats to our emotional well-being. The emotional implications of "dirty" are far more threatening in media fantasies than are the physical, such as disease or infection.

Dirt with its related fantasies is vastly profitable. "Not clean" in advertising, means bad breath (halitosis), obesity, dandruff, greasy hair, psoriasis, unbright teeth, unwhite clothing, and constipation. Clean is often used to describe virtually anything of significance in American life—including, not least of all, concepts of morality and sin. People and clothes are clean-cut, we breathe (or we used to breathe) clean, fresh air, our political, athletic, and military victories are described as clean sweeps. The incessant claims of the Clean corporations is often couched in the language of patriotism and national loyalties: "Look at what we are doing for you! America is the cleanest nation on earth."

Unilever, Procter & Gamble, Colgate-Palmolive, and their smaller competitors annually pump via the public information media over $10 billion in soaps and detergents of a hundred varieties which promise to deodorize, sanitize, antibacterialize, whiten, brighten, bleach, blue, sterilize, hygienize, and—as an important, though unspoken psychogenic byproduct—*dehumanize*.

Clean, as a viable selling technique, is rooted in each individual's psychosexual development. Roughly between the first and third birthdays, children's primary concern shifts from the oral to the anal areas of their bodies. Infants experience erogenous pleasure from passing or withholding bowel movements. Children value their anal product and find enjoyment in both its odor and its feel. The child holds back the stool until its accumulation brings about violent muscular contractions. As the stool finally passes through the anus, the mucous membranes are powerfully stimulated. The experience, though sometimes painful, is also highly pleasurable.

This is probably the only time in their lives that most Americans consciously enjoy their bowel movements. Many children's later conflicts with authority figures have roots in this early anal period where their need to conform and comply focused upon bowel training. A clear relationship exists between the erotic gratification, conflict over bowel training, and various adult personality traits.

Bowel training is not biologically necessary during the second year of a child's life. It serves only as a convenience for the parent. Many cultures permit children to bowel-train strictly on their own with no parental coercion. Most children appear to develop control over their bowel movements at about the same time—during the third year—whether or not their parents have trained them. However, America's advertising-managed culture demands that bowel training be introduced as early as possible, during the second year or even earlier.

Mothers have been taught over many generations to fear and reject dirt, a symbolic concept which basically implies feces or feces particles. With the American mother's preoccupation with bacteria, germs, and other microbes, her disgust with dirty toilets and kitchens, her anxiety whenever her floor or laundry is less than white or clean, there is no way she can possibly tolerate a child who pumps out odorous, contaminated excrement several times each day.

The media perpetuated heritage teaches that if they are to avoid guilt, American mothers must train their children in cleanliness at the earliest possible moment.

American Regularity

Furthermore, if children can be programmed to respond with mechanical predictability in their bowel movements, mothers can enjoy a much greater degree of personal freedom and convenience. Like adults, children are carefully educated to fear constipation, one of clean America's most pernicious foes. The mechanical enema, or its chemical counterpart the laxative, is standard procedure in many, if not most, American homes. Many Americans train themselves and their infant children to defecate on time, much as they condition themselves to eat on time. Deviations from regularity produce extreme anxiety.

It does not take most infants long to discover they can control maternal reactions to a large degree by letting go or holding in their excrement, counter to Mother's expectations and coercive demands. Eventually, of course, the child loses the game, but the training course may leave scars far deeper than even those experienced in a Marine boot-training camp.

Later, as an anally compulsive adult, the individual may see excretion as symbolic of enormous power.

The ominipresent barrage of advertising that harps upon "regularity" will in itself subliminally program certain individuals to feel themselves freaks if they are irregular, often imposing guilt over the body's inability to comply with the pharmaceutical houses' admonishments. The industry creates its own market by inducing constipation through guilt and anxiety, then providing a simple and profitable solution for it.

As children grow to adulthood, their anal eroticism is repressed more deeply into the unconscious by the daily barrage of anal-oriented media content. Children between two and six perceive an average of fifty-five hours weekly of television in North America—much of it jammed with anal-oriented Clean Product advertising, virtually all of which is subliminally reinforced by hidden SEXes and other techniques.

The prevalence of widespread anal fixation is sharply apparent when the American culture is compared with primitive cultures, or those of less industrialized nations, where time-oriented anal and oral preoccupations are either nonapparent or much less emphasized. A number of anthropologists have referred to the American culture, however, as strongly anal-oriented—much more so than any national culture on earth at the moment. If we were to rank national anality, the British would likely be second.

Psychiatrists have pointed out that adult anal erotics often unconsciously enjoy their bowel movements and their perspiratory and salivary mechanisms (bodily secretions). The anal-erotic typically overemphasizes body functions, however, and may consciously repress these as pleasurable feelings. Chronically constipated individuals tend to stubbornness, showing covert hostility by withholding affection from others in a silent and determined way—as they probably did during their early bowel training. They also display varying degrees of miserliness, pettiness about details, meticulousness, and pedanticism.

This so-called anal personality has problems over holding or letting loose, about keeping or sharing both possessions and information about themselves. They tend to ambivalence on love and hate, both of which they have learned to conceal. Ironically, individuals overtly concerned with cleanliness and neatness are very often covertly quite dirty and messy. The apparent manifestations of these fixations often turn out to be merely superficial camouflage displayed for the benefit of others.

Overcontrolled children, especially at the critical anal phase, are quite likely to become individuals who need to hide hostilities and aggressions, who unconsciously feel they will be rejected, hated, or endangered if their real feelings are discovered. The anal character often believes others are always trying to get something from them, or that they will be shamed, embarrassed, or exposed if they communicate natural feelings or needs.

Anal Syndromes

Media bombardment, reinforced with subliminal technique over many years after starting in infancy, could result in an unreasonable fear of dirt, germs, or contamination—in its extreme manifestation—mysophobia, the so-called housewife's neurosis. In this pathological example of anal preoccupation, some men and many women develop phobias about dirt. They become obsessed with scrubbing, washing, and sterilizing their bodies, homes, and possessions. Many mysophobes surround themselves with as much white as possible upon which they can detect the slightest suspicion of dirt—white rugs, clothes, even automobile upholstery. Ritualistic handwashing is usually performed dozens of times daily, until quite frequently their hands become chapped and inflamed with pathological dermatitis.

This phobic reaction to fear of dirt (i.e., feces) is widespread in America and extremely difficult to treat. With great ingenuity, sufferers will go to virtually any extreme necessary to maintain their phobia, often sacrificing mates, children, and friends.

An opposite process appears in a symptom labeled *coprophilia*, another form of conditioning also believed the result of childhood anal trauma. The coprophilia-oriented adult consciously desires involvement in excrement, subliminally recalling the power once derived from free-flowing bowels. Humiliation and discipline through the use of strong enemas often become a technique of sexual gratification. There even exists a national "swingers" organization dedicated to coprophilia.

Most Americans would like to convince themselves that such "perversions" exist only within corrupt deviants who are so few they are not even worth comment. But telephone calls to eleven practicing psychiatrists in a midwestern city revealed that each was treating between one and nine patients monthly who could be described as mysophobic or coprophilic. These conditions appear to be far more prevalent than anyone inside or outside of medicine apparently suspects. Phobic compulsions appear very closely related to addictive behavior. Literally, American culture as expressed in the mass media does not include bowel movements. Even toilet bowls are omitted from bathroom scenes in television and movies. BM's are forbidden in public, hidden from both sight and smell. Bodily functions are first suppressed, then later consciously repressed.

Foreign visitors to America comment frequently upon the ingenious ways in which Americans disguise any reference to excrement. Euphemisms for bowel or urinary movements are elaborate, though apparently unnoticed at the conscious level. Like so many other cultural entities that involve various forms of perceptual defense, the techniques used to avoid dealing with body elimination processes (a euphemism, of course) become invisible to people within the culture.

One of the most elaborately disguised excretory industries in America sits upon a low, carefully landscaped bluff which overlooks the Los Angeles beach area. Perched upon the summit is a magnificent, modern, green tiled temple. When the smog is not too heavy, the building appears from a distance as a lovely architectural expression of man's dedication to higher inspirations and ideals. The lovely, almost poetic, name popularly applied to this noble structure is Hyperion Outfall, suggesting it may be a monument to America's most treasured dream for a better, more beautiful world.

But alas, Hyperion Outfall is the central sewage disposal plant for the City of Los Angeles. Inside the graceful structure are powerful, though invisible, pumps which transport via huge aqueduct pipes the collected excrement of three million people, depositing the liquid sewage five miles out in the blue Pacific and the solid sewage seven miles out into the mouth of the very deep Santa Monica Canyon.

The number of words that describe various natural phenomena are often displays of what a particular culture considers significant. The Eskimo, for example, has roughly twenty words in his vocabulary that describe different types of snow, while in English there is only one.

Other languages, especially the Latin, are rich in popular words for shit, feces, caca, or what have you. In Spanish, for example, there are at least two dozen popular—mostly quite humorous—words that seek to describe excrement of various consistencies. Yet in modern English there are only two popular words for excrement—*shit* and *crap*—both vulgar, abrupt, hard four-letter words of profane rejection. Of course, one can always use the Latin medical euphemism for excrement and call it *feces*, or revert to baby talk and call it *caca*.

Though human excrement is often the subject of gut-level humor in Spanish, Portuguese, and French folklore, Americans take their shit most seriously, hiding and camouflaging this simplest of all human functions as though some repulsive form of criminal behavior might be involved.

Soft Is Best

Even toilet paper is sold on the basis of how the soft roll squeezes, rather than how well the paper wipes. There is never the slightest suggestion in these ads as to the real use of toilet paper. A viewer might justifiably conclude that toilet paper is used for some other function than merely cleansing one's anus.

Delsey or Scott commercials even seem to propose some new form of predigested food carefully wrapped and sealed in plastic. Few foods are packed so hygienically. Subliminally, the ads are selling soft, clean bowel movements—implanting a symbolic projection where good, soft toilet paper substitutes for good, soft feces. Mr. Whipple, the supermarket manager who protects the Charmin tissue from being squeezed, is an anal stereotype. The TV audience will know he uses laxatives along with Charmin to maintain regularity.

Even a cursory review of national magazine and television

details clearly how clean products are huckstered via the anal-erotic tendencies and fixations of the American consumer. The messages are devastatingly simple: Get rid of all that dirty, unsightly shit, both inside and outside—even if you can't actually see it. Remember that dirt, germs, bacteria, stains are always there waiting to get at you! Don't let it touch you or your loved ones. Scrub, spray, mop, wax, polish, disinfect, etc. Be safe, be Clean! A plethora of products compete dynamically for the privilege of guarding Americans from this filthy, unsightly, contaminated pollution.

Once the Clean Syndrome is well established in a culture it will persist generation after generation if reinforced by media. Passed on from parent to children, it is inherited almost like a genetic mutation and capable of similar long-term effects upon life. This is apparent in market research where large numbers of women as well as men continue to purchase brands of cleaning products preferred by their mothers or fathers.

Some writers have compared the American preoccupation with *clean* to a religious movement whose parish priests include Mr. Clean, the head-shaved symbol of dominant sexuality; an armor-clad, ghostlike apparition described as the White Knight, who charges about the neighborhood with his lance straight and erect; and the omniscient, muscled giant who materializes from walls or ceiling with a dome-topped, cylindrical spray can in his hand, introducing himself to the awed housewife as Big Wally. New priests of Clean are introduced every year or so by corporations who have built vast empires through ads for air fresheners, toilet bowl cleaners, toilet paper, laxatives, and acid-indigestion remedies.

Clogged Sexuality

The *Liquid-Plumr* TV production is a thirty-second fantasy trip into the world of symbolic open bowels and unclogged sexuality, finally leading to the ultimate state of Clean. An opening scene portrays the ever-searching American housewife beneath her sink, exploring for germs and contamination. As her eyes gaze fondly and longingly at the stiff, upright drain pipe, an expression of euphoric affection and admiration spreads across her face (see figure 28). But the background music strikes an ominous chord: all is not well back up in the sink. With the bowl (or bowel?) half full of dirty, foamy, repulsive water, the drain is clogged.

Liquid-Plumr, in the long cylindrical phallic container with the domed top, is caressingly held in the housewife's delicate fingers as she confidently pours the life-giving fluid into the wastes and impurities that float disgustingly in her sacred sink. LP goes to work instantly.

The ad's final scene is a triumph, an epic, a heroic masterpiece, as all impure thoughts together with unclean sources of contamination are sucked deeply down the drain, out of the sink and out of sight, leaving behind a sparkling pure kitchen—the housewife's throne room.

The four-second sink draining segment of the thirty-second commercial was videotaped and replayed a frame at a time. There are 72 frames per second in videotape compared with 24 in film. As the contamination began to swirl slowly around the drain, almost as if God had willed it, a large letter "S" appeared in the water (see Figure 29).

Then, as the drain further uncloged and the water rapidly bubbled down through the pipe, an "E" (the letter is brown) appeared floating agitatedly upon the bubbling filth (Figure 30). Finally, as the last of the ugly mess sucked its way down the drain, the letter "X" appeared over the drain opening (Figure 31). The entire subliminal sequence happened in roughly four seconds and is completely invisible to the conscious eye. The SEX, nevertheless, was recorded in the unconscious perceptual systems of millions of viewers instantly.

As an added subliminal feature, a face appeared on the bubble just above the final "X." Though the eyes are slighly offset, the nose and tooth-filled smiling mouth was readily apparent. The bubble face, above the "X," formed the ancient skull-and-crossbones symbol of death.

In the commercial's final scene, (Figure 32) the phallic LP container rested triumphantly in a bouquet of flowers (symbolic of the reproductive organs) and sparkling clean plumbing (symbolic of clean bowels). In this final placid, relaxed scene, Liquid-Plumr posed victoriously on the sink. To the left of the "L" in Liquid, above and left of the red band on the bottle, is the letter "E," which forms the center of a SEX mosaic The letter "S" appears to the left of the "E." The letter "X" appears on the white bottle to the left of the blue seal and just above the red band. Another "X" appears in the shadows below the "E."

The LP commercial was played at full speed for over a hundred test subjects. Even though they knew the SEX was embedded in the film, only about one third could consciously perceive the "S" after the second or third viewing. The other letters were completely invisible to conscious perception.

The next time you view a floor, window, or table wiped or mopped on television, or something being poured, watch the filmy surfaces carefully. You are probably being subed. Also watch the strained body-language positions from which the housewife models mop their floors. Appliances, brooms and mop handles usually point toward genital areas. Often the model has twisted her posture into an absurd contortion to achieve an appropriate genital relationship with her kitchen equipment.

Free-Flowing Media

The sound track was recorded from a recent TV Drāno commercial. In the story line, two sinks and two struggling housewives are heard. One woman, of course, clears her stopped-up sink with Drāno; her voice is bright, sparkling, happy, triumphant. The hapless woman using the "other" brand, however, could not free her stopped-up sink. She spoke in a low, strained, guttural, almost painful voice. When the audio portion of the commercial was replayed several times without video, the second woman's voice unquestionably portrayed a woman straining unsuccessfully to evacuate (an admitted euphemism).

In a clever application of subliminal anality to food advertising, one ten-second radio commercial for a dairy association was classic. The announcer's smooth, low, sexual voice instructed the listener to "take a minute, have a beautiful experience, pour yourself a cool, pure, fresh glass of milk. . . ." As the deep voice droned sensuously on with the soft, warm sell, liquid was heard swirling in the background while the voice described the appearance of milk and how it makes your life more meaningful (i.e., sex life). When isolated and magnified, the pleasant, swirling sound of liquid presumably being poured appeared to be the recorded sound of a toilet being flushed. The subliminal logic—if it can be called logic—of the commercial is that milk will loosen up those tight bowels.

Be Clean With Vaseline

Vaseline, today in America, has an almost archetypal symbolic significance as a vaginal and anal lubricant. The product has been a part of American folklore for over half a century in the form of several hundred obscene jokes.

Vaseline Intensive Care Cream, an intensively advertised product, reaches into millions of American homes. The concept of "Intensive Care," however, is never really explained on the label or in the advertising.

Except for certain dermatological situations that involve very minute portions of the population, human skin does not really require intensive care, nor would it benefit even if such care were available. The phrase was purloined from hospital parlance and describes care for critically ill patients. The phrase means to be taken care of, naturally, but also implies placing oneself under intensive management and control.

Vaseline Cream is a multisensory product: visual, olfactory, and tactile. From the label and advertising (see Figure 33), the cream's visual and conscious image involves protection against "chapped, irritated, rough, dry skin."

The cream is, the claim implies, so protective that water or other solutions will not rinse the substance off. The hands are symbolically sealed off from the threat of contamination and damage. But the source of all this danger is left unclear. Attempting to explain the motivating power behind the product's merchandising technique just does not make sense in terms of any factual reality.

The subliminal implications in Vaseline Cream go much, much deeper than merely chapped hands. Visually, VC appears to have a viscosity, texture, and color similar to that of seminal fluid.

Readers can visually examine the cream in the palms of

their hands. The symbolic parallel is instantly obvious. The tactile experience of VC communicates a feeling of smoothness, again not unlike the texture of seminal fluid. But after rubbing several seconds, the oily feeling disappears and the lotion develops a dry, moderately sticky sensation before it disappears. Rubbing seminal fluid into the skin produces a very similar feeling and experience.

The tactile illusion presented, of course, is that the cream was absorbed by the skin—an illusion that is pure nonsense since the cream merely evaporates. Nevertheless, in terms of the visual and tactile illusion, Vaseline Cream appears to have vanished into the skin, forming a protective fantasy barrier against contamination.

The aromatics of Vaseline Cream are also revealing. The smell is sweet, light, with a subtle touch of lemon. The container's light yellowish color visually reinforces the aromatic experience of lemon. The multisensory appeal of the symbolic product is thoroughly integrated. In consumer aromatic tests, the flat, acid smell of lemon is often identified with seminal fluid. When you recall the enormous variety of viscous, lemon-smelling cosmetic and soap products merchandised today, it appears that seminal fluid has become as symbolically important to our modern economy as it used to be for human reproduction. Olfactory symbols may be even more powerful at the subliminal level than the visual.

The Seminal Cosmetic

Discovery of reproductive sperm in seminal fluid was a quite recent event in human history—perhaps two centuries ago at the most. The history of man's symbolic relationship with seminal fluid, however, is packed with incredible confusion, awe, wonder, superstition, and fantasy. Even in some societies today, the fluid is believed to have magical, supernatural powers to prolong youth, fertility, beauty, and sexual desirability. Wealthy medieval and Renaissance women employed alchemists to collect the fluid for use as a cosmetic. Seminal fluid, sometimes scented, was once applied lavishly to women's bodies and faces as a fertility ritual.

The sperm whale was hunted for centuries primarily for

what appeared to be its seminal secretions which were used in expensive cosmetics and perfumed products. It is curious how, when the whaling industry is discussed, this tradition is today repressed—certainly not a suitable subject for conversation among polite, educated people. The most valued portion of the whale was traditionally spermaceti, not blubber. This seminal tradition, though thoroughly repressed from consciousness, is very much alive today in modern cosmetic products such as Vaseline Cream, tubed and bottled shampoos and soaps, liquid cleaners, face creams, treatments, etc.

In Herman Melville's *Moby Dick*—perhaps the greatest of all whaling stories and literary probes of the American psyche—the author played with the archetypal meanings of sperm or seminal fluid when he wrote in Ishmael's final vision of love:

> *As I bathed my hands among the soft, gentle globules of infiltrated tissue . . . as they richly broke to my fingers . . . as I snuffed up that uncontaminated aroma . . . I forgot all about our horrible oath; in that inexpressible sperm, I washed my hands and heart of it . . . I felt divinely free from all ill will or petulance, or malice of any sort whatever. . . .*

In symbolic sperm, therefore, Ishmael cleansed himself of the contaminations of evil. He calls upon the entire world to unite in love:

> *. . . nay, let us all squeeze ourselves into each other; let us squeeze ourselves universally into the very milk and sperm of kindness.*

Melville's humor was not at its most subtle when he alluded to "the angels of paradise, each with his hands in a jar of spermaceti."

Subliminal Pets Are Different

In the *Ladies' Home Journal*, read by upper-middle-class, middle-aged housewives, an ad portrait of a jar of VC is held suspended between a woman's thumbs and middle fingers—highly significant parts of the female hand in many ad illustrations (Figure 33). Every woman who has ever lived knows, at both conscious and unconscious levels, how these fingers are used in masturbation or in caressing the vulva and clitoris. The symbolism would certainly qualify as a universal archetype.

To assure the message does not become confused or remain ambiguous within the reader's unconscious, the hands, jar, and blue background are covered with mosaics of embedded SEXes. A large, obvious SEX is embedded horizontally at the top and to the left of the stream of water directly above the right middle finger when the more or less than thin straight line of water crosses the wider splash. The "E" is, perhaps, the most obvious letter. The "X" is within and at the top of the water stream. The "S"—a large capital letter—is to the left of the "E." There are at least a dozen SEXes hidden in the water-splashed blue area above the hands.

The concept, often experienced in dreams, of "saved from the waters" (as it is designed into the Vaseline ad) symbolizes fertility and is a metaphorical image of childbirth. Water, remember, washes away original sin in baptismal rituals as well as in shower, soap, or Vaseline advertising. Water, when portrayed as drops, splashes, or running streaks, can also be symbolic of ejaculation. The closed jar is also an important symbol, representing the woman, the womb, and when the jar is full, virginity.

The Vaseline ad's basic symbolism—fingers, water, jar, and embedded SEXes—should easily sell thousands of gallons of cream. But there is more, much more (see Figure 34).

Hidden in the water, just below the top margin, to the left of center, is the rather large head of a cocker spaniel. Just to the left and below the cocker's right ear is the head of a cow—something like the cow's profile on the Pet canned milk label (a canned milk brand, incidentally, used primarily in infant's formulas). Below the cow's profile is another dog's head—possibly a fox terrier or beagle. The head is tilted, the eyes looking at the reader with love and longing. A wild dog is symbolic of a dreaded father, a domesticated dog a beloved father. The cow, of course, is an obvious symbol for mother.

A careful study of the blue area above the jar reveals several faces embedded in the flowing water. The faces could be human, even though the representations are as grotesque as something out of a nightmare. These faces may appeal to some bizarre sodomistic sexual fantasy believed common, by the advertiser, to women.

In the spray on top of the jar—directly above the "S" in "Vaseline" on the label—is a white bird with wings outstretched, as though frolicking in a subliminal bird bath. Birds have often symbolized the female genitals or vagina. A white bird, of course, would specifically represent purity or cleanliness. The 1960s euphemism "bird," meaning a young girl, is symbolically quite meaningful. The white bird—perhaps a pigeon or dove—is also symbolic of the soul, spirituality and, according to Carl Jung, the power of sublimation. The flying bird symbolizes release from sexual fear or inhibition.

Animals, generally, appear to play important roles in the human unconscious. The anthropomorphism (giving human attributes to animals) of animated cartoons, children's fairy and folk stories, and in such things as Halloween costumes and masks is highly meaningful.

Nothing appears to have been overlooked by this most profitable industry which is dedicated to making America the cleanest nation on earth.

6

That Clean,
Odorless Smell

*Olfactory [odor] sensations
awake vague and half-
understood perceptions, which
are accompanied by very strong
emotions.*

P. FRIEDMAN
Observations on the Sense of Smell

Smelling Is Big Business

International Flavors and Fragrances, Inc., a mammoth New York-based international corporation, is in the business of managing sensory experience for millions of individuals throughout the world. In their laboratories are roughly 60,-000 fragrances (smells) and 20,000 flavors. IFF candidly brags that its business is sex and hunger—the two drives most basic to human survival over the past million years or so of human evolution. Many of their smells and flavors would be classifiable as subliminal as they are undectable at conscious levels.

IFF (perhaps the largest, but only one of many companies in the business) has annual sales in excess of $112 million. Their 1971 profit was $17 million. Sixty-eight percent of IFF products are sold outside the United States to customers that include the so-called French perfume industry. The corporation manufactures in fourteen countries and sells to over one hundred. IFF President Henry G. Walter, Jr., expects to be selling over $500 million worth of smells and tastes annually before 1980. Thirty percent of their current business is in flavor, while seventy percent involves aromatic chemicals.

Spending $11 million on behavior research in 1971, IFF had sponsored research at Masters and Johnson's Reproductive Biology Research Foundation where several years of intense study was devoted to the relationship between odors and sexual behavior. In the summer of 1972, IFF announced the discovery of a subliminal odor exuded by women during their monthly ovulation which they planned to synthesize and sell. The discovery itself was not startling. Most female mammals exude such odors though they are usually undetectable by other specie. The announcement originated through the IFF corporate offices and appeared in *Newsweek* and other publications. The subliminal chemical is by now probably already a part of food, food packaging, cosmetics, clothing, and what have you—invisible odor stimuli supplying purchase motivations for millions.

If aromatic and flavor enhancement resulted in an increased capacity for intimate human relationships, IFF might be considered one of mankind's great benefactors. This possibility, however, does not appear to be the case.

Nature's Way?

One of the current cosmetic claims is fascinating when looked at critically—the natural look, with its accompanying natural smell. It requires more cosmetics for a woman to achieve the natural look than it does to achieve the made-up look. In order to become natural, you must become more unnatural.

In one national TV commercial, Mother Nature is shown walking through a fruit market. She ignores, even snubs, the fresh piles of oranges, apples, grapefruits, cherries, pears, etc., selecting a can of Del Monte fruit cocktail as "the real thing" or as "nature's own flavor." Coca-Cola's recent product self-image makes the drink appear as a life necessity. Caramel-sugared soda water as "The Real Thing" might even be hilariously funny except that millions of consumers apparently respond to the nonsense.

To be natural in America, one must carefully avoid natural states of existence. In fact, part of the conditioned concept of Clean implies that natural odors are inherently evil, morally objectionable, and unhealthy. *Natural* odors, that is, not synthetic-natural odors. American advertising demands virtually everything in nature be deodorized—then reodorized by synthetic aromatics: pine for bathrooms and kitchens, leather for plastic upholstery, charcoal for steaks, etc. With the human body, the basis for "good" smells is either a synthetic chemical odor or a total absence of odor—produced by plugging the bodies' sweat glands with gluelike deodorants or by anesthetizing the nose's olfactory bulbs with sprays or volatile chemicals.

Aroma as Data

A brief review of animal experiments provides some insight into the significance of smelling to various species. Mammals living in water generally have poorly developed senses of smell. Fish, however, appear to both smell and taste with extraordinary sensitivity. Minnows and salmon, for example, distinguish by smell between males and females of their own species.

Canadian naturalist A. D. Hasler discovered that streams retain their own specific odors for years. Minnows retain these odors in their memories for several weeks after birth. Salmon and sea trout memories for odors related to reproduction are even more remarkable. High proportions of salmon return to stream locations where they hatched from distances of even thousands of miles after up to five years. In tests, roughly 2.5 percent (11,000 out of 470,000) of salmon survive their spawning migration, laying and fertilizing their eggs in exactly the same location in which they were hatched years earlier and then, of course, dying.

Salmon hatched in an inland stream were flown out to a connecting river from which they migrated to the sea. They returned to the exact stream in which they had been reared years later when they were ready to spawn, traveling a route they had never traveled before. The experiment suggested that olfactory memory traces may even be inherited genetically. These remarkable, though quite natural, memory feats appeared based entirely upon the fish's highly developed ability to remember specific odors.

Rats, as well, have highly developed abilities to differentiate odor. Guinea pigs have been shown to possess an olfactory acuity a thousand times or more greater than man's. Dogs communicate with each other through smell stimuli, primarily emanating from their mouths, noses, and genital areas. They have been demonstrated to have olfactory acuity (smell sensitivity) 1 million to 100 million times greater than man. Whereas man distinguishes only a few thousand smells, dogs can distinguish about half a million, easily distinguishing one individual human scent out of thousands. Experiments with tracking dogs suggest that each individual human has a completely unique body odor. Dogs can identify a stick touched by a specific human finger for only two seconds. Further, odorous liquids such as alcohol and strong-smelling oils applied to the hand or stick do not prevent dogs from correctly selecting the one individual scent for which they are searching.

Evolutionary theory suggests that the olfactory bulbs, which are believed to collect aromatic molecules from air as it is breathed, appear to have been the evolutionary origin of what—in the highest developed specie of life—we call the human brain.

The two halves of the brain appear to have originally been buds that evolved from the olfactory stalks. In the human foetus of six months and in adult lower animals, there are three pair of rhinencephalic nerve complexes (the smell portion of the brain). The relatively undeveloped human olfactory bulbs replace the foetus's highly developed bulbs and rhinencephalon (or smell brain). These highly developed bulbs and nerve structures completely disappear before birth. They exist only in the foetus as vestiges of our evolutionary predecessor's highly developed organs of smell.

Putting Smell in Its Sensory Perspective

Aristotle first defined the five senses of man over three hundred years before Christ. During the twentieth century, the list of senses was slowly extended to include nearly eight times Aristotle's original list and the discovery of additional human sensory inputs into the brain continues. These senses are all interrelated and interconnected. No portion of the brain appears isolated from other portions. The way food "tastes," for example, is partially determined by how it looks, smells, feels, etc., at both conscious and unconscious levels. At the conscious level, the multiple senses appear to operate with a fluctuating bias that continuously shifts from one sense to another while we taste, hear, feel, etc. This bias does not, however, shut off the momentarily unfavored senses, which still convey information to the brain.

Of all senses, smell appears to have the best memory. Virtually anyone perceiving an odor he had not perceived for ten years might very likely recognize the perception instantly, bringing to conscious awareness an avalanche of memories and emotional associations.

Studies of both primitive peoples and unsighted individuals suggest that their olfactory sensitivities are very highly developed. When individuals are forced to depend upon alternative senses, many develop astonishing powers. The sense of smell, of course, cannot be turned off in the way we close our eyes, rinse our mouths, or remove our fingers from an uncomfortable surface. In a way, smell turns itself *off* or *down*. Odor intensities diminish after prolonged exposure. This diminishing effect is often referred to as "olfactory fatigue." Virtually any human could comfortably live adjacent to a garbage dump or an open septic tank. Within a few days (or only hours for some individuals), the stench would not be considered objectionable and would soon pass unnoticed.

Smells just do not lend themselves to neat, clear, analytical measurements such as we have constructed for sound and light, though several classification systems are useful in perfumery or other olfactory production areas. A perfumer, for example, must have an intimate working knowledge of between six and eight thousand aromatic substances. Perhaps three thousand odors intermix to form a virtually endless number of possibilities. Futher, each mixture may vary—in the way it is perceived—in relation to sex, age, and physical condition. Heavy or light aromatic concentrations vary perceptual response, as well as such factors as temperature and humidity. Odor intensity increases, for example, as humidity decreases.

Large dung hills from a distance often smell strongly of musk—a pleasant, sexually stimulating aromatic. But at close range, the excremental stink is unbearable. Skunk aroma, for another example, is also a pleasant scent for many people if experienced at a distance.

Several general conclusions appear to emanate from the large collection of animal studies. The sense of smell is vital in food selection and in the avoidance of danger and enemies. And, perhaps most significantly, virtually all species—even those whose sense of smell does not appear highly developed—utilize odors as a basis for social and reproductive behavior.

Origins of Human Odor

There are two known types of sweat glands in the human body: *eccrine glands*, which emit an odorless fluid 99 percent water and 1 percent salt; and the *apocrine glands*, distributed over the body but concentrated in areas such as armpits, genitals, feet, hair, etc., which secrete a sticky, milky fluid that rapidly decomposes, becoming odorous.

Perspiration does not serve to rid the body of wastes. The some 3 million eccrine glands in each human appear to have one major function—the regulation of body temperature. Eccrine sweating, however, can also occur from emotional arousal when the body is not actually overheated.

The infinitesimally smaller number of apocrine glands, on the other hand, are activated only by emotion. Men and women produce about the same quantity of apocrine secretion and odor, though there are subtle differences (sometimes not so subtle) in the odor produced by each individual. The apocrine glands in different parts of the body also produce different odors.

Experimenters have demonstrated that tracking dogs follow

human scents that diffuse through footwear. Man, like many mammals, has heavy concentrations of apocrine scent glands on the feet. In a tracking situation, of course, persons under emotional strain perspire more than they would normally.

Apocrine-gland-produced solutions serve to communicate emotional states from individual to individual. And throughout evolution this system of odor communication appears to have had considerable survival value for man.

Sexually mature humans have body odors quite distinct from the immature. Odors are basic to the relationship between child and mother. Heavy concentration of apocrine glands in the mother's nipples strongly stimulates the child in sucking and attachment behavior. Infants can identify their mother's breast and genital odors during their first few weeks of life. Naturalist Charles Darwin collected evidence that odors sensed by infants are capable of producing changes in heart rate and respiration. Three groups of individuals will place any object within reach into their mouths in response to smell stimuli—lobectomized monkeys, healthy infants, and schizophrenics regressed to early childhood.

When a small child thumbsucks while holding on to a baby blanket, the blanket must smell of human odors. Children carefully examine their blankets for a portion with a tranquilizing human smell. Most small children will reject a newly cleaned blanket.

Male silkworms can scent a mate as far as seven miles away. Females of the species, however, are odor-blind to their own powerful aromatic. Females of virtually all species, including humans, appear unaware that their bodies produce powerful, natural, olfactory sexual stimulants.

Physicians often utilize body odor as a basis for medical diagnosis. Many verified cases have been recorded where doctors detected the approach of death through odors, even when pulse, temperature, and patient feelings were not unfavorable. Patients with acidosis and uremia have quite distinctive odors. The odor of leukemia patients has been described as similar to that of "a freshly opened corpse." Chronic schizophrenic patients emit a sweetish odor.

One most curious phenomenon, observed by many scientists, is that sensitivity to smell is often much greater or much less in the United States than in other areas of the world.

Odors appear much more extreme in the U.S. Again, the specific causes are unknown, though they do not appear to involve such things as temperature and humidity.

Odor Sensitivity

In adult human females, apocrine glands concentrate around the breast nipples and genitals, and secrete butyric acid—an odorant also found in butter and feces. Freud was not the first to recognize that aromatics from hair, feces, and blood have sexually exciting effects upon both male and female children and adults. Recall the *Playboy* cover (Figure 5) where the disguised little boy sits with his head near his mother's genital area, a pose frequently observable with male children.

Conscious sensitivity to smells increases with age until roughly the sixth year, and appears stronger among girls than boys. Odor sensitivity greatly diminishes in old age (seventy-five and above), but females remain more sensitive than males in old age as in childhood. Usually, however, by the fourth or fifth year, initiation of the Oedipal conflict produces repression of body and other odors associated with the mother. It is an almost universal experience to repress memories of odors related to parental intercourse. Odors heavily charged with sexual implications appear the most completely repressed at each level of psychosexual development.

Asthmatics are usually hypersensitive to smells. One major theory of asthma suggests such attacks are defenses against odors that reactivate conflicts that originated in the anal phase of childhood—between the first and third years.

Odors are also known to play a potent emotional role in fetishism. The fetish is often selected because of its odor, usually anal or genital in origin. All this may suggest a theory to explain at least part of the American preoccupation with suppressing and repressing body odors.

Breast worship via such manipulative media as *Playboy*—and the media induced control or abolition of female body and genital odors—appear as attempts to erase, avoid, or camouflage conscious memories from the early maternal relationship in the interest of commercial product merchandising.

Among the thousands of odors recognized and described by man, perhaps the single most powerful odor known is that of musk. Musk odor, which both consciously and subliminally affects humans, was originally found in the anal glands of the civet cat and musk deer. The odor is detectable by man in quantities as small as .000,000,000,000,032 of an ounce and appears to have aphrodisiac effects upon both animals and humans. Musk odor was later discovered in many plants, more than twenty animal species, birds, mammals, molluscs, reptiles, at least one insect, and is encountered in synthetic chemicals from six or more classes. Musk, of course, is used in many food and cosmetic preparations. Natural musk odor extracts can be detected only by humans who have the animal hormone estrogen in their blood, excluding children and older adults. Perceptual defenses against sexually oriented pleasure through smelling are media encouraged to continue throughout life as a corollary of consumer conditioning. These defenses may take the form of repression as in the conscious unawareness of certain odors, by denial through the use of deodorants, antiperspirants, smell deadeners (anesthesias), or by camouflage—masking with perfumes, colognes, etc.

Cultures Smell Differently

People's personal odors also vary in relation to their culture. Diet may have something to do with the observable differences, but causes are still uncertain.

A Japanese writer, Adachi, observed that Europeans appeared unaware of their characteristic pungent and rancid odors. European children and old people, he observed, were almost free of the repulsive odor, but he found it especially strong in women. Asiatics seldom have this strong, pungent body odor which originates primarily in the armpits. Japanese young men found to have armpit odor were once exempted from military service. Over the past several centuries, many French writers have alluded to the "odor of the English," which some describe as "most persistent and long-lasting."

Of course, much of human perception, what we take for reality from our sensory inputs, is culture-bound. As the senses and brain appear to perceive the totality of what is going on around an individual, culture will determine what is consciously perceived and, likewise, excluded from consciousness—what is designated significant and irrelevant.

Most humans seem to prefer floral and fruity odors and dislike odors of putrefaction, though agreement is by no means universal. Many individuals thoroughly enjoy odors of decay in meat and cheese. But what smells "good" among one people may be considered "bad" among another.

It is doubtful that modern, synthetically reprogrammed man could ever completely comprehend the aromatic preferences of primitive man. Anthropologist Claude Levi-Strauss recorded that Amazonian Indians are particularly susceptible to the natural smells of the human body which civilized man suppresses or camouflages.

In one Urubu tribal myth, Levi-Strauss recorded that God created woman after smelling a rotten fruit full of worms. In the Tacana tribe, a mythological jaguar decided not to rape a woman after perceiving the smell of her vulva which seemed to him to reek of worm-ridden meat—which is, incidentally, an Urubu delicacy. A Mundurucú tribal myth explained that after animals had made vaginas for the first women, the armadillo rubbed each organ with a piece of rotten nut, another dietary delicacy.

These Brazilian Indians appeared to find female odors a source of what could be called affectionate humor. And these putrefaction odors were considered sexually stimulating and not at all "bad." It is even doubtful these primitive peoples (who have survived centuries in environments that would destroy civilized man within days) would find a woman desirable whose vulva was odorless.

The entire rich spectrum of human odor has long been a cherished and meaningful human experience. In the Song of Solomon (7:8) the poet wrote, "Oh, may the scent of your breath be like apples." The scent of natural apples would today most likely be found objectionable, and it would be masked by Binaca, Listerine, Dentine, or Wrigley's. Psalm 115:6 explains why one God is supreme while the many idols are fraudulent: the idols "have ears, but do not hear; noses, but do not smell."

In one of history's most famous love letters, Napoleon

wrote his beautiful Empress Josephine, "See you next Thursday. Please don't bathe in the meantime!"

Prior to World War II, deodorants were strictly women's products. There was only one major brand in the limited market—Mum, a symbolically significant brand name. Mum (Mother, of course) was the one who trained her children in infancy to handle their body excretions. In the finest tradition of anal management and control, Mum could now be with the American woman throughout life—always available to protect her from the evils of perspiration.

During World War II, I recall two soldiers, bunking at one end of an Army Air Force barracks, who were discovered using Mum. These soldiers were, because of their concealed jars of Mum, seriously suspected of being homosexuals. At the time, no one knew that a new world of odor fantasy had been initiated. All that was needed for the chemical companies to change our lives was time and heavy advertising budgets.

The Education in Cleanliness

Pupilometer and Mackworth are two-camera devices which photograph the eye track across a picture or scene as well as the increase or decrease in the size of the pupil in response to what the eye perceives. Studies with them have shown primary focal points in a TV scene are invariably mouths, noses, and eyes (in that order).

As a child (or anyone else) follows the slick continuity of a 30-second commercial, their emotional involvement appears far more intense as they view reaction shots (facial expressions which respond to the action portrayed) than when they are viewing the actual objects or actions portrayed. In other words, Kitty's reaction to something said or done by Matt Dillon creates a much stronger level of emotional involvement within the viewer than does Matt's action itself. (For comparison, note that most cartoons show not merely "funny" behavior, but a character reacting to these events. An on-stage observer somehow is needed to make the joke amusing to an audience.)

In a commercial, an actor's facial reaction to a bad smell projects the smell into the viewer's living room with great emotional intensity rarely perceived at the conscious level by the audience. When an actor's facial expression in a reaction shot portrays annoyance, disgust, rejection, or pity toward someone with—horror of horrors—body odor, the instantaneous subliminal effect upon viewers is to program their unconscious with a virtual post-hypnotic suggestion for them to react similarly in similar situations. A similar real-life reaction effect, of course, occurs as mothers change diapers or attend the child's needs during infancy.

Likewise, when we are incessantly told by ads, "Don't take chances with body odor!" the conscious fear of body odor is being emphasized as some mysterious danger which threatens our social survival. Constant repetition of the theme will act upon the unconscious much in the same way as would a post-hypnotic suggestion. We will soon, under such a symbolic barrage, become sensitive to others who take chances with body odor. And, though we cannot consciously smell our own bodies (a frustrating problem of body image well understood by the chemical companies), the mere thought of taking such a chance will strike terror deep into the staunchest American heart.

In effect, smell advertising has actually created a widespread sensitivity to body odor. As far as "objectionable" body odors are concerned, *apocrine* secretions require twelve or more hours to produce heavy decomposition odors—depending upon the body's emotional experience during the period.

Media reinforcement or conditioning is not insignificant for American children between two and six who receive an average of fifty-five hours weekly of television—much of it saturated with advertising for cleanliness or hygiene products aimed at their mothers. It is estimated that an average North American child spends about 11,000 hours in classrooms through grammar, junior high, and senior high schools. During this same period, however, the child will receive over 25,000 hours of TV loaded with subliminal sell techniques.

"Ban takes the worry out of being close," announces their advertising. The statement also initiates or reinforces worry about being close. It might never have occurred to us that we *had* anything to worry about in being close until several million dollars' worth of subliminally loaded advertising has hammered the fear into our unconsciouses.

Deodorants that kill or inhibit bacteria can prevent this odor by not permitting the apocrine fluid to decompose. Antiperspirants, which seal off both types of sweat glands, simply remove the warm moist skin surface where bacteria can multiply. Antiperspirants are merely gluelike chemicals that paste up the sweat gland pores. Odorous perspiration is thus contained in the body. In physiological terms the chemical sealer is probably harmless to most people—though a persistent minority react with allergic reactions or recurrent irritations and infections. Roughly 85 percent of American adults use some form of chemical odor suppressant.

Deodorants as Necessities

According to most medical authorities, a shower once, or possibly twice daily will be entirely adequate to control body odors in a healthy human without recourse to chemical suppressants. But any reader who doubts that deodorants are a necessity to the American life-style is challenged to conduct a simple experiment. Spend a week of your life without deodorants of any type.

A group of volunteer students agreed to stop using deodorants for a week and record their daily reactions. Over half dropped out of the experiment by the third day. They simply couldn't take it. The students admitted to fears of getting close to anyone. All felt very conscious of a sensitivity toward other people's body odors. Throughout their experience, they were "up-tight," "anxious," "apprehensive," "worried," "afraid," "self-conscious," etc., over being rejected by others because of their body odor.

This was, indeed, strange, for each member of the experiment bathed carefully twice daily, in the morning and in the evening. In reality, their bodies were quite clean—soap-and-water clean, that is, but not psychological-fantasy clean. Bristol-Myers, makers of Ban, have actually referred to human perspiration as "obscene," pointing out that people become upset over the sight of a wet armpit—either their own or someone else's. Once you have had it explained by a high

91

credibility source, the thought of a wet armpit is, in itself, provocation for many to break into a cold sweat.

More than mere perspiration is hidden by deodorants or antiperspirants: the elimination of body odor actually hides our emotional responses from the perception of others, a sure way to avoid letting others know how we feel.

God's Most Grievous Error

The battle of body odor and unwanted hair, fought diligently these past forty years by chemical and razor-blade companies, has been won in America. American women, with the enthusiastic support of their men, today react nauseously, or uncomfortably at least, even to a discussion of armpit or leg hair.

It is not unreasonable to assume that body hair, like all biological entitites, serves some useful function. Evolution has been quite severe in eliminating unnecessary appendages both inside and outside the human body. Neuron endings, within the skin, are unique in areas covered by hair. Haired skin has high concentrations of Krause genital and Iggo corpuscle nerve receptors. The latter, located between hairs, are so sensitive they respond to pressures less than one thousandth of an ounce—about the weight of a mosquito.

Hair, especially underarm hair, persisted throughout evolution as a device for retaining body aromatics related to social and reproductive communication. Hair provides a retention device to hold the aromatics produced by apocrine glands. This may also be the function of leg hair.

Most of the world's women do not shave or use chemical hair removers. Even if they could afford expensive hair-removal products, most women would have a difficult time convincing their men to accept their hairless bodies.

Several years ago, a major razor-blade company probed Latin American women's resistance to body shaving or hair removal. The enormity of ad budgets, the intensity of media saturation, and the creative insights of the most talented writers and artists—after years of trying—had been generally unsuccessful in converting Latin American women into body hair neurotics willing to regularly endure the cuts and burns necessary in order to become "clean." This situation, of course, seriously limited the company's sales and profits. Several thousand consumer interviews began to produce data with unsuspected implications. Hair, in Latin America, has much to do with ethnic identity.

Indians, as is true of many Asiatic peoples, have very little body hair. Indian men usually have light beards. And Indian women's bodies are quite lightly haired.

Many Latin Americans still consider the Indian inferior. One's degree of *sangre español* (Spanish blood)—the degree of white ancestry any individual possesses genetically—is an important cultural consideration in mating games, social acceptance, and economic opportunities. Many Latin American women displayed their *sangre español* via the hair on their legs. In ranking ethnic or racial physical determinants among Latin Americans, hair was most important, facial features secondary, and skin color of much less significance.

At last contact, marketing specialists were hard at work on a way to convince Latin Americans that body hair removal was the "natural" way to determine white ancestry or *sangre español*. It is only a matter of time and advertising media pressure until Latin Americans become culture-trained to perform daily hair-removal rituals in the service of corporate profits.

It might be easy to conclude that maybe all this sexual manipulation is a good thing, considering the already dangerous overpopulation of the world. Sexual behavior, however, involves human emotional health as well as biological reproduction. No one, however, least of all the corporations that have milked millions out of managing America's odors (the United States deodorant market exceeded $3 billion in 1974) has ever considered the consequences of long-term changes in social and reproductive behavior.

Odorlessness—the Real Thing?

Air or space deodorants are another technique of culturally managing America's ability to perceive odor. Most of the spray or evaporative air deodorants contain a chemical preservative such as phenol or formaldehyde, volatile chemicals that do not in any way remove odors from the air. They simply anesthetize human olfactory bulbs. Lysol's curious advertising claims provide an insight into the sterile aromatic environment modern Americans have built for themselves:

"Destroys household germs and odor-causing bacteria. Prevents mildew and mold. Deodorizes and disinfects garbage cans, diaper pails, toilet areas, under sinks, nurseries, sickrooms, basements, musty corners, and other places where odor-causing germs are a problem.

"To eliminate cooking, smoke, tobacco, bathroom, and other unpleasant household odors ... Leaves a clean, fresh scent. Antigerm actions lasts for days."

Even in an antiseptic operating room environment, germs are reduced, perhaps, but not entirely eliminated. Nor, in the interest of health and resistance to infections, is it *desirable* to eliminate germs, bacteria, molds, mildew, and other microorganisms that permeate our atmosphere. These organisms are very necessary to human survival.

Uncomfortable though the thought may be, the human digestive tract is loaded with bacteria, germs, and the like—extremely necessary to human health and digestive processes. The assortment of odors that Lysol advertising claims to destroy or eliminate might include some which are vital to emotional as well as physiological health.

Lysol, of course, does not eliminate odors, only an individual's ability to perceive them. Lysol contains phenol, a cell preservative. Enough Lysol in the air will kill or anesthetize cells in the olfactory bulbs and prevent anyone from smelling anything.

Smell dullers or anesthesias involve a large assortment of chemicals—including gasoline, ether, camphor, oil of cloves, and ammonia. Ether and oil of cloves are common scents used in colognes, aftershave lotions, and other cosmetics. The effect of the highly advertised Old Spice cologne aromatic is a reduction in smell sensitivity or olfactory acuity—so that all odors but its own are blotted out for the user.

Ammonia, presently in wide use as an ingredient of household soap, is also claimed to have extraordinary cleansing powers. Nonsense! Ammonia is a deadly poison and in the very minute quantities used in household cleansers, ammonia's primary purpose is to make the product smell clean by anesthetizing the consumer's olfactory bulbs. Just one whiff of ammonia reduces olfactory acuity by 50 percent for as long as twenty-four hours.

Another antismell product goes even further. Nilodor claims that "if you can smell it, you've used too much." A strong olfactory anesthetic, Nilodor doesn't even include a strong antiseptic smell to camouflage odor molecules that leak through the partially anesthetized olfactory bulbs, as with Lysol. Nilodor extends its advertising claims to include the odor control of such objects of aromatic horrors as "kitty toilet boxes."

These smell-dullers, or so-called space deodorants, have been banned by the Federal Aviation Agency from the flight decks of commercial aircraft as they inhibit the pilot's ability to perceive the plane's odors, which can often warn him of developing danger. Applying an anesthetic to the human smell machinery will, of course, influence all the other senses and their ability to perceive the world around an individual. Flavor, an obvious example, is inextricably connected with smells, as are the other senses. Foods or drinks taste much differently in a room sprayed with formaldehyde.

As a large portion of North America's population has lived in a chemically induced state of bulbectomization or olfactory anesthesia for several generations, it is somewhat unnerving to review the behavior of laboratory animals after their sense of smell was removed through an operation called olfactory bulbectomy—removal of the two smell bulbs.

Bulbectomized gerbils, for example, became docile and refused to fraternize, copulate, or display any kind of aggression, even when attacked by other gerbils. The gerbils' territorial exploration and mating behavior were completely eliminated. Rats, after bulbectomies, sharply reduced their copulatory behavior. Learning behavior also virtually ceased, and female rats became highly emotional.

Some rats kill mice on sight; others do not. After bulbectomizing both killer and nonkiller rats, nonkillers became killers.

In both nursing and virgin female mice, maternal behavior was eliminated. In fact, all eighteen of the nursing female mice studied ate their young after bulbectomies. Sexual behavior in both male mice and golden hamsters was totally eliminated after bulbectomies.

Many qualifications were placed upon the findings from the bulbectomy experiments. Results appeared consistent in one species, but reversed themselves in another.

Nevertheless, one specific conclusion was most abundantly clear—*social and reproductive behavior in all the test animals were severely upset by removing their sense of smell.* Readers should carefully weigh the obvious conclusion: By reducing the American aromatic environment to a flat level of barely perceptible or imperceptible smells, the full, natural range of human sensory experience and the subtle—though important—nuances of olfactory communication are severely inhibited.

Unless further research proves otherwise, it seems likely that bulbectomy or olfactory anesthesia will induce (or may have already induced) major changes in human social and reproductive (sexual) behavior. The Federal Food and Drug Administration, Federal Trade Commission, Federal Communications Commission, and the other agencies of government charged with protecting the public health have their hands full simply trying to keep profit-hungry corporations from chemically poisoning the population. As yet, no one has even remotely considered psychogenic damage.

Early No-Smell Conditioning

It would not be at all unreasonable to conclude that many millions of North Americans have little, if any, knowledge of what they or the natural environment smells like. In our society, babies are usually born into sterile, disinfected, deodorized hospitals. The baby's first breath in the delivery room is air well synthesized with artificial aromatics and smell-dullers. Even their mothers are carefully shaved, washed, and deodorized with hexachlorophene and other chemical antiseptics and deodorizers.

Once the baby is at home, the acculturation process begins in earnest. The baby is immersed in an environment of synthetic aromatics and smell-anesthetizers. Advertising-trained mothers, whose own mothers were advertising-trained must reject their child's natural smells. The advertising culture will not permit a mother to accept the natural scents of the child to which she gave birth. Fathers, of course, have been similarly brainwashed.

Under the adult's flow of baby talk and verbal adulation, a child will easily sense parental anger, frustration, or disapproval. Should a parent even slightly express disappointment, the child is quite likely to perceive the negative reaction. And, it is impossible for such odor-trained adults to avoid negative reactions.

Many observers have pointed out that children under five in America find sweat, fecal, and urinary aromas quite pleasant and appealing. After five years, however, they appear to succumb to cultural conditioning and react negatively to aromas, which they have been conditioned to fear as unclean.

Negative Self-Images

Body image is something each individual develops from birth. Children raised in the American Clean are indelibly imprinted with a negative view of themselves as producers of unpleasant odors. By capitalizing upon the created fear of what we cannot perceive with our unaided senses—germs, viruses, and bacteria, those invisible, omnipresent enemies always out there somewhere waiting for a chance to spring at us when we least expect an attack—a form of olfactory paranoia has been nourished.

This one giant step toward the dehumanization of mankind was taken years ago with everybody congratulating themselves upon how good their world smelled once it was rid of odor.

7

The Exorcist Massage Parlor

> *Necrophilia, the attraction to*
> *what is dead, decaying, lifeless,*
> *and purely mechanical, is*
> *increasing throughout our*
> *cybernetic industrial society.*
> *The Falangist motto, "Long live*
> *death," threatens to become*
> *the secret principle of a society*
> *in which the conquest of nature*
> *by the machine constitutes the*
> *very meaning of progress, and*
> *where the living person*
> *becomes an appendix to the*
> *machine.*

> ERICH FROMM
> *The Anatomy of Human Destructiveness*

Audience Priming

The Exorcist dramatically proved—if this needed proving—that the motion picture industry was not averse to making a fast buck with subliminal technology. Director William Friedkin maximized the return on the film's capital investment, reportedly in the neighborhood of $14 million, through a brilliant repertoire of visual and auditory subliminal innovations.

The Exorcist was not the first motion picture to use subliminal techniques. In 1957, the Precon Process and Equipment Corporation of New Orleans produced two experimental films heavily saturated with subliminal devices—*My World Dies Screaming* and *A Date with Death*. Neither film was ever publicly released. Friedkin must have used these films as a textbook.

The Exorcist audience was first primed or preconditioned for the subliminally induced emotional trip by the film's publicity: "*The Exorcist* is more than just a novel. A nightmare novel of demonic possession. See the movie! It's the most shocking thing that will ever happen to you!" warned Warner Brothers' promotional materials.

Preconditioning was apparent while audiences waited for the show to begin. Virtually everyone was on the edge of their seats. Conversations appeared nervous, laughter forced, and talk was often quite loud. Interviews indicated almost everyone had the same apprehensive thought, wondering how they would be affected by the film. When the lights finally dimmed and the curtain parted, the audience seemed to be holding their breaths in anticipation.

In technical terms, this priming experience is important to produce the most ideal perceptual conditions for subliminal stimuli. Yet, most of the priming publicity was absurd, the usual contrived nonsense—in this case overtly appealing to childlike fantasies of witches and evil forces. However, the public's reaction—as the film opened in major cities across the nation—*was* genuine. People really *did* faint in large numbers, many more became nauseous in varying degrees, a great many more had very disturbing nightmares. Several theater employees—in the theaters where interviews were taken—were actually placed under the care of physicians, and a few quit their jobs. Employees frequently had to clean up floors and rugs when nauseous patrons (mostly male, for some reason) did not quite make it to the rest rooms. In the several cities that were checked after the film had run several weeks, every major hospital receiving department had dealt with dozens of fainting, nausea, and hysteria cases. Hospital emergency room physicians reported patients who appeared to be both hallucinating and extremely distraught.

Nine psychiatrists in a midwestern city, who agreed to be interviewed, reported they had all counseled disturbed patients who displayed "hysteria" as a result of the movie, ranging from one to eighteen patients for each psychiatrist.

There is virtually no way cognitive or consciously perceived stimuli could have produced this intensity of emotional disturbance. Human perceptual defenses are very well organized and will protect individuals from most potentially disturbing experiences. Even the dramatic illusions of *Cinerama*, when first introduced some years ago, produced only mild nausea or dizziness among a small handful of theater patrons.

The Poetzle Effect

Out of fifty individuals in a test group who saw the movie, only three could recall subsequent dreams that in any way appeared related over several weeks after the screening. Dr. O. Poetzle, one of Freud's contemporaries, postulated in his Law of Exclusion that dream content was comprised of subliminal or unconsciously perceived experiences. He demonstrated that dream data was often transformed or disguised within a familiar setting, but the dream's "real" content was derived from subliminal rather than cognitive or conscious perceptions.

Around 1917, Poetzle developed his subliminal stimuli theories from studies utilizing tachistoscopic displays and hypnosis. He was the first scientist to demonstrate the apparently close relationship between subliminal stimuli and posthypnotic suggestion. The Poetzle Effect involves a delayed action, or as he called it, a "time clock" phenomenon. His studies revealed that subliminal perceptions could evoke dreams and actions days, even weeks, after the original percept.

When individuals perceive a subliminal stimuli in print or in television advertising, they are consciously unaware of the percept. These hidden devices usually involve taboo sex or death content which program some individuals for the delayed reaction. Several weeks later, these *sensitive* individuals will notice the brand label in a supermarket. This second conscious percept serves as a cue for action. Applying the Poetzle theorizations, a statistically significant proportion of consumers will purchase the product or dream about it after the second percept.

Several weeks after our test group had seen *The Exorcist*, photographic slides taken of the screen during the movie were shown.

Scenes included the actors' faces, staircases inside and outside the house, and the exorcism. The slide show lasted an hour, during which time several people left the room, reporting they had become nauseous. Almost the entire group reported severe depression after the showing. Many were openly annoyed at having to experience the slides. Comments included feelings of "agitation," "anger," "rage," "persecution," "fear," "extreme annoyance," "upset stomach," etc.

During the following week, well over half the group reported nightmares—unusual and vivid horror dreams clearly related to the movie. Many dreamed they were tortured and persecuted by the devil in one way or another. Several young women reported dreaming of sexual experiences involving the devil.

These effects were remarkable because this entire group had been involved with studies on subliminal phenomena for nearly two years. They generally knew how to discover and assess subliminal embeds and, at least from theory, understood the process and how it operated. Even so, it appeared they could not defend themselves from subliminal stimuli effects.

Media Psychopathology

The Toronto *Medical Post* reported, after *The Exorcist* had been shown for several weeks in that city, at least four young women had been confined for varying periods in a psychiatric hospital as a result of viewing the film. Subliminal induction techniques are capable of inducing various levels of depression and hysteria among some individuals. A majority of the film's audience would probably experience only momentary emotional unpleasantness. It might appear to some as even exciting. For a small minority, nevertheless, *The Exorcist* could indeed be threatening or even dangerous.

There is little psychological threat to an individual from anything consciously perceived. At the conscious level, humans can decide alternatives and rationalize their involvements in terms of morality, self interest, or conscious motives. The whole pornography issue, for example, is totally absurd. As long as an individual can decide consciously whether he will *accept*, *reject*, or *consider*, there is really no such thing as "harmful" information content.

Subliminal stimuli, on the other hand, are far more insidious and believed responsible for attitudinal frames of reference, moods, emotional predispositions, and residual value systems. There is no possibility of rational decision making or defense, since consciousness is bypassed completely.

One of the most dramatic visual subliminal stimulation techniques in *The Exorcist* featured full-screen tachistoscopic displays. Numerous times during the movie there was a sudden flash of light and the face of Father Karras momentarily appeared as a large, full-screen death mask apparition—the skin greasy white, the mouth a blood-red gash, the face surrounded by a white cowl or shroud.

Muriel Schwartz, owner of the Capitol Theatre in Dover, Delaware, refused to permit a public examination of the film, but "out of curiosity" agreed to check it out herself. She had a projectionist unwind the reels to Father Karras's dream sequence and discovered a subliminal cut. "The face was a ghostly white," she explained, "with red outlines around the eyes and mouth." One of her employees saw the cut as "the face of the devil." She said the subliminal cut consisted of two frames spliced into the film.

Warner Brothers, who produced the film, refused to comment about the subliminal cuts but admitted their existence, claiming, "We thought everyone knew." One of Director Friedkin's assistants, Albert Shapiro, conceded, "It's not common knowledge that the film contains subliminal cuts." He denied their use in *The Exorcist* was a secret, however.

Despite their claim that they had nothing to hide, I was refused permission to reproduce six photographs for this book, taken in the theater during the movie. Warner's Chief Legal Counsel responded, "You are hereby notified that no license or permission is given for the use of any . . . photographs taken of or from our motion picture 'The Exorcist.' You are further notified that Warner Bros. will take all legal steps necessary to prevent any such use of materials from 'The Exorcist,' whether such use is made by you or others."

The death mask was most often consciously perceived in two specific scenes. It appeared in the dream sequence, when Father Karras's mother came out of the subway entrance as he watched from across the street, and near the end of the exorcism after the older priest died and Karras attempted to murder Regan. The display flashed at 1/48 of a second. Many viewers believed the death mask flashes occurred at least four additional times, but there was disagreement over precisely in which scenes the flashes had been inserted. At the movie's climax, when Father Karras was finally possessed by the devil, his face turned white—closely resembling the tachistoscoped death mask.

After interviewing nearly a hundred individuals who had just viewed *The Exorcist*, it appeared that roughly one third consciously did not perceive the flashing death mask. One third were strangely uncertain whether they had seen it, and one third consciously recalled the display. Two thirds of the audience did not perceive the death mask. Many who consciously perceived the death mask, commented about forcing themselves to deal with their memory of the experience. Perhaps strangely, the movie's strongest emotional impact was among the one third who repressed the perception and consciously believed they saw nothing.

Tachistoscopic technique is long established and frequently used in television commercials. In a recent case, presently under investigation by the FCC and FTC, half a dozen single frames in a sixty-second commercial for a child's toy called "Hūsker Dū?" were inserted with the command "Get it!" The commercial was nationally broadcast during children's programs before Christmas in 1973.

Two patents on subliminal induction equipment—including the tachistoscope—are owned by Dr. Hal Becker of Tulane University's Medical School. Dr. Becker, a biological communication engineer, has used these induction techniques to treat psychoneurosis. He claims to have lowered diastolic blood pressure (hypertension) with subliminal tachistoscopic displays. Slow-speed consciously perceivable tachistoscopes, ranging from 1/10 to 1/150 of a second, are regularly used in language training programs. High-speed tachistoscopes, however, flash images or commands at 1/1,000 to 1/4,000 of a second, repeating the flash every so many seconds. Currently, these machines are employed in universities, research corporations, and advertising agencies, but are generally considered obsolete as a practical tool of market manipulation. Subliminal messages can be induced into an audience in much simpler, cheaper, and far less detectable ways.

Perceptual Threshold Management

Director Friedkin and his behavior experts would have found it dangerous to their $14 million investment if they had brought a tachistoscope anywhere near an American theater. They arrived at a much better solution.

Buried within the experimental literature of psychology are experiments dealing with what is called perceptual threshold, an imaginary line that divides a percept into either conscious or unconscious awareness in the brain. This line appears to move about continuously. As we have already considered, humans perceive much information about which they have no conscious awareness.

Theorists speculate that as little as 1/1,000 of a total, single percept registers at the conscious level. The division of information into conscious and unconsciously perceived information is separated by what we can call the perceptual threshold. Substantial experimental data suggests physiological tension, anxiety, fear, and apprehension control perceptual thresholds. As tension within a person increases, he perceives less and less at the conscious level and becomes more and more susceptible to subliminal stimuli. As these tensions decrease, individuals perceive a wider range of information at conscious levels, and appear less susceptible to subliminals. The harder you strain to perceive subliminals, for example, the less likely you are to perceive them.

The tension phenomenon is easily demonstrated. When ready for bed, adjust the radio volume to a comfortable level—neither too soft nor too loud. Lie down and turn off the light. During the next half hour you will readjust the volume lower and lower every few minutes to maintain a comfortable volume level. As you relax, the radio volume appears to increase, but it is actually your conscious perceptual ability that changes, becoming more sensitive, not the radio. Should you turn on the light, get up, and walk about the room, you would discover the radio will have become barely audible.

The subliminal death mask cut in *The Exorcist* passes through the projector at 1/48 of a second, a speed quite visible at the conscious level to most people who are relaxed. However, the audience's tension or anxiety level was intensified just before the display was used. As mentioned earlier, two thirds of *The Exorcist* audience did not consciously perceive the death masks. Further, what is *not* consciously perceived appears far more significant to emotional and attitudinal predispositions than what is consciously evaluated.

Symbolism's Subliminal Induction

Another embedding technique used frequently in *The Exorcist* was demonstrated in the scene where the old priest is sitting on the bed in the cold bedroom. As his breath condensed, a ghostly face appeared momentarily in the cloud. The face, apparently drawn on several frames, was also consciously invisible to the audience.

There was much more in *The Exorcist*, however, than merely tachistoscopic and embedded death masks.

In a society where science and technology had become generally accepted as the new religion, it was astonishing how easily the writers and director discredited science and established the devil as an almost preferable alternative. Many viewers described the fantasy destruction of neurological medicine in the clinic scenes as the most "horrifying" portion of the movie. Count was made in several theaters of patrons, leaving for the bathroom or the street during this scene, and in packed theaters, it was never fewer than fifty.

The white, sterile operating rooms, the spinal tap, the injection of radioactive iodine in Regan's neck artery, and the overamplified and quite overdramatized clanking of the X-ray machines helped portray Regan as a pale, trembling, weak, and helpless child in the clutches of impersonal, mechanical contrivances. After the clinic scene, the audience was prepared to accept the devil by comparison as a kindly, even though a somewhat dirty, old man.

The scene that supplied the coup de grâce for science involved the various physicians with their stilted, insincere jargon, lightly camouflaging their ignorance and pedanticism. Unfortunately, there was enough truth in the caricature of modern commercial medicine to make the scene plausible.

The Wipe-out of Reason

One strong factor supporting the movie's success involved an almost primal urge in modern man to believe in the forces of mercy, goodness, and God—even though faith in these concepts has become increasingly difficult to maintain. Many viewers responded to criticisms of the film's fantasy devil being childish nonsense as though their belief in God had been attacked. Though most churches in North America publicly took a strong, antagonistic position toward the movie, many viewers strangely perceived *The Exorcist* as a denouement of material values and a return to religious faith.

The *Exorcist* writers established greater credibility for the devil by representing the story's lead characters as agnostic. Had Regan or her mother, Chris MacNeil, been Catholic, for example, many Protestants, the primary North American audience, might easily have avoided accepting the story. On the other hand, had these two characters been Protestant, it would have put them in the position of being saved from the devil by Catholics—hardly an acceptable idea for most American Protestants.

Further establishing the mother as a credible image in the audience fantasies, the writers made her a glamorous movie and television star who had dined at the White House. Her home was compulsively clean and neat. Though objects were heavily scattered throughout the house on shelves and tables, they were always neat, precise, and never handled or disturbed. In contrast, the urination scene was even more upsetting in this overly neat, tastefully decorated home where toilets never appeared—even in the several bathroom scenes. The urine, of course, was heavily soaped out of the rug by a cleaning woman immediately after the party.

The downstairs was always orderly and clean, and events

that occurred downstairs appeared reasonable and logical. Upstairs, however, was another story. Regan, in her solitary confinement with the devil, was in chaotic surroundings where vomit and drooling spit played upon audience disgust and revulsion toward bodily secretions. This was truly the North American fantasy of what the devil's world would be like. Some, at the unconscious level, however, might have found the disorder attractive.

Between Heaven and Hell

Stairs were important props in *The Exorcist*, symbolic of limbo—the connection between the lower and upper worlds of hell and heaven. Stairs appeared in Father Karras's dream sequence where his mother emerged from a subway station (symbolically hell), behind the house where the motion picture director and Father Karras fell to their deaths, and as the link between the troubled upstairs world invaded by the devil and the downstairs world of reason and sanity. The attic stairs leading up to a dark room cluttered with half-forgotten junk carried Chris to her first contact with the devil.

The outside death stairs were inspected by the detective who climbed from the dark shadowy bottom, where the director perished, to the top which is portrayed in sunlight and openness (symbolically heaven). The priest finally committed suicide by throwing himself out the window, falling at the foot of these stairs. Suicide, of course, is a mortal sin for which the Church must deny the sacraments. Father Karras had, indeed, surrendered himself to the devil.

The staircase in the house, however, was the symbolic fulcrum around which the story evolved. The ascendant devil was living, temporarily, upstairs in Regan's body. The priests had to climb up to do combat with him. And they had to wait on the stairs until the devil was ready.

Various sexual perversions, strongly taboo in the American culture, were cleverly incorporated into the film. Pedophilia, for example (the use of children for sexual stimulation), was a paramount subliminal theme carefully arranged so the audience would not consciously deal with the forbidden subject. Unconscious perception, as pointed out earlier, is peculiarly sensitive to both sex and death taboos.

In the movie, Regan was twelve years old. Her language and actions—genital exposure, masturbation, etc.—were sexually provocative. Throughout much of the movie, she was posed spread-eagled and tied to the bedposts in bondage. Her movements were often quite purposely sensual. As the wounds opened on her arms and legs, they appeared as lash cuts inflicted with a whip. There was even the sound of a whiplash as these wounds appeared. The cut on her leg, however, was also reminiscent of a vagina—the slang terms "gash" and "slit" suggest that the unconscious may associate wounds with the female genitals.

Sadomasochistic themes were quite obvious and shocking, though most viewers repressed the highly taboo real meanings of these scenes. The use of strong taboo sexual symbolism throughout *The Exorcist* was striking. In the attic scene Regan's mother held a candle that ejaculated a burst of flame when the caretaker surprised her. The bedposts in Regan's room cast phallic shadows on the walls.

Other subs simply emphasized supernatural themes. Some bedroom shadows appeared as dark silhouettes of hooded figures like the statues in the Iraq archaeological museum. Many ancient beliefs persist that creatures of hell, such as vampires and demons, cast no reflection. The house was full of mirrors. They appeared in every room, yet Regan's reflection never appeared as she walked in front of the mirrors.

While Father Karras prays in church, a skull-shaped shadow appeared on the white wall behind him. In the hospital scenes Regan's skull appeared repeatedly in the X rays forming the scene's background. During the exorcism scene, Regan rises from the bed with her arms outstretched in the symbol of the cross.

The Devil in Pursuit

Director Friedkin confronts the audience with figure-ground actions that keep them in constant uncertainty and tension. Many viewers approached hypnotic states because of the concentration required to follow the ambiguity. In many scenes it was impossible to be completely certain as to which action was intended as figure and which was intended as ground.

Jantzen looks for you.
To make a joint statement in patriotic red, white and blue. Now, on the wings of CP Air, go capture yourselves a piece of beach where you can watch the sun go by Matching Jantzens of Print Stretch Nylon. The All-Canadian statement at better stores everywhere. About $7.00 for his and $22.00 for hers.

April 72
Rdrs Digest

Jantzen

figure 1

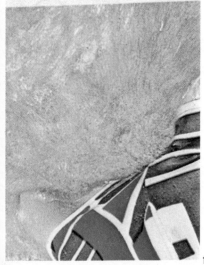

figure 2

figure 3

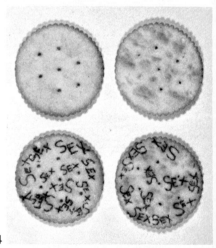

figure 4

figure 5

figure 6

figure 7

figure 8

figure 9

figure 10

Monet

figure 11

figure 12

figure 13

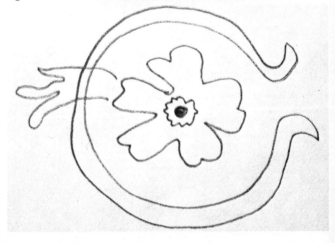

figure 14

figure 15

figure 18

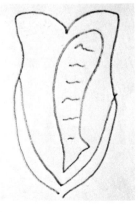

figure 19

figure 20

figure 21

figure 22

figure 23

figure 24

figure 25

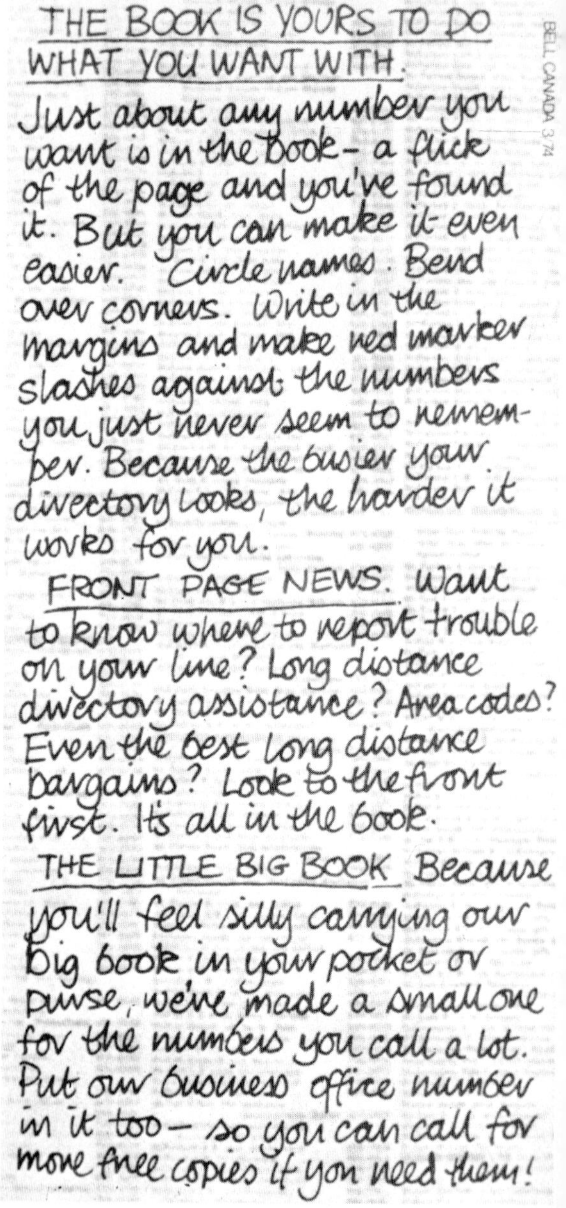

THE BOOK IS YOURS TO DO WHAT YOU WANT WITH.

Just about any number you want is in the book— a flick of the page and you've found it. But you can make it even easier. Circle names. Bend over corners. Write in the margins and make red marker slashes against the numbers you just never seem to remember. Because the busier your directory looks, the harder it works for you.

FRONT PAGE NEWS. Want to know where to report trouble on your line? Long distance directory assistance? Area codes? Even the best long distance bargains? Look to the front first. It's all in the book.

THE LITTLE BIG BOOK Because you'll feel silly carrying our big book in your pocket or purse, we've made a small one for the numbers you call a lot. Put our business office number in it too— so you can call for more free copies if you need them!

figure 26

If you don't take care of this tooth,
the permanent one might not be so cute.

Somehow, a lot of people figure it doesn't really matter if a "baby tooth" gets a cavity. After all, it's just a little temporary tooth.

But it really does matter. First, the tooth is so small, a cavity in it can be a big problem. So, the tooth might have to be pulled.

Then, the space left by the pulled tooth can cause bad spacing of the permanent teeth which can affect anything from your child's bite to his appearance.

So it makes sense to take care of those first little teeth just like you would big teeth. With the right foods, regular checkups, and brushing after every meal with a good toothpaste.

We hope that toothpaste will be Crest.

Crest

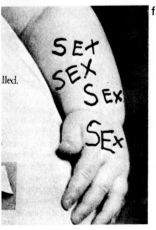

figure 27

lled.

SEX
SEX
SEX
SEX

figure 28

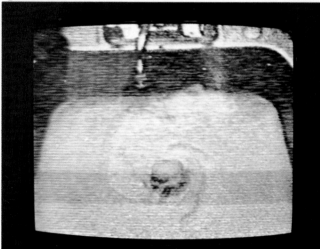

figure 29

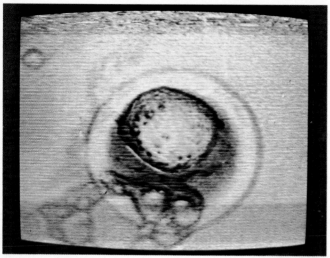

figure 30

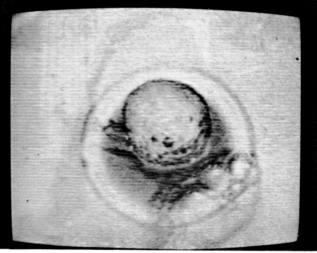

figure 31

figure 32

NEW...
FIRST SKIN CREAM
THAT EVEN PROTECTS
YOUR HANDS IN WATER

figure 33

figure 34

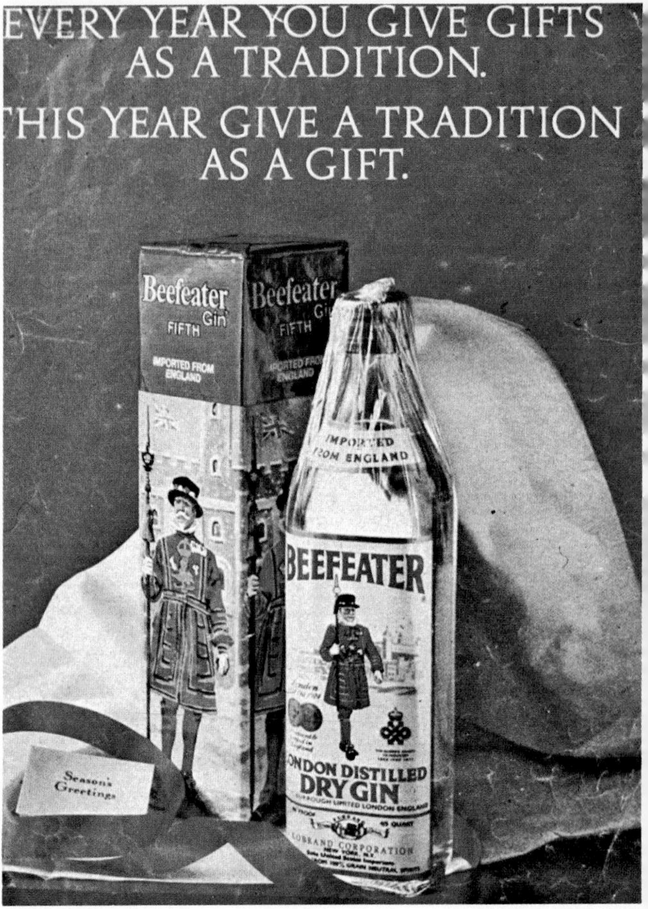
EVERY YEAR YOU GIVE GIFTS
AS A TRADITION.
THIS YEAR GIVE A TRADITION
AS A GIFT.
Beefeater Gin
FIFTH
IMPORTED FROM ENGLAND
IMPORTED FROM ENGLAND
BEEFEATER
LONDON DISTILLED
DRY GIN
Season's Greetings

figure 35

figure 36

figure 37

figure 38

figure 39

figure 40

figure 41

figure 42

figure 46

figure 47

figure 48

figure 49

For example, Father Karras walked through the streets to his mother's apartment. Children were playing in the road and in wrecked cars, symbolizing the end of technology. As these scenes cut back and forth, the viewer became quite distracted and more intensely vulnerable to the specific mother-and-son scene that followed. In this scene, introducing Father Karras's guilt over his treatment of his mother, appeared the final justification for the devil's pursuit of Father Karras through the child Regan.

The quick-cut transitions in and out of seemingly unrelated scenes formed a mosaic of visual impression that in the advertising business are called the McLuhan Effect or *perceptual overload*. Familiar examples of the technique are Coca-Cola TV commercials where as many as four scenes are shown in a single frame, different actions continuing in each element of the frame. It is impossible to consciously make sense out of what is going on. The audience's consciousness has been overloaded in order to bypass it into the unconscious, which easily processes very large quantities of data, storing it for later feedback into consciousness.

Director Friedkin heavily utilized subliminal continuity devices that tied the entire film together, in the audience psyche, into a tight, integrated package. For example, the old woman in the carriage that almost ran down the old priest, Father Merrin, had a quickly exposed face similar to Regan's during the exorcism. Father Merrin took a pill after the incident with the carriage, presumably for a cardiac condition, just as he did later in the Georgetown bathroom before the exorcism.

When the old priest moved toward the stopped clock in the Iraq museum, a single pink rose appeared in a white teapot on a table. In the apartment of Father Karras's mother, the wallpaper was covered with pink roses, as was the wallpaper in the bedroom of Regan's mother. There was a single pink rose in the sugar bowl in the apartment of the priest's mother. When Regan urinated on the rug, her mother, Chris, was holding a pink rose. The downstairs of the Georgetown house was full of flowers, suggesting a funeral was taking place. Flowers, of course, are the plant's reproductive organ and symbolize both death and resurrection. In Renaissance art, flowers often represented the soul.

Auditory Archetypes

The Exorcist was remarkable in the way both audio and visual were integrated and mutually reinforced. The sound track, for which the movie won an Academy Award, was a brilliant example of creative subliminal sound engineering. Similar techniques have been used for years in other movies and by the popular music recording industry.

In several dozen interviews with theater employees—refreshment stand attendants, ushers, and ticket takers who had only heard the movie's sound track for several days before actually viewing the film, all reported extreme discomfort from the sound. The discomfort could not be verbally explained, but all agreed it was directly related to the sound track. Each of the theater staffs interviewed reported employees who became ill after finally seeing the film in its entirety—from mild to extreme nausea and hysteria.

Friedkin openly admitted he had used several natural sound effects in the movie's auditory background. One of these, he explained, was the sound of angry, agitated bees. After provoking a jar of bees into excited anger, he recorded their buzzing, then rerecorded the buzzing at sixteen different frequencies. He finally mixed the sixteen frequencies of buzzing together in what might be consciously heard as a single sound—a super buzzing of infuriated bees virtually unrecognizable at conscious levels. This sound of angry bees wove in and out of scenes throughout the film.

Virtually all humans (some much more strongly than others) respond with hysteria, fear, and intense anxiety to the sound of angry, buzzing bees, even if they have never in their lives experienced the actual sound. Many animals respond similarly. Perhaps the strongest verbally definable emotion triggered by the bee buzzing is fear or fright—a near panic-filled desire to run, flee, and escape from the threat. Carl Jung's theory of archetypes suggests that this sound—as the emotional reaction appears to cross cultures—could qualify as an archetypal symbol.

In many cultures the bee has been symbolically associated with death and immortality. In several ancient civilizations, dead bodies were smeared with honey as food for the soul. Indeed, honey was often used as an embalming fluid. Over

110

many centuries in Europe, bees were prohibited from use in barter for fear they might take offense and destroy crops and flocks in retribution. Bees appeared as symbols of death, fear, and power in ancient Egypt, Germany, China, Greece, Italy, and Japan, in early Christian art, in both Hebrew and Moslem traditions, and in Norse mythology. The Hindu god Krishna was often described as hovering in the form of a bee. Souls have often been thought to swarm as bees migrating from hives.

There is never any conscious awareness, of course, within *The Exorcist* audience of angry bees buzzing. However, there are easily observable levels of anxiety produced by the sound as it weaves in and out of various scenes. The bee sound appeared, for example, in the scene where Father Merrin first visits Regan's bedroom while he removed various objects from a pouch, symbolically letting the invisible bees out of the bag.

Symbols of Evil

Another auditory archetype mixed subtly into the sound track was the terrified squealing of pigs while they were being slaughtered. Few sounds strike terror so deeply into the heart of man. This sound will affect virtually all humans even though they may never have experienced the squealing or sight of an actual pig. The expression "squealing like a stuck pig" has even gone into the language.

Pigs have been portrayed in various symbolic relationships with man for at least half a million years. Even today, the pig is considered one of the most intelligent of domestic animals—by human standards, of course. The pig, at least for modern man, was cursed by bad table manners that emphasize the pig's filth, greed, gluttony, and lethargy. Nevertheless, in many ancient cultures, pigs were often substituted for human victims during religious sacrifices. A black pig has often been symbolic in Christian art of the devil and Satan. In many civilizations the pig was thought to be a demon that injured fertility heroes in the groin, rendering them sterile. In Celtic mythology pigs were even portrayed as returning to life after being eaten. And, of course, in one of the New Testament's most celebrated exorcisms, Christ drove a legion

111

of devils into a herd of swine which, maddened, threw themselves into a lake much as Father Karras flung his possessed body out the window.

In addition to the pigs' squealing hidden in *The Exorcist* sound track, Regan's grotesque, filthy face during the exorcism scene often resembled that of a pig. Further, subliminal reinforcement for the pig symbol is obtained by the word PIG written as graffiti on a ledge at the left side of the stairs looking down behind the house where the deaths occurred. This staircase, and the consciously unnoticed word PIG, appeared many times throughout the movie. Friedkin explained how the sound track often mixed the angry bee buzz with the pig squeals. The two sounds wove in and out of the film, coordinating with the visual.

Embedded in the sound, under the voices and surface sounds apparent in the exorcism scene, was what seemed to be the roaring of lions or large cats. A third of the audience surveyed described a feeling of being devoured or struggling against being devoured. There were also orgasmic sexual sounds in the exorcism scene that appeared to involve both males and females.

Sound is extremely important in the management and control of any group of individuals, certainly for those in a theater. Famed movie director Alfred Hitchcock ranked sound as more vital to the success of his famous suspense movies than his visual illusions.

In a recent Muzak Corporation advertisement, the company actually presented its services, background music for stores and offices, as an "environmental management" technique.

In Western society surprisingly little is publicly known about sound and its effect upon behavior. The consciously available portion of sound frequency ranges from 20 to 20,-000 cycles per second—or so advertise the high-fidelity appliance manufacturers. Most theaters have sound equipment that will produce audible sound in this range. As a practical matter, however, few individuals can consciously hear over 17,000 cps or under 200 cps, especially young people whose hearing has been permanently dampened by high-volume electronic amplification.

Sound, nevertheless, can be perceived at each end of the

spectrum beyond the consciously perceived frequencies. Resonance and other sound qualities also play parts in the subliminal perception of sound. To illustrate, some Moog synthesizers are capable of producing sound at 20,000 cps or higher and under 20 cps. You can consciously hear nothing at these high or low frequencies, but if volume or resonance is increased, most people become extermely agitated. If information is included in these subliminal frequencies, it will instantly be perceived at the unconscious level.

Hypnotic Inductions

When normal voice volume levels in *The Exorcist* were reduced, the audience was required to strain or increase attention or concentration upon the dialogue. This is almost a standard hypnotic induction technique, compelling the subject to concentrate upon one sensory data source. The audience uniformly leaned forward in their seats to hear, for example, the charming conversation between mother and daughter in the bedroom scene at the film's beginning. Similarly, many scenes throughout the movie were momentarily out of focus. Again, the audience—like puppets being manipulated with strings—leaned forward, concentrating on the visual images as they tried to correct for the blurred focus. Much of the dialogue between shock scenes was muted or whispered, so as to regain audience involvement.

When humans are led toward hypnosis, they become highly suggestible. Their emotions become more easily manipulated, managed, and controlled the further they proceed along the induction path.

Friedkin utilized little music in the sound track, though he credited works by Hans Werner Henzle, George Crumb, Anton Webern, and five other composers. Like all good background music, the themes were purposely designed for subliminal consumption. The consumption of music and sound generally followed two patterns. One pattern built slowly from plateau to plateau, always intensifying the audience's emotional response. Indeed, in a sample of roughly fifty women who had seen the movie, over half candidly admitted *The Exorcist* excited them sexually. Most cited the sound track as the apparent source of this excitement.

The other general sound pattern abruptly jarred the audience into a tension state. Loud, sharp noises—bells ringing, doors slamming, dogs barking—preceded and followed by extended periods of electronic silence. The sound would gradually increase to a crescendo, then abruptly trail off to nothingness, or cut off sharply. This technique is primarily an attention-holding-tension-building device. Physiological tension was also increased by silences. For example, the early scene in the attic—which was abruptly broken by a loud, sharp noise.

Jumping the sound from one scene to the next—as a continuity and tension-building device, quite similar to the pink roses used visually—was done throughout the film. An important sound jump occurred during Father Karras's first visit to the house. During the preceding scene, in the dream sequence where Karras's mother climbs the subway stairs, the street sound was unrecognizable as a rather high frequency, moderately loud-volume sound. In the next scene where Karras visited the house, the sound was the same except a truck gear shift was heard and the sound increased in frequency. The gear shift identified the background noise, reducing audience tension for the priest's first visit with Regan, where the tension again built toward a tense climax.

Loud Silences

The Exorcist silences were not completely silent. They were electronic silences, with low-frequency background hums. The silences were only silent in contrast to high and increasing volume sequences. These silences also formed a series of plateaus which gradually increased in volume and decreased in time interval as the story moved toward various climactic situations. Silences, like the sounds, were used to produce within the audience a series of emotional plateaus. These silences became louder and louder and more and more rapid as each segment progressed. The tension and release, tension and release, tension and release, always building higher and higher and higher, induced—by itself—exhaustion and even nausea for many in the audience.

Another manifestation of tension management in the audience was coughing. The audience coughed heavily at predictable intervals throughout the movie. Audience coughing was recorded at several theaters and always appeared at roughly the same points in the story. This was compared with cough reactions in several other action-type films, *The Sting, Executive Decision*, and *Papillon*. *The Exorcist*, in comparison, produced notably stronger and more predictable cough patterns. There were, apparently, subliminal cues in the visual or auditory stimuli that motivated the coughing.

Coughing is a tension release and appeared to occur roughly within thirty seconds after the auditory tension peaks were released. The first sounds of the evil force in the attic sounded like coughing, followed by a rasping bronchial sound. Coughing, of course, can lead to an upset stomach.

The changes of Regan's voice—from that of a twelve-year-old girl to that of the devil—were carefully synthesized with the visual changes in her appearance. At some point during this transition, the girl's voice was replaced by the voice of Mercedes McCambridge, an actress with a deep husky voice. Friedkin admitted to putting the actress's voice through a filter to produce a voice unidentifiable as either male or female.

In other words, the devil's voice was consciously perceived as androgenous, or hermaphroditic. This voice quality would not be meaningful at the conscious level, but would be subliminally apparent. No matter how natural voices are disguised, hypnotized humans are able to identify male or female voice characteristics. It would not be an exaggeration to state that *The Exorcist* visual effects were only props for the sound. A large proportion of the audience recalled the sound with great discomfort weeks after leaving the theater.

Stranger Than Fiction

These pages have included only a handful of the behavioral engineering techniques utilized in *The Exorcist*. Many of the techniques described in this chapter go far beyond merely playing yo-yo with an audience's emotions, during an afternoon or evening's entertainment. They endure far beyond the commercial lifetime of a single movie. What was done to *The Exorcist* audience could endure in some memory systems throughout a lifetime.

115

On December 8, 1972, a two-paragraph note appeared in *The New York Times* business section, announcing that In-Flight Motion Pictures, Inc. would initiate the sale of subliminal advertising commercials embedded in the film they distribute. In-Flight is a monopoly corporation that distributes movies to every major airline operating in and out of North America.

Considering the exponential growth patterns of Western behavioral science and technology, we can reasonably assume this is still only the beginning. As a society, we prefer to think of *1984, Brave New World, A Clockwork Orange,* and *Soylent Green* as science fiction and fantasy. But as *The Exorcist* abundantly demonstrated, modern media-induced truths and realities may have already become far stranger than any fiction ever written.

8

Subliminal Rock

*To ignore your environment
is to eventually find yourself
a slave to it.*

WYNDHAM LEWIS
The Art of Being Ruled

A Subliminal Hook

This chapter probes those subliminal techniques engineered into popular records that almost anyone can find. The subliminal messages are hidden in relatively simple verbal or musical illusions. Subliminal technology sells records by the tens of millions each year in North America. No one apparently knows or understands as yet, however, the consequences of this sensory bombardment upon human value systems.

Buried within the April 1974 list of top-thirty record sellers was a song called "Hooked on a Feeling" recorded by a rock group billed as Blue Swede. Like so many hundreds of other such rock ballads, relentlessly merchandised each year across North America, "Hooked" was a passed-over item a few months later. But during its brief glory peak, the record sold several million copies, producing a small fortune for its promoters. Most of the singles were purchased by gum-chewing, long-haired teen-age girls who first heard it being plugged by disc jockeys on the AM band wasteland.

Not one of the rock biggies, "Hooked" did well. Though few fans could consciously decipher the banality in the song's lyrics, the melody was whistled and hummed by both teen-

117

agers and even by some of their parents who picked it up unconsciously.

"Hooked on a Feeling" has a curious chant, sung by the chorus, which is sustained behind the lyric. The repititious background phrase sounds like "ooh-ga-shook-ah." Considering the lyric and chant in a figure-ground relationship, the audience consciously listened to the lyric's meaningless banality, not the background chant. Roughly a hundred teen-agers who owned the record, both male and female, were asked what the background phrase "ooh-ga-shook-ah" meant. No one had any idea. They also had no conscious idea what the lyric was about, even though all had heard the song dozens—if not many, many dozens—of times.

At several points in the continuity of the background chant—consciously ignored because attention was focused upon the foreground lyric—the chanted phrase "Ooh-ga-shook-ah" smoothly and very distinctly converted into "Who got sucked off?" The technique has been called *metacontrast* or *backward masking*, much like the magician who tricks you into watching his right hand while he picks your pocket with his left.

Several weeks later, many in the group interviewed stated all they could hear now in the song was this embedded obscenity. Most appeared disgusted and disillusioned with both the record and the recording artists. Several pointed out, "We've been had!"

North America is a visually oriented culture. Americans are more consciously concerned with *visual* form, experience, color, movement or the lack of movement, depth illusions, and other visual experiences than are many other cultures. Russians, for example, appear strongly biased toward *auditory* experience, putting far more trust in what they hear than in what they see. Because Americans tend to consciously ignore or consider auditory experience insignificant, there appears little indication that we are aware of either music's power or its pervasiveness.

Two thousand years ago, Plato demanded strict censorship over popular music in his utopian *Republic*. He feared citizens "would be tempted and corrupted by weak and voluptuous airs and led to indulge in demoralizing emotions." Fears of music's power to corrupt have been expressed by many

hilosophers and scientists. In modern America, even with all
he media criticism published, very little mention has been
made of the behavioral effects of music or lyrics. Popular
music, in all its happiness and horror, is an invisible dimension of today's environment.

Divide the Market and Conquer

Popular music is skillfully marketed to specific groups and
subgroups within the society with an intensity that would
make an underarm deodorant salesman blush with envy. A
record may be produced and marketed for several young
markets, but producers usually aim at specific targets: the
preteen, eight to twelve; early teen, thirteen to fourteen;
midteen, fifteen to sixteen; late teen, seventeen to nineteen;
and postteen, over twenty. Rarely will a single recording artist or group hit across the board, selling to all the markets.
The Beatles were, in their later years, one of the few groups
who appeared to cross virtually all demographic groups. As
some successful music groups aged, however, their audiences
sustained their enthusiasm as they, too, grew older. This is
rare. Most of the groups hit hard, saturate their markets, and
disappear.

The teen-age rock market has been studied for years by
commercial researchers, much like any marketing target:
purchasing patterns, life-styles, psychosexual development,
mating customs, aggressions, costuming, drive systems, pa-
ternal-maternal relationships, the whole range of complex
needs within individuals and the groups to which they belong.

These music consumers are highly discriminating in what
they purchase, and usually buy strictly within their market
segments. The soul sounds of James Brown will not likely
reach the same market segment supporting Bobby Sherman.
Rock music, for example, breaks down into "rock 'n' roll,"
"jazz rock," "bubble gum," "commercial rock," "acid (or
psychedelic) rock," "heavy rock," etcetera ad infinitum. The
category list constantly changes, divides, and subdivides.
Teen-agers generally listen to top-forty music stations an
average of six hours daily. They purchase an average of four
new records weekly. They buy 60 percent of all 45-rpm
singles, while the under-twenty-five age group buys 80 per-

cent. The music merchandising business is aimed at the young, especially those in the upper-middle income group with high discretionary incomes supplied by indulgent parents.

Marketing technicians have been extraordinarily successful in managing teen-age music markets. More millionaires are believed to have emerged from the popular music industry during the past two decades than in any other segment of the American economy.

Paul's Early Death

One very profitable use of subliminal manipulation technique involved the Beatles' multimillion-dollar publicity stunt over the supposed death of Paul McCartney. For never-explained reasons, McCartney avoided public appearances over an extended period. Rumors swept the world, "Paul is dead!" Headlines questioning the fate of Paul appeared in every major world capital.

Had they really wished to resolve the question, the rumor could quickly have been turned off by simply permitting a wire service to interview the musician. This, of course, was never done. When you can make more money by staying home than appearing in public, you stay home. The Beatles milked the rumor for all it was worth—and it was worth millions. They embedded material on Paul's death in their recordings. One of these was in the *Magical Mystery Tour* album in the last few grooves of a song titled "Strawberry Fields," A voice inexplicably appeared at low volume and said, "I buried Paul." In the hysteria of the time, similar sound embedding appeared in many other recordings. These embeds would not be consciously perceived, but would subliminally—because of their strong emotional impact—reinforce the album's value and emotional significance far more powerfully than could a million dollars' worth of network television commercials.

The death rumor was also reinforced on the covers of albums such as *Sergeant Pepper*, where on the cover the four Beatles were pictured with Paul McCartney's back turned to the reader. The *Abbey Road* album cover even showed Paul in a burial costume. The cover layout on an album titled *The*

Beatles in the Beginning also included a four-candled candelabrum with one of the candle's flame extinguished.

The success of these strategies is attested to by virtually any parent who has witnessed the glassy-eyed hypnotic stupor in which they find their youngsters absorbing highly amplified stroking via the latest hit record. The highly visible effects of these promotions are a compulsive purchasing of singles and albums and endless hours of repetitive listening.

Music as Sex Substitute

Very strong subliminal sexual stimulation is at least part of what is being massaged into the young psyches. In one survey of about fifty male high school students, almost a third openly admitted masturbating while listening to rock music. Most young Americans are highly secretive about their sexual behavior. This implies that the actual percentage of those who obtain vicarious sexual stimulation from auditory stimuli is much higher.

Most clearly, neither record addicts nor their parents who support the addiction have any conscious idea of what they are so deeply involved with. In a survey of over four hundred students in metropolitan Detroit and Grand Rapids, Michigan, psychologists John Robinson and Paul Hirsch found that only about 20 percent of these teen-agers—from the eighth and eleventh grades and varied in social class, race, and religion—could reasonably explain the meaning of lyrics from such super-hits as "Ode to Billy Joe," "Incense and Peppermit," "Heavy Music," and "Lucy in the Sky With Diamonds." A third to one half of these students had no conscious idea whatsoever as to the meaning of these lyrics. And the rest had only vague or partial explanations of the various songs' verbal meanings.

The teen-agers surveyed uniformly tried to avoid any discussion of meaning, many maintaining there was no real meaning—"just a good sound!" Seventy percent emphasized they liked a record more for its *beat* or *sound* than for its message. None appeared certain just what "beat" or "sound" meant, nor could they even specify what they meant by "message."

In the above Michigan study, as well as many others, what

appeared was a consumer repression from consciousness of lyric meaning. If the mind-massagers who produce the music were as vague and uncertain about what was going on in their markets as are the consumers, widespread bankruptcy would be in store for every major record producer in America. Consider the king's ransom these companies have had to pay writers such as Paul Simon. Yet few of their fans appear to either understand or consider significant what these writers produce. This is, to put it mildly, a strange paradox—unless the song's lack of conscious meaning becomes highly meaningful at the unconscious level, and song lyrics, like poetry and other art forms, are purposely produced for unconscious perception.

Tommy's Invisible Sell

The Who's *Tommy*, a so-called rock opera, was released during 1975 as a feature motion picture, starring Ann-Margret, Oliver Reed, Roger Daltrey, and Elton John. Based upon a record album first distributed in 1969, the movie provided audiences with a visual bath in sensation.

Every visual trick in the book was thrown into the film by director Ken Russell—sacrilegious spectacles such as a rock communion procession escorting a fifteen-foot plaster statue of Marilyn Monroe with her skirt blown high and a communion offering to the faithful of booze and amphetamine (speed) capsules rather than the more traditionally symbolic wafers and wine. In one powerful scene Tommy's sensual mother (played by Ann-Margret) hurled a champagne bottle into a TV picture tube where soap and bean commercials were appearing. A flood of soapsuds shot into the room from the damaged tube, followed by a torrential outpouring of beans, and finally a surging river of excrement in which the actress erotically rolls and bathes.

The film, however, had very little to do with the record album. Marshall McLuhan's notion of "hot and cool media" well illustrates the point "Cool is involving, hot is not." The film version was "hot." Audiences could consciously perceive virtually everything the director and actors tried to express. The involvement was, for the most part, conscious.

The Who's original album of *Tommy* was another story.

Mostly designed for subliminal interpretation and involvement, the album was, in McLuhan's terms, "cool," deeply involving subconscious levels. The album, of course, initially programmed the audience for the film at least five years in advance. The album of *Tommy* sold roughly 2 million copies during the first year of its distribution.

An event like *Tommy* is usually dismissed as meaningless by adults, especially parents who usually finance the album's purchase. If they were consciously aware of the event at all, it was only in terms of a background-noise distraction in their living rooms.

In late 1969, a group of fifty adults in a university adult education class, many of them parents of teen-agers, were requested to write out briefly what they believed was meant by the story of *Tommy*. The record was played for them in its entirety. After hearing the record, the group sat with universally bewildered expressions. Some liked it, some disliked it, but most were uncertain how they felt. No individual in the group was able to even vaguely answer simple questions such as, "What is *Tommy* all about?" "What does the story mean?"

Tommy was played for the group a second time with the lyrics displayed on a projection screen so the group could read what they were hearing. But end results were identical—no one was able to specify anything about the story. However, feelings toward the album appeared to intensify after the second playing. More people strongly liked or disliked the album, and fewer were uncertain about their feelings. Nevertheless, even then no one in the group could describe what was going on.

Analysis of the lyrics was now undertaken by the group on a line-to-line basis, much as one might attempt to analyze an Elizabethan sonnet. Meanings for each phrase, line, and stanza were accepted only if a majority of the group agreed the meaning was a valid possibility. When the group disagreed significantly, alternative explanations were included as possibly valid.

The results of this experiment were, to put it mildly, shocking—especially as the primary market appeared to be teen-age boys and girls in the thirteen to nineteen age group. The following is a synopsis of what the group felt *Tommy* was all about:

A Romantic Fantasy

Tommy's mother was a prostitute whose husband died in World War I. After Tommy was born, she continued with her clients and eventually married a man who became her pimp. As an infant, Tommy had witnessed the sexual relationships between his mother and her lovers. He was told repeatedly by his mother and father to wipe these "absurd" memories from his mind. "To know the truth" by forgetting what had happened. The Oedipal implications of a young man and his step-father were, of course, basic to Shakespeare's play *Hamlet*. Now, complicate the situation by making the step-father a pimp. Tommy became autistic—blind, deaf, and dumb, unresponsive and unaware of everything. He "sits silently, picks his nose and smiles, and pokes his tongue at everything."

Cousin Kevin taught Tommy about life. Kevin described himself as "the school bully, the classroom cheat, the nastiest playfriend you could ever meet." He put glass in Tommy's food, spikes in his seat, pins in his fingers, treads on his feet, tied him in a chair, called him a freak, held his head under water and laughed, shut him outside in the rain to catch cold and die, burned his arm with a cigarette, dragged him around by the hair, and pushed him down the stairs.

Uncle Ernie baby-sat with Tommy. A homosexual, he became drunk and sexually assaulted the autistic child. Autistic Tommy was, then, left by his mother with the Acid Queen—a friend of the family—who introduced him to both drugs and sex. "Watch his body writhe," she screamed excitedly.

Tommy, described as a deaf, dumb, and blind freak, eventually developed great skill with pinball machines. He "becomes part of the machine." A wizard at the game, he was not distracted by buzzers, balls, and flashing lights. He played by "sense of smell."

Tommy was finally taken to a doctor who discovered he could see, speak, and hear, but had become a machine that did not feel. The doctor's prescription was, "Go to the mirror, boy!" The mirror was the mirror of Narcissus which reflected only idealized illusions. When Tommy attempted to probe beneath his superficial image, his mother attacked him for peering into his inner self. In desperation, she smashed the mirror. His cure was miraculous.

From that moment, Tommy became a popular sensation. He left a devastating trail of people hypnotized by his messianic power. Everyone marveled at Tommy's seemingly supernatural ability to make his own images, to define his own illusions and realities, and to make his inner hidden reality match in appearance the exposed outer illusion.

Tommy became a gospel singer and preacher surrounded by disc jockeys, guards, and his loyal fans. A girl, Sally, was infatuated with Tommy and tried to touch him during one of his sermons. She was thrown from the stage by guards and her face was cut, requiring sixteen stitches. She, in the end, married a rock musician. Tommy was finally free—a messiah followed by many disciples. He founded Tommy's Holiday Camp, run by Uncle Ernie, where "the holiday is forever."

But this manipulation of society's illusions made everyone turn against Tommy in the end. "We forsake you," the crowd yelled. "Let's forget you—better still." Tommy's fate seemed typical of that in store for anyone who steps through the broken mirror of mass illusion to probe the inner world—from Socrates through Freud to McLuhan.

The Repression Mechanism

The complete line-by-line analysis of *Tommy* required several hours' work by the group. As the meanings developed, several women, who in the earlier test of their feelings had indicated strong aversion to the recording, became nauseous. Many reported agitation, anger, a sense of outrage and frustration. One mother reported she had refused to permit her thirteen-year-old daughter to purchase the album. At the time, she had not been certain as to why she felt so strongly against *Tommy.* The woman described her daughter's reaction to the denial as "near hysteria." When the idea of a drug-deprived addictive response was suggested, the mother reluctantly agreed to the similarity. This mother could not believe her daughter consciously understood what the album was all about—even though the young girl had heard it several times all the way through.

Since the album *Tommy* was much discussed among teenagers at the time, interviews with roughly fifty were undertaken by college students several months after the record appeared in stores. Less than 2 percent of the teenagers were able to give a coherent, even partial explanation of the lyrics' meaning. Yet 20 percent owned the record, another 40 percent planned to buy it, and 98 percent had heard the album at least once. All the teen-agers interviewed reported *Tommy* was one of the most significant album productions of the year.

Two years later, another survey of a hundred teen-agers was again made. Teen-agers were asked to explain what *Tommy* was all about. Roughly 25 percent of those who had heard the record gave a reasonably detailed account of Tommy's tragic and bizarre life. Their interpretations were remarkably close to the one developed a year earlier by the adult group. It appeared that when these teen-agers first purchased or heard the album, they were consciously uncertain as to what the story involved. The learning process, apparently, took several months. Once they were more or less consciously aware of what was going on in *Tommy*, they generally lost interest in the album.

All the students interviewed agreed they would never, under any circumstances, discuss what they knew of Tommy's adventures with their parents or any other adult. These young people identified with Tommy quite strongly—an autistic, ravaged child forced not to feel, hear, see, or speak the truth. Parents might well give these identification structures some careful thought.

What appeared to be occurring in *Tommy*, and in many similar rock music albums and singles, was planned ambiguity. Lyrics, orchestration, recording effects, the whole production—most of which required hundreds of hours of skilled labor—was designed to communicate meaningfully only at symbolic subliminal levels.

Teen-agers seem to "buy" the feelings produced by subliminal stimuli without any conscious awareness of specific meanings. A few eventually do discover what is going on, but the cognitive process appears to take weeks, even months, as the message slowly rises to consciousness. At the point where the market, or a substantial portion of it, can consciously deal with the message, the record is commercially dead. But there are always new singles and albums being born to replace the fallen. As many as five hundred new recordings a week hit the promotion fan.

Who Tells the Story?

The question of *who is saying what to whom* in rock music is one of the most intriguing aspects of lyric symbology. Ostensibly, boy vocalists dominate the industry and often appear to be singing to girls—possibly the ones who might reasonably be the marketing targets. But this would seem to leave the boy audience out in the cold. In fact, both girls and boys identify with the vocalist, however, suggesting something far more complex and devious is involved.

The boy singer does not aim his lyrics directly at the gum-chewing, vacant-eyed teeny-boppers. This would invite disaster at the record shops. The singers and their lyric writers often project their sentimentality at the singer's mother—a symbolic subliminal identification. The girl record buyers can then unconsciously identify with their hero's mother, whom their hero worships and loves. The boy record buyers support the records as they unconsciously perceive the singer suffering the same maternal rejections they believe themselves to have suffered. They have no reason, therefore, for jealousy or envy when girl friends boost the record.

The technique appears often on million-seller recordings. Elvis Presley's 1957 hit pleads with a subliminal mother to "Let Me Be Your Teddy Bear."*

> . . . *Put a chain around my neck*
> *And lead me anywhere,*
> *Oh let me be your teddy bear.*
>
> *Baby let me be around you any night,*
> *Run your fingers through my hair,*
> *And cuddle me real tight.*
> *Oh let me be your teddy bear.*

* Copyright © 1957 by Gladys Music, Inc. Used by permission.

This hardly describes a popular teen-age mating ritual. Even in America's maternally dominated society, few boys would submit to such a relationship with a girl friend. Humans often describe loved ones in verbalisms they project upon themselves—idealized realities, wishes, or fantasy fulfillments. Presley's "baby," then, became an unconscious synonym for mother while the highest paid star in the history of motion pictures assumed the role of a small infant.

The designation "baby," as used in popular music, is often a direct maternal reference. The euphemism for mother, sung by a quivering, immature male voice—pleading an unresolved Oedipal conflict intimately familiar to millions of young Americans—is frequently at the bottom of a song's financial success. These are the plaintive puberty pleadings of a maternally starved generation. The girl consumer identifies with the singer's love object—his mother. The boy consumer identifies with the singer and his sufferings. The formula is well proven and successful. Dad, of course, is totally ignored in this matriarchal game.

Bobby Curtola, another rock superstar, sang his way into early retirement by skillfully manipulating young America's Oedipal conflicts. "Call Me Baby" was one of his early best-selling records.

> Call me baby, honey baby
> Put your loving arms about me honey baby
> Say it tender when we meet
> Say it soft and say it sweet
> Call me baby, baby, honey baby.

Is it conceivable a young man would want his sweetheart, girl friend, or lover, to call him "baby" and deal with him as though he were an infant child? Hardly! The song is aimed at Mommy, providing subliminal identification for the market.

Mommy's Many Pseudonyms

Paul Anka's first recording, "Diana," sold in excess of 8½ million copies—the third largest-selling single record of all time. A national publicity campaign was launched over the enigma of Diana's identity. Several girl vocalists and actresses of the

128

early 1960s were considered as fantasy possibilities in publicity releases. Like most publicity department fantasies, however, these were simply nonsense—designed only to milk that high discretionary income from the pockets of teen-ager's parents.

Paul Anka, serving the Oedipal conflicts of North American teen-agers, serenaded his symbolic mother:

> *I'm so young and you're so old*
> *This my darling I've been told*
> *I don't care just what they say*
> *'Cause forever I will pray*
> *You and I will be as free*
> *As the birds up in the trees*
> *Oh please stay by me, Diana**

A handful of the hundreds of lyrics which utilize maternal identifications include Elvis Presley's "(You're So Square) Baby I Don't Care," Joe South & the Believers' "Walk a Mile in My Shoes," Bobby Vee's "Rubber Ball" and "Sharing You," and Frankie Avalon's "Welcome Home." Only once in a while does Mother get into a song at the conscious level as in Jo-Anne Campbell's "Mother, Please!" and Roy Orbison's "Mama."

Father, as a symbol of dominance, authority, respect, and love, plays a limited role in mainstream popular American music. When he appears it is most frequently in the country and western field. One recording superstar, Jimmy Dean, made a fortune out of an idealized father projection in his "Big Bad John," followed by "Little Bitty Big John," and finally "P. T. 109," which dealt with John F. Kennedy's wartime experience. When the trilogy was completed, Jimmy Dean could have retired for three lifetimes to the French Riviera. All of which seems to prove that there is money to be made out of paternal, as well as maternal fantasies in the American dream.

* "Diana" words and music by Paul Anka © copyright 1957 by Pamco Music, Inc. © copyright assigned 1963 to Spanka Music Corp., 445 Park Avenue, New York, N.Y., for USA & Canada only. Used by permission, all rights reserved.

For many years, American culture has been discussed as a matriarchy. Women—both real and symbolic mothers—have long dominated the society, especially the children. Long-haired teen-age boys are precisely what mothers would have endorsed thirty years ago if their husbands had permitted them to get away with it. Long hair on male children used to be cut when the boy finished the Oedipal stage, rarely later than the fifth year.

Beatles Followed Bobbies

No discussion of popular music in America would be complete without mentioning the Beatles. The Beatles emerged from an evolution of musicians and composers that between 1956 and 1958, culminated in Elvis Presley. During a military service eclipse in Presley's career, a small army of Bobbies were hatched by the industry—Bobby Curtola, Bobby Vee, Bobby Darin, Bobby Rydell, Bobby Freeman, *ad infinitum*. The Bobby phenomenon died slowly during the early 1960s when a brief, though intense, dance-fad period developed with Chubby Checker's "Twist." Dee Dee Sharp, Bobby Rydell, Little Eva, The Orlons, and the Dovells promoted dance songs such as "The Fly," "The Pony," "The Hully Gully," "The Mashed Potato," "The Locomotion," "The Bristol Stomp," "The Hitchhiker," "The Limbo Rock" and "The Wah-Watusi."

These dance fads came into vogue after large investments and heavy promotion expenses, but few stayed alive long enough to yield either high or sustaining profits. Market segmentation and segment isolation began to evolve as a more dependable music merchandising strategy.

Teeny-boppers are young teens, thirteen to fourteen and preteens, eleven to twelve. Their music is called *bubblegum,* designed for fans still young or innocent enough to chew gum rather than smoke tobacco or pot. Toward the end of 1963, no bubblegum music appeared on national U.S. hit surveys. The market was wide open.

Already a phenomenal success in England, the Beatles' skilled marketing technicians invaded America. By January 1964, songs such as "I Saw Her Standing There," "I Want to Hold Your Hand," "From Me to You," "She Loves You,"

"Please Mr. Postman," "All My Lovin'," and "Hold Me Tight" appeared in the top ten. During February, Ed Sullivan captured 94 percent of the Class A time Sunday night television audience when he featured the Beatles for only fifteen minutes on his national variety show.

The craze was on. Teeny-boppers drove their parents into distraction over the purchase of Beatles dolls, records, T-shirts, etc. The Beatles sold everything that could be attached to their name and image.

It is impossible to determine how much of the Beatles fad was actually created (in the sense of adding something new) and how much was merely a reflection of psychosocial dynamics already operating in Western society. Very likely, the Beatles both innovated as well as attached themselves to the undercurrents of the past.

Though the four Beatles were the only visible portion of the empire, there were several hundred skilled—though invisible—technicians behind the scenes who created and manipulated the illusions. No one will likely ever know for certain which portions of what the public perceived as the Beatles was actually produced by the four young men or their staff. For example, the Beatles often recorded separately, and their four (or more) recordings were mixed electronically for the final album. The technique gave their engineers complete control over what finally appeared.

Plaintive Puberty Pleadings

An entire book could be devoted to a study of the lyrics written for the early Beatles music. It would probably make dull reading, however, as the puberty agonies portrayed become highly repitious. These songs did, nevertheless, tell the teeny-boppers what they most wanted to hear. And many parents probably felt a sense of relief when their kids dropped the ass-bumping sexuality of pre-Beatles groups.

Once established, the Beatles became one of the few groups engineered to transcend market segmentation and achieve almost universal appeal. According to Beatles biographer Hunter Davies, every Beatles album, even before 1968, sold in excess of one million copies. The retail price became higher and higher as they milked the market for all it was worth. One multimillion-seller album, *Abbey Road*, sold for ten dollars. A publicity release from the Beatles' management had the temerity to state that fans should be grateful they could obtain the record even at that price.

In 1968 the industry's most successful album was released by Capitol Records—*Sergeant Pepper's Lonely Hearts Club Band*. As a monument to electronic gimmickry, *Sergeant Pepper* was a work of art. The album—by the producer's own admission—required over four hundred hours to record. Perhaps strangely, the album reflected despair, hopelessness, and the futility and hypocrisy of modern life's illusions. To the uninitiated parent, however, the record appeared gay, light, and even humorous. Minor portions were perceived by the teen-age audience consciously, but the largest portion was heard only at subliminal levels.

Side One concerned illusion and means by which people hide truth from themselves. The side began with the business of show business, the greatest illusion of them all. Drugs were dealt with in the songs "Fixing a Hole" and "Lucy in the Sky with Diamonds"—a not so hidden reference to LSD.

Lush verbal imagery and musical phrase distortions conveyed the hallucinations from an acid trip:

"With tangerine trees and marmalade skies . . ."

Refusals by parents to face the truth or deal with realities were caustically dealt with in "Getting Better," the parental illusion of their idealized relationship with their children in "She's Leaving Home," which pictured parents after their daughter had run away from home:

> *We gave her most of our lives . . .*
> *We gave her everything money can buy. . . .*

The song's narrator sings in counterpoint to the lyrics:

> *She's leaving home after living alone*
> *For so many years**

---

* "She's Leaving Home" by Lennon/McCartney © 1967 Northern Songs, Ltd.

Side One concluded with a return from disturbed family relationships to the illusions of show business.

Side Two opened with a song by George Harrison, "Within You Without You," which summarized the meaning of Side One.

> *The space between us all, and the people who*
> *Hide themselves behind a wall of illusion.**

The next three compositions considered life without drugs or hypocrisy—the sterile, ritualized roles people play. The first "When I'm Sixty-four," ridiculed the life of an elderly couple; the second, "Lovely Rita," made fun of romantic love, extolling the tribulations of a Liverpool whore who procured through her respectable job as a meter maid. The third, deceptively titled, "Good Morning, Good Morning," desolately described the futility and banality of life.

The reprise of *Sergeant Pepper's* theme changed dramatically. Sergeant Pepper was no longer the outrageously funny character who promised smiles and entertainment. Repeating the line four times, the Beatles sang "Sergeant Pepper's lonely." In summary, the final song, "A Day in the Life," questioned whether man could live without his illusions.

A Literature for the Young

Heady stuff for teen-agers? Jon Eisen in *The Age of Rock* compared *Sergeant Pepper* with T. S. Eliot's *Wasteland* in its near desperate reflections upon contemporary life. Dealing—for most of the fans—at subliminal levels, the Beatles became spokesmen for their generation who resisted the status quo. Their record company simply attached their resistance, quite normal resistance among the young at least since the times of Socrates, to the mass merchandising of music. The Beatles even, at one point, exposed themselves as illusions or put-ons created by their early manager Brian Epstein. They declared publicly that from *Sergeant Pepper* onward, they planned to be themselves both off stage and on. Their fans believed

* "Within You Without You" by George Harrison © 1967 Northern Songs, Ltd.

them, to the tune of tens of millions of dollars in record purchases.

At the subliminal level, *Sergeant Pepper* was heavily integrated with sex, drugs, and revolutionary politics. It is difficult to determine where the line or threshold lies between conscious and subliminal perception for any stimuli as complex as *Sergeant Pepper*. One thing is certain, however. Parents never got the message, though most of them strongly rejected *Sergeant Pepper* without consciously realizing why. Of course, this parental rejection played right into the marketing technique, virtually assuring the record's success.

"Jude" Hits Jackpot

One of the most popular recordings of 1968 was the Beatles single "Hey Jude"* and "Revolution." "Revolution" dealt with politics and was sung by John Lennon—the symbolic father of the Beatles' archetypal family. Paul McCartney, who consistently portrayed a maternal role in the family, sang "Hey Jude," providing spiritual advice in the form of drugs as an escape route for pain.

Two meanings for "Jude" appeared as likely symbology in the song. "Jude" could have referred to Judas who betrayed Christ under the guise of friendship. Heroin, of course, at first seems to be a friend before it betrays the user into addiction. The second possibility involved the Apostle Jude who warned against those who call themselves Christians while living hypocritically in a morally loose society.

The haunting voice of McCartney sang, "Let her into your heart," "Her" meaning the drug and "heart" the pump that circulates drug-laden blood through the body—so "you can start to make it better."

During the lonely opening verse, the drug injection occurred. In the second verse, musicians joined to make the sound (life) more full and complete. The lyrics tell us, "Don't be afraid." "The moment you let her under your skin, you begin to make it better."

* "Hey Jude" by Lennon/McCartney © 1967 Northern Songs, Ltd.

The third verse said, ". . anytime you feel the pain, Hey Jude—refrain."

"Refrain" means, in one sense, leave it alone. But, the inverse symbology means repeat the chorus or repeat the injection at the end of each good period when the pain returns. The verse explained that only a fool pretends there is nothing wrong with empty feelings and avoids being helped by the heroin. The reference to "cool" and "a little colder" is curious. A common symptom of the deprived addict is being continuously cold. The message here is why be cold when "she" or "her" is available.

The narrator, or drug pusher, repeats his plea in the fourth verse, asking "don't let me down." All you need do is "go and get her" and "let her into your heart."

The fifth verse advised, "Let it out and let it in." Let out inhibited emotions and feelings, let the drug or syringe into your body. "You're waiting for someone to perform [synonym for trip] with." "Don't you know it's just you." You are all that is necessary. "The movement you need is on your shoulder," suggesting either the arm used for the injection or the monkey on your back or shoulder.

The final verse counseled, "don't take it bad"—a bad trip should be avoided. "Make it better," by releasing inhibitions and fears. Toward the end of the song, a scream is heard for "Mamma!"—a cry for help, a plea for rescue from the drug addiction.

As the song progressed, a screaming, maniacal chant is heard in the background—providing a contrapuntal theme to the lyric. The chorus chanted, "you gotta break it"—an apparent reference to the habit—"you know you can make it," "don't go back," or in other words, Stay clean!

Jude's future at the conclusion is uncertain. The audience never found out whether Jude had kicked the habit or gone on to another fix. The probability that the addiction continued, however, appeared far more likely. "Hey Jude" could, to put it conservatively, reinforce a tendency toward addiction, making it appear a logical solution to a young person's normal conflicts with authority, society, and the maturation process.

Immortality May Be Forever

Any hope the Beatles would eventually run their course and disappear into limbo is purely wishful thinking. Their pervasive influence upon young people all over the world persists.

In 1973 two anthologies were released: *Beatles 1962–1966* and *Beatles 1967–1970*. Both albums were million sellers within three weeks. A year later, both albums were still among the top hundred in Current LP Sales, according to *Billboard*. George Harrison's *Living in the Material World* and Paul McCartney's *Red Rose Speedway* were also released in 1973 and were instantly successful.

In interviews with young record purchasers in 1974, many admitted that in spite of the high cost of new Beatles records, they purchased them usually without hearing the music. None could explain why. Their behavior resembled that of either robots or Pavlov's dogs responding to bell stimuli.

Keeping the Beatles myth alive with manufactured rumors or pseudo-news about an eternally promised Beatles reunion, the news media helped perpetuate the mythological image. For example, a well-engineered publicity release in *Newsweek* of March 26, 1973, commented upon the new record releases of the folk heroes of the American dream-marketing industry:

> It was, as producer Richard Perry noted, the first time the three have played together since the Beatles. But any future reunion is pure conjecture. An awful lot of impure conjecturing was going on including the possibility, encouraged by business manager Allen Klein, that the three Beatles would remain in L.A. to record a real John, George, and Ringo album.

The above logic is much like the old question "Will she or won't she?" As long as no one is certain, she will be courted, pursued, indulged, and kept alive in our fantasies.

No one today questions the Beatles' impact upon Western society. They were successful in many languages, even reaching into the collective unconscious of such tradition-oriented cultures as the Russian and Japanese. The mythology follows each of the four young multimillionaires as they grow older and journey from wife to wife and from one misadventure to another. They are viewed as the initiators of an important epoch of history, the founders of popular culture, and the beginning of an entire army of popular music heroes who exploited their tradition.

However, when anyone asks direct questions as to the Beatles' contribution to Western society, the answers are always vague, unspecific, and usually involve some aspect of the mystique. During several hundred interviews with both children and adults, no one appeared to have any exact idea about the specific differences in their lives that might be directly attributed to the Beatles. Every answer given by these respondents could have been said of other musical groups going back into the 1920s, 30s, or 40s.

A Value System Changed

The answer was amazingly simple and so shocking that no one had apparently put it together. *The Beatles popularized and culturally legitimatized hallucinatory drug usage among teen-agers throughout the world.*

Hallucinatory and addictive drugs had never before been a part of any society's main cultural value system. Even in places like Indochina, where the French legalized opium as a technique of population management and control, drugs were confined to a minority of users—usually the economically or politically disenfranchised. Certainly, drug usage had never before in the world's history been advertised heavily—as a record promotion technique—by popular music directed at adolescents.

An examination of best-selling music lyrics during the five years preceding the Beatles failed to turn up many song lyrics that could even remotely be interpreted as drug ballads. Pre-Beatles lyrics were crammed with overt and covert sexual symbolism. Death was not an infrequent symbolic entity celebrated subliminally in popular song. But drugs were simply not being pushed, even though drug usage was, as it had always been, apparent among American society's disenfranchised fringes. The Beatles became the super drug culture prophets and pushers of all time. Drugs, of course, ultimately involve self destruction, and death, or withdrawal from reality.

Western society, especially England and North America, had been well primed for expanded drug usage through years of conditioning by pharmaceutical, alcohol, and tobacco advertising. Media long ago established a culturally accepted legitimacy for the use of chemical solutions for problems of emotional adjustment. For the music industry to expand one step beyond household psychogenic products to hallucinatory drug utilization by teen-agers was so simple that even a child should have been able to figure it out. Children did figure it out, of course. No one outside the industry got wise to what was going on, nor did they even suspect how the marketing plan worked.

The Bridge to Happiness

According to *Billboard*, "Bridge over Troubled Water" sold over 5 million copies during 1969 as a single recording. The album sold over 4 million copies—the second highest seller during a single year in the history of record sales. (The Beatles' *Sergeant Pepper* was the first.) "Bridge," however, as single and album, received a total of five of the recording industry's Oscar equivalents—the Grammy Awards—in 1969.

Paul Simon and Art Garfunkel won best-selling single, best-selling album, best-engineered single, best-engineered album, and best composer.

Paul Simon, the composer, claimed he took a month to write "Bridge" and another month to record the composition. The rather simple, unassuming final recording lasted four minutes and fifty-two seconds—rather long for the average single. For Simon, this was a major project. His other hit records were composed, so he claimed, in only a day or two.

As Simon explained in an interview with *Jazz and Pop Magazine*, "I wanted to create a feeling of comfort. The words are relaxing, warm, almost euphoric. My music has always been different from what's normally on the top ten. I've been quite successful. I hadn't recorded for about a year and a half. The listening public wondered where I was. I knew the song would be successful. I don't buy the American Bandstand success formula. I've always done my own musical thing. The secret to me has been a genial fusion of music and lyrics."

Whether the above statement was written by Simon or one of his many publicity writers is irrelevant. The usual vague, meaningless euphemisms for reality—*relaxing, warm, euphoric, musical thing, genial fusion*—says nothing really about what the composer was doing in "Bridge."

As a very skilled merchant of symbolic values in both words and music, Simon knows better. Illusions are a tough business. In order to reap the millions of dollars he has taken from teen-age record buyers, in the most competitive business in the world, Simon must be a skilled professional. He, his financial backers, musicians, arrangers, and electronic technicians must know precisely what they are doing—or they simply won't succeed. The hundred or so invisible specialists who surround them put everything they had into the song, along with the quarter of a million dollars of capital investment required to launch a new record nationally.

"Bridge," at first hearing, *is* crude—almost amateurish. The beat is weak and undanceable, even phlegmatic. Neither cracking drums, electric guitars, nor a hard-driving bass were utilized. At the beginning, a weak, psalm-playing piano appeared. After the initial verse, faraway violins, vibraharp, softened bass, and echoing drums formed the background. Indeed, at the time "Bridge" was released, it seemed to have done everything wrong—just the opposite of current trade practices. There is simply no way to explain the success in terms of what was cognitively perceived by music fans. (See Appendix A.)

A Feeling Massage

"Bridge" dealt primarily with feelings in its target audience, massaging these feelings with subliminal stimuli. When trying to probe the subliminal level of the lyric, the first question was simply, *Who is talking to whom about what, and why?* Specifically, who was "I"—the person singing? A list of people representing both personal and occupational relationships for teen-agers was prepared. All those included were individuals with whom teen-agers were likely to have a close, familiar, intimate, and trusting relationship—the kind and quality of relationship suggested by Art Garfunkel's voice on the recording. Included were twenty-two possible designations for "I"—mother, father, motel owner, brother, sister, drug pusher, hairdresser, boyfriend, girl friend, sweetheart, mechanic, minister or priest, gas station attendant, teacher, etc. The list was presented to roughly fifty teen-agers who were asked to check off the single most likely candidate for the "I" in "Bridge."

After they learned what they were supposed to do, roughly 30 percent of the teen-agers refused to play the game. Many rationalized that they could not make up their minds. Others in this group simply refused to try. Avoidance behavior was clearly apparent.

Roughly another 55 percent provided varied answers—mother, father, etc. These appeared random and spread out across the entire list.

Roughly 15 percent of the students cited drug pusher as the "I" in "Bridge."

The reader may consider this possible interpretation as absurd. For a moment, however, consider the hypothetical possibilities.

If the "I" or the singer is a drug pusher, what he is describing in the song is a drug trip. His customer—or addict—is the young audience bewildered by the fast-paced, automated, depersonalized, lonely, complex, and powerful society.

> *When you're weary, feeling small,*
> *When tears are in your eyes . . .**

"Bridge," therefore, becomes symbolically a drug user's guide to withdrawal into a syringe-injected hallucinatory drug experience—most probably heroin—but this could be also interpreted as speed or amphetamines. The lyric extols the promise of drug relief from depression, loneliness, and uncertainty. The music symbolically forms the trip itself. The verses are sung in two-part harmony, indicating to the audience subliminally that two people are on the trip—the listener and their drug-peddler guide.

* © 1969 Paul Simon. Used with the permission of the publisher.

The pusher is talking, much like a physician on a television pharmaceutical advertisement, to weary and alienated young people whom the world forces into tears. He is "on your side" when "times get rough" and when "friends can't be found."

The pitchman drug pusher claims he acts as "a bridge over troubled water"—a support to help the audience over the turbulent rapids of day-to-day life. The first verse provides a come-on, an opening pitch, much like the warmup used by insurance or encyclopedia salesmen. The second verse is a stronger focus upon the product through symbolic archetypes and imagery. The third verse really gets down to business, presenting a hard sell, deep in meaning and subliminal significance.

The musical arrangement during the first and second verses suggested a feeling of agitation, discomfort, imbalance, and insecurity. As the music moved into the third verse, parallel with the lyric story line, it conveys a feeling of euphoria, security, and relaxation as the drug takes effect.

A Search for Security

In the first verse the music begins with a lone piano chording, as Simon specified in the published arrangement, "moderato . . . like a spiritual." The spiritual piano is sustained throughout the arrangement, alternately dominant and passive in the background. The piano symbolizes unconscious remnants of childhood feelings such as love and protection derived from Mother or the Sunday School sense of security in being watched over by Jesus.

As Art Garfunkel's voice begins in the first verse, he sings of "being weary, small, of tears, of being down and out." In the published arrangement the piano is directed to play "rubato"—a rhythmic give and take, a lingering or hurrying over notes. Time (meter) is bent. The piano reflects the audience's unstable state of mind or emotion.

In the second verse the listener is still "*down* and out," but now "on the street." The street of life is where the troubled water swirls, the place where society rushes frantically to nowhere. The street is loud, impersonal, and cold. The pusher promises. "when evening falls so hard, I will comfort you."

Evening is symbolic of death and darkness, perhaps the color lessness of American society.

The pusher declares his willingness to "take your part"—become the audience, suffer for them while they escape through drugs. "When darkness comes and pain is all around," the pusher will provide "a bridge over troubled water." The line, as sung, includes a brief pause before and afterward.

"And pain is all around." Pain in the young audience's minds must be avoided at all costs. Harsh realities and dark images of death must be somehow put aside. As the second verse is sung, the orchestration produced a vague discomfor and feeling of uneasiness.

The rhythmically unstable piano joins a low-key, quiet vi braharp at the beginning of the second verse. The discord literally jars audience attention, as the chord is in a different key from the song. At this point, the electronic bass plays a series of dominant notes which slide from a low E-natural up two octaves to an A-flat. The sliding notes move from an ex treme low to an extreme high, unconsciously elevating the au dience to a higher plane in the arrangement's subliminal background.

And Finally the Needle

The third verse involves the actual syringe injection and the comforting assurance that—if needed again—the pusher will be available with more. A long pause appears between the second and third verses, suggesting the time it takes to prepare for a drug injection.

To "sail on" is to be free of fear and inhibition, to achieve the escape sought in the second verse. "Sail" conveys a feeling of light, liveliness, grace, and freedom—as opposed to the second verse's death imagery. "Sail" even suggests the flight of a bird—the release from reality and its pain, free of the social gravity that forces individuals into the dirt of the second verse's "street," energy—not weariness; feeling big, tall, significant—not "feeling small." "Sail on by" is opposed to the second verse's "Lay me down."

"Silvergirl," in the first line of the third verse, is one of the teen-age euphemisms used to describe a hypodermic syringe.

In "Bridge" the pusher speaks to the syringe as he injects the drug, "Sail on silvergirl." "Silver" refers generally to the shiny needle and "girl," of course, to youth, fertility, rebirth through drugs, and the narcotic itself.

"Sail on by" carries the drug from body into mind. "Your times has come to shine," the pusher says to both the audience and the syringe—time to work or "shine."

"All your dreams are on their way" is a separate sentence, yet on the record sounds like a subordinate clause, part of "Your time has come to shine." Simon, apparently, handles the phrasing like this to catch the audience off guard and more easily reach into their unconscious.

The pusher vocalist speaks to his audience after the injection. "All your dreams are on their way." He is heavily pitching the drug, emphasizing its miraculous results. "See how they shine" described the audience's fantasies and dreams as these illusions come alive and true.

"If you need a friend, I'm sailing right behind." The pusher and his drug-loaded syringe are right there with you, audience, so don't feel alone.

The last sentence of the third verse differs from the last sentence of the first and second verses. The drug pusher pitches, "I will ease your mind." This might be called the punch line of the drug pitch.

After the users (audience) have tried the drug, after their fantasies have become realities, after they have escaped from the harsh brutalities of life, and after the drug trip is over, the pusher will ease their minds by relaxing their anxieties about drug usage, coming down off the trip, and assure a drug source for the next trip to ease the "troubled water."

After the electric bass's low to high slide in the second verse, the bass works throughout the rest of the song, serving as subdued background. At the start of the third verse, the drums are consciously apparent at the beginning of the drug trip. The drums produced a muddy and unreal tempo, quite different from straight timekeeping. The drums, however, usually remained buried deeply in the background under the other instruments.

Only the snare drum intruded upon consciousness with any clarity, but it also remained an unclear, though steady, background echo. The snare copied the heartbeat at seventy-two beats per minute (4/4 time) during the first two verses. The snare tempo induces a state of prehypnotic suggestibility as the listener perceives the snare only subliminally.

Bass and drums work similarly during the third verse—a thumping seventy-two pulses per minute, carried into the fantasy of "the shining dream" during the third verse.

Violins entered the third verse, adding another fantasy dimension to the music. By increasing the volume of musical background, the subliminal dimensions of the drug trip expanded. The faint piano, however, presented a constant nagging reminder of the audience's once stable and secure past. The at first subdued, then dominant bass, drums, violins, and vibraharps carried the audience along on their trip where "all your dreams are on their way."

Loneliest Scene in Town

In response to subliminal meanings for words and music, one of America's most repressed forms of sexual communication appears in teen-age dancing. One of the readily observable effects of highly amplified sound or music is isolation. People in a crowded room can be totally isolated from one another by simply increasing the music amplifier's volume level. No one communicates even through eye contact. Speech is not attempted. There is very rarely physical touching. Each individual sits staring into an empty space—usually a very small, unoccupied space. Communication disappears. Each appears carried away by his or her very own, very personal, and very secret fantasies.

When couples dance to highly amplified rock, a similar isolation occurs. Many of the dance movements—pelvic actions, self-touching, and leg and body movements—are frankly sexual. Everyone appears not to notice, however, and the secret is well kept. No touching is permitted, not even with eyes.

The partners skillfully avoid looking at or physically touching their companion. Each appears entirely alone. This isolation is often described by the phrase "doing your own thing." Any overt gesture that involved touching, intimacy, or gentle caressing during these dances would be considered crude, uncouth, and annoying—a violation of both privacy and protocol.

There is a strong resemblance to these teen-age dances and the relationships observable at a drug party. Anyone who believes marijuana is a party turn-on makes a serious error. Hallucinatory drugs are more accurately described as *turn-ins*. One of the most effective ways to wreck a party is to introduce pot or hash. Individuals rapidly end up doing their own thing alone. The party fragments quickly from group interaction to individual trips deep inside each person's head. The participants sit on the floor giggling nonsense to themselves. The inside fantasy deludes individuals into believing they are eloquent and sensitively communicative, but it is only another fantasy.

Even today, Americans' unwillingness to deal with the realities of drug usage is astonishing. Should the reader still believe the power of a popular record is insignificant, consider how much advertising media would have to be purchased by an advertiser to reach the audience for any of the records cited in this chapter. Then compare the selling power of the most creative, subliminally loaded, powerful, and most expensive ad possible to create. The selling power would still not even begin to approximate the high-credibility source impact of a single release by an established music group.

Why these drug fantasies, designed to appeal only to the unconscious, sell records is not entirely clear nor is it logical or reasonable unless you are willing to accept Freud's notion of the human "death wish" or "death instinct." Nevertheless, death and self destruction are clearly successful subliminal merchandising techniques in alcohol, tobacco, drugs, and other products. Why shouldn't they sell records?

Just think—it all began with the Beatles.

9

Cultural Conditioning for Addiction

> *The subject was no more trying to learn something from television than she would be trying to learn something from a landscape while resting on a park bench. Yet television is communication. What shall we say of it, a communication medium that effortlessly transmits huge quantities of information* not thought about at the time of exposure, *but much of it capable of being stored for later activation?*

> HERBERT E. KRUGMAN
> *Electroencephalographic*
> *Aspects of Low Involvement*

Addiction as a Marketing Objective

Among the small army of public health specialists who concern themselves with addictive behavior, a new perspective has begun to emerge. Narcotics has turned out to be only the tip of the addiction iceberg. The pathetic heroin user is the obvious, extreme end of the spectrum, involving a usually atypical deviant group within the general society. Narcotics

146

addicts are apparent only because eventually they must involve themselves in criminal activities to support their habits.

Much less obvious, the twentieth century has spawned a whole range of behavioral responses that can only be described as addictive. On an enormous scale, involving billions of invested dollars annually, Americans are induced into a value system that applauds addictive behavior almost as a patriotic duty. This wide spectrum of addictive behavior is socially acceptable and invisible for the most part. The American addict behaves precisely as he has been instructed since birth to behave.

America's most honored, celebrated, and profitable forms of addiction involve alcohol, tobacco, and drugs—the three highest-profit products manufactured and marketed in modern society. The list extends to a whole range of other products. The cost of selling these three products, of which advertising is only a portion, is also the highest for any manufactured product in America. As addictive substances, these three products are mutually reinforcing—heavy drinkers are invariably heavy smokers, and almost always heavy consumers of psychogenic drugs such as analgesics, tranquilizers, antidepressants, etc. These three products all propose chemical solutions for problems of emotional adjustment.

According to Morris Chafetz, former Director of HEW's National Institute of Alcohol Abuse and Alcoholism (NIAAA), "Alcoholism among both youths and adults has at last been recognized as a modern plague." NIAAA statistics revealed that roughly 10 percent of the over 100 million Americans who drink are already either "problem drinkers" or full-fledged alcoholics. "Problem drinker" is merely a polite way to describe an incipient alcoholic or anyone compulsively involved in alcohol consumption. A teen-ager can develop an alcohol addiction in as short a period as eighteen months. An adult might take ten years or more.

The Payoff Outside the Corporation

In a July 1974 study of alcoholism, HEW made some startling disclosures about drinking. The annual subsidy paid by all Americans to support the distilling industry is roughly $25 billion—$9.5 billion lost in absenteeism, $8.5 billion lost in health care directly attributable to alcoholism, $6.5 billion in motor accidents, and $.5 billion in research. And these are not just cold financial statistics. During 1973, nineteen thousand Americans were killed in alcohol-related accidents. There is overwhelming evidence that alcohol contributes to heart disease, brain damage, homicide (in 50 percent of U.S. murders, either the victim or the killer had been drinking) and suicide (25 percent of suicides in the United States have high alcoholic content in their blood). In one Ontario study of 22,600 deaths of persons between twenty and seventy, alcohol was responsible for 38 percent of cirrhosis deaths, 22 percent of peptic ulcers, 18 percent of suicides, 15 percent of pneumonia, 16 percent of deaths from cancer of the upper digestive and respiratory tracts, and over 5 percent of heart and artery disease deaths. Alcohol was also involved in 45 percent of deaths by poisoning, 43 percent by accidental fire and nearly 25 percent of falls and other physical trauma deaths.

Of total deaths in Ontario for the year of the study, 11 percent were clearly alcoholic-related. The alcoholic, it was discovered, had twice the chance of premature death than the nonalcoholic. The average alcoholic's life-span is shortened by ten to twelve years.

Heavy drinkers are seven times more prone to marital separations or divorce than the general U.S. population, and nearly half the annual 55,000 automobile deaths and the 1 million major injuries involve alcohol.

About 13,000 people die each year from liver cirrhosis. The HEW study revealed a close correlation between heavy drinking and cancer of the liver, mouth, and throat. Heavy drinkers have a fifteen times greater probability of cancer than do nonsmoking teetotalers. The nondrinking smoker has only a four times greater probability of cancer than the nonsmoker.

Teen-Aged Drinkers

Lowering of the drinking age to eighteen, occurring in various states with the strong though subtle support of the distilling industry, has had disastrous effects. The HEW study revealed that one out of four American teen-agers now classifies as "alcoholic" or "problem drinker." Michigan reported a 141 percent increase in arrests for drunken driving the first year after its legal drinking age was reduced to eighteen.

Parents, strangely, are leading the pressure groups now demanding a lowering of the drinking age in every state. Many are often relieved to find their children involved with drinking rather than drugs—though the two are consumed in combination by most teen-agers today.

In San Mateo County, California, only a few miles south of San Francisco, school officials discovered in 1970 that 11 percent of ninth-grade boys (thirteen- to fourteen-year-olds) admitted drinking alcoholic beverages fifty or more times during the year. By 1973, when the county repeated the survey, the figure had jumped to 23 percent. Among seventeen- and eighteen-year-old seniors, frequent drinkers rose from 27 percent to an astonishing 40 percent. Fewer seventeen- to eighteen-year-old girls drank, the study reported, but were catching up fast—29 percent in 1973, compared with 14 percent in 1970. It would be obscene to translate this suffering and degradation merely into dollars—the usual criterion of value in North America. But if you did, the cost would be far in excess of the $25 billion price for alcohol consumption.

Addicts Are Just Like Everyone

In the past, middle-aged men appeared the most prone to alcoholism. The pattern is rapidly reversing. During the early 1970s, there appeared a sharp increase in alcoholism among the twenty to thirty age group and among women. During the 1960s, roughly 20 percent of alcoholics treated were women, but by 1974 over 25 percent were women. In certain localities such as Miami, Florida, the ratio reached 50-50.

Skid row derelicts account for less than 5 percent of U.S. alcoholics today. The other 95 percent include everyone—most of whom pass unnoticed until they become involved in sickness, accidents, suicides, or marital and employment problems. Perpetuated by the alcohol industry and society in general is the age-old myth that alcoholics are special people with some basic defect in personality or character. If so, no research over the past fifty years has been able to substantiate the mythology. So far, no one has discovered any common denominator of personality, character, biology, education or income among alcoholics.

To provide even a conservative measure of the power and affluence of the alcohol industry, the U.S. Commerce Department listed total alcohol industry revenues (after federal, state, and local taxes) at nearly $18.5 billion in 1973. This is far below the amount paid by Americans to subsidize the industry.

Alcohol, tobacco, and drug advertising are presently the heaviest in print media—so heavy, in fact, that if alcohol, tobacco, and drug ads were suddenly banned, very possibly about half the advertising dependent publications in the country would go out of business. America's economically hard-pressed newspapers would suffer severely if they lost their ad lineage for any of these three products. Many would simply collapse into bankruptcy.

The Consumption Addict

The media know their drinkers well and have studied them in great detail for many years. Though they rarely admit it, the knowledge that the media, distillers, brewers, and winemakers have about their consumers is vastly beyond anything available at NIAAA or in any university library. Perhaps the best description of *heavy users*—the so-called market within a market—was supplied by the Brand Rating Index (BRI), one of the fanciest and most expensive of media's national research organizations:

"Purely and simply, *heavy users* are the *most important customers* you have. They are the men who consume well beyond the average ... the men who account for a markedly disproportionate share of product purchases and usage. As a rule, these *heavy users* represent an unusually small percentage of the total population. In other words, this active buying minority is the *vital purchasing core* of the prime market for luxury products and quality merchandise."

BRI, as well as many other commercial research organizations, can supply incredibly detailed information on heavy consumers for virtually every major product sold in America.

These heavy consumers can be easily correlated and analyzed into complex psychographic and demographic profiles.

The statistical data goes on and on and on—boring facts for most of us, but they form a sales-strategy bible for anyone in mass merchandising.

Over 85 percent of all adults in the United States use alcohol. But that's not specific enough. Media—in behalf of advertisers—aim at highly specialized groups. For example, if you are selling only vodka, you are not interested in how many rum drinkers might read a particular magazine or newspaper where your ad appears.

The modern advertisers' needs are highly specific. He must seek out the medium that offers him the best deal: minimum cost per thousand reader/vodka drinkers. Media's prime content function is to deliver a suitable number and quality of readers or audience at a competitive price. And the advertiser is not interested only in just plain everyday vodka drinkers.

The advertiser knows, for example, that 8.1 percent of the total United States adult male population accounts for 83.3 percent of all male vodka consumption. Further, the vodka advertiser knows—and can check the data validity from several sources—that only 2.8 percent of adult males in the United States are heavy vodka drinkers, consuming four or more vodka drinks weekly on the average. U.S. vodka drinkers combine vodka with other beverages. But this 2.8 percent of U.S. male, heavy vodka drinkers accounts for 63.3 percent of all vodka consumed by men.

Heavy product users are the most desirable readership or audience for any medium. These heavies often perform an interpersonal leadership function, especially in alcoholic beverages. If you wish to know of a good Scotch, just ask someone who drinks a lot of Scotch.

BRI defines "heavy alcoholic beverage user" as one who drinks "fifteen or more distilled spirit drinks per week," or roughly two drinks (3 ounces) per day. The "problem drinker" and "alcoholic" are in the upper end of the heavy-user spectrum, accounting for the heaviest alcohol consumption of all.

One very elaborate and expensive study commissioned by *Esquire* magazine gave a detailed picture of how publishers deliver to the advertiser the heavy consumers for an enormous range of products. The cost per thousand for heavy consumer readers was compared for most major publications in America. For example, 4.7 percent of *Esquire*'s readers during 1969—something just under 1 million total circulation—were heavy vodka drinkers. *Esquire* sells them to vodka advertisers on a cost-per-thousand basis for a full black-and-white page at $42.91. Not bad for a thousand heavy vodka drinkers, especially when compared with their competition. They would have cost $58.92 per thousand in *Look* magazine.

HEAVY VODKA USERS (4 or more drinks per week)

Publication	% of Total Readers	Cost per Thousand Readers (for full-page black and white)
Life	4.2	$57.20
Look	3.9	58.92
Newsweek	4.9	36.45
New Yorker	4.4	56.58
Playboy	5.2	41.75
Sports Illustrated	4.4	42.55
Time	4.6	48.35
U.S. News & World Report	5.7	39.19
Esquire	4.7	42.91

Source: BRI Study, *The Market Within a Market*

The value of the deal, of course, must take into consideration other elements in the size and quality of their various readerships. The main reason the general circulation publications such as *Life* and *Look* ceased publication was their inability to compete in these specialized readership consumer categories. They had the two highest costs per thousand readers in most major product categories of any publication in the country. Television is a much more efficient and cheaper medium for advertisers who pursue general rather than specialized consumers.

Addicts Are Cheaper by the Thousand

BRI provided similar information and prices per thousand readers for heavy drinkers of Scotch, bourbon, rye or blended whiskey, gin, rum, wine, brandy, cognac, cordials or liqueurs, beer and ale, and ready-to-serve and prepared-mix cocktails. It might be helpful to review the cost-per-thousand ratios for heavy drinkers of *all* alcoholic beverages—many of whom would be included among the 10 million alcoholics and problem drinkers in the United States today.

ALCOHOLIC BEVERAGE HEAVY USERS (15 or more drinks weekly):

Publication	% of Total Readers	Cost per Thousand Readers (for full-page black and white)
Life	9.7	$24.82
Look	8.9	25.39
Newsweek	11.2	15.94
New Yorker	15.3	16.29
Playboy	11.4	19.21
Sports Illustrated	11.5	16.21
Time	10.6	21.03
U.S. News & World Report	12.5	17.89
Esquire	13.6	14.74

The above information is only a small porportion of the total data available to editors and publishers on U.S. drinking and drinkers. *Esquire* paid a very large research fee in order to brag to its potential advertisers about the high proportion of heavy drinkers among their readership and their low cost-per-thousand delivery rate.

Subliminally Massaged Addicts

Virtually all alcohol advertising employs subliminal stimuli. One reason, certainly, is that heavy consumers of any product—at whom most media content is directed—*are likely to be highly susceptible to subliminal stimuli used in relation to that product.*

One of the booze industry's more cynical attacks upon the vulnerable young (toward whom they are strongly discouraged from directing their advertising by several government agencies and national media associations) appeared recently in an alcohol industry public relations poster distributed widely throughout the world. Portrayed were two eighteen-year-olds—clean-cut, clear-cut, neat, forthright, and mature youngsters who peered challengingly from the poster. The caption reads, "You're old enough to drink. Are you mature enough?" What teen-ager could resist replying, "Of course I'm mature enough. My parents think I'm only an irresponsible immature child. I'll show *them* by drinking. . . ."

That the alcohol industry should disguise their advertising to the young consumer behind a facade of concern for alcohol abuse should not surprise anyone. It is not illegal and it is most profitable.

Most of the early life conditioning to accept alcohol is media-induced. Part of the American culture, used cleverly by the alcoholic beverage industry, involves the identification of masculinity with drinking. Virtually all American young men are taught to believe that being able to "hold your liquor" is a sign of manhood. This is believed by many parents, as well as their children. It costs the alcohol industry very little to sustain widely accepted cultural myths.

The Myth of Moderate Drinking

Very infrequently, on television (which still competes heavily for beer and wine advertising) a news special or dramatization deals—sometimes eloquently—with alcoholism. Generally, though, as a residual background to the nation's illusion about itself, media keep the drunk well out of sight. In a drunken society, drunks are almost completely invisible.

Media is deeply indebted to the alcohol industry for millions in advertising support. These figures are extremely conservative estimates by the U.S. Commerce Department. In 1970 newspapers alone received well over $121 million in advertising from the alcohol industry; magazines received $98 million; and television—just for beer and wine advertising—

$67 million. These amounts have vastly increased over the past five years, now totaling over $600 million annually, a massive media environment.

The allegation by publishers and broadcasters that media content is unaffected by advertising is sheer nonsense. In behalf of their advertisers, American news media often softpedal or rationalize such problems as pollution, alcohol and drug abuse, and cigarette smoking. Audiences are conditioned to accept these calamities as "The price of progress," "You can't change human nature," or "We must maintain a reasonable position." During 1972, when cigarette advertising was banned from television and heavy ad budgets were up for grabs, many "respectable" newspapers across America ran editorials defending the right to publish cigarette advertising as "freedom of the press" in a most cynical disregard for the public interest.

Alcoholism has all but disappeared from media content. Back in the 1930–40 era, alcoholism was of a much lesser magnitude, and the alcoholic was visible and very obvious— even joked about. Drunks as objects of humor frequently appeared in print, flims, radio programs, and in the theater.

There are vastly more drunks around today than thirty years ago—both in total number and as a proportion of our population. Yet they have become the invisible men and women of American society. When they infrequently surface, they are perceived as pathetic aberrations to be avoided or dealt with only through professional or institutional intermediaries. In the media fantasies that presume to show American life, alcoholism appears an insignificant problem.

A curious example of media's concern for its heavy advertisers appeared when the HEW 1974 study was announced. In every mention of the research on radio-TV newscasts or publication in magazines or newspapers, a clause or phrase was inserted into the story to make it clear that the pathological alcohol consumption was unrelated to "normal," "social," or "light" drinkers—implying that excessive drinkers were a special type of people.

According to a recent public health survey, media conditioning leads most Americans to conclude that alcohol is much less harmful today than it was before. In America, at least, just the opposite is true.

Another oft-repeated media myth often reminds us, "Europeans know how to drink." Europeans do, indeed! In France, where you rarely see a drunk on the street because of the tolerance levels developed from the world's heaviest alcohol consumption, 42 percent of total health expenditures involve alcohol-related diseases, 50 percent of total hospital beds are occupied by patients with alcohol-related sicknesses, and nearly 10 percent of France's adult population is chronically impaired due to alcohol.

Saturation Life-Styles

The United States appears rapidly headed toward the saturation levels of France, where increases in consumption long ago leveled off. France's national alcohol disaster has been exhaustively studied. And yet, in the name of making a buck, the media continue to lead American consumers down this misery-drenched path.

In stories widely publicized by news media, the U.S. Cooperative Commission on the Study of Alcoholism (an industry public relations front) recommended, ". . . the convivial use of beverage alcohol and drinking with meals should be encouraged, the so-called 'beverage of moderation' [beer] should be stressed, and drinking should become an incidental part of routine activities."

The above statement was the typical rationalized garbage published by Nixon-appointed commissions investigating the public welfare. Such recommendations, often heavily publicized by news media, totally ignored the epidemiological evidence on alcoholic consumption levels. Numerous studies have unequivocally established that neither beer nor wine is a a drink of "moderation" (whatever that may mean). In alcoholism, the *type* of beverage is irrelevant. Domestic wine is the cheapest source of alcohol in American society, beer—quite possibly—the most expensive. Most U.S. hospitals have patients waiting to die from terminal liver disease who have never drunk any alcoholic beverage except beer and wine.

The United States Government gains an annual king's ransom in taxes from consumer taxes on alcohol. But the Nixon Administration appropriated a miserly $138 million in taxpayer dollars to HEW's National Institute of Alcohol Abuse and Alcoholism for 1974 to be applied in research, training, community health services, and public education—not even a good-sized drop in the bucket.

This $138 million is *less than a quarter* of what the industry spent on advertising during 1974 (over $600 million) to create and sustain an extraordinarily successful marketing system. The nearly 10 percent of the North American adult population who are now alcoholics or problem drinkers constitutes a calculated (and apparently acceptable) casualty rate that sustains corporation profits for such organizations as Schenley's, Seagram's, and United Distillers.

To further illustrate the cynical involvment of media in alcohol merchandising, the April 22, 1974, issue of *Time* devoted a cover story to "Alcoholism: New Victims, New Treatments."

The story, like so many major editorial efforts by the affluent and powerful national magazine, was well written and factual as far as it went. The story emphasized the distilling industry's concern over alcoholism, especially among the young. The theme that drinking in moderation is good for the society was clearly apparent.

The story emphasized the $250,000 spent annually by the liquor industry to combat excessive drinking and that the industry had "awakened to the problems caused by excessive use of its products." No mention was made of the over $600 million spent in advertising that year to increase both alcohol consumers and the quantities they consume. The article was a public relations piece for the distilling industry.

As with the food advertisers who fight to place their ads adjacent to articles on dieting and weight reduction, *Time* had no trouble selling liquor advertising in its alcoholism issue. That particular issue was jam-packed with full-page, four-color advertisements for alcoholic beverages—easily approaching a half-million dollars' worth.

The most skillfully executed—and expensive—advertising artwork is utilized in these ads. With their high profits and heavy proportion (6 percent) of sales invested back in advertising, the liquor industry can afford the most creative artists available in America. A single page of advertising art can easily cost $10,000 or much more, not counting display space. But if that ad sells several million dollars' worth of product or brand, it is well worth the price. Several excellent examples of subliminal artwork in alcohol advertising were included in my earlier book, *Subliminal Seduction*.

Merry Christmas From Beefeater

The subliminal themes of love and death still slyly decorate alcohol advertising in magazines, newspapers, and on billboards. One four-color, full-page Beefeater gin ad that appeared in *The New Yorker, Newsweek, Time,* and many other publications just before Christmas 1972 displayed the dignified, foil-capped carton just unwrapped—the white gift-wrapping paper crumpled in the background (see Figure 35).

The stalwart Beefeater stands at ease on the label, firmly grasping his ornamental phallic lance. Embedded mosaics of SEX were lightly etched into the surface of the ad in numerous places. These faint embeds may not be completely visible in the reproduction, but there is much more to perceive that will be visible. By the way, the reader might give some thought to how the word *Beefeater* relates subliminally to American culture. At the conscious, ego-flattering level, the suggestion is a hearty, robust, virile man who eats *beef*(?).

We can see from the BRI study (which defined heavy gin drinkers as those who take four or more drinks a week) that only 2.6 percent of adult male heavy gin drinkers account for 52.5 percent of all gin consumed by men. These heavy drinkers constitute 5.8 percent of *Time* readers, which has 4.4 readers per copy, or over 26 million total readers who are 55 percent male (14.5 million). The space cost of the ad would have been in the neighborhood of $60,000. According to BRI, *Time* magazine merchandised their heavy gin drinking readers at a cost per thousand of $38.46. This figure is based partially on 1969 costs. Heavy gin consumers are unquestionably more expensive on a cost-per-thousand basis today.

Just looking at the Beefeater ad, it is difficult to tell how this very heavy transaction could be triggered by a layout so simple, ordinary, and undistinguished. These banal qualities in the ad are precisely guaranteed to elicit complete *conscious* indifference.

But look! In the paper wrapping beside the bottle—if you follow the line of the label's BEEFEATER to the right, just a fraction of an inch to the left of where the line would intersect the right edge of the white wrapping paper, is the tip of a faintly etched nose. Following the nose upward and to the left, there is an eye socket—a dark, faint shadow. The eye socket shadow appears in a straight line from the top gold border of the label within the white wrapper. From the eye socket downward to the right, it is quite easy to locate the nose, mouth, and jaw of a skull or death mask. The Beefeater death mask appears to be under a shroud formed by the white wrapping paper. Merry Christmas anyone?

Skulls, as well as a wide variety of other death symbols, have been discovered in the advertising of most major alcoholic beverage brands sold in North America. Some readers may find this fact disturbing or unsettling, especially if they have been brand-loyal boozers. But it is time they discovered that distilling corporations know far more about their real motives for drinking than they do themselves.

The Self-Destruct Syndrome

It is difficult to rationalize death symbols' ability to sell booze. One theory might be that drinkers sufficiently saturated with gin may not care if they live or die. Another theory might arise from the Freudian concept of death wish or death instinct. Then again, perhaps defying death—even subliminally—may enhance a drinker's self-image of masculinity and virility. No one knows *why* for certain, but death sells extremely well.

Responding to the Poetzle Effect (discussed in the Exorcist chapter) the consumer never even suspects how his unconscious motives or drives were tapped by media manipulators. Worse, the death appeal is likely to be much more intense an unconscious purchase motivation among the young, especially those experiencing puberty.

After several years of dealing with skulls, genitals, and taboo sex embedded in advertising, the simple themes become highly repetitious and rather dull. After all, love and death have been a basic part of human existence for over a million years. Every once in a while, however, a Madison Avenue artist outdoes himself and develops a new twist to the subliminal flimflam.

One curious subliminal slip of the copywriter's Freudian tongue appeared in national advertising for Canadian Mist whisky. For years, these ads have been published regularly in such periodicals as *Playboy* and *The New Yorker*. The ad series is titled simply, "Canada at its best." The art usually portrays a wilderness scene, a lake or forest, often reminiscent of the Canadian image, which, of course, is different in the United States than it is in Canada. The copy head's play on words is interesting when you simply move the space from between *at* and *its* to between the *a* and *t* in *at*. The subliminal line then reads, "Canada a tits best."

Again, in a tit culture, there is no greater security or source of oral gratification than a tit (symbolic or otherwise), preferably mother's but most any tit will do. The subliminal identification between whiskey and milk must also be a source of financial security for the distilling corporations. The connection is reinforced at Christmas with eggnog ads, and throughout the year with other "milky" drinks such as an Alexander or pink lady—not "pink girl," mind you, but "pink lady." (Ladies are mothers, girls are not.)

Where Is Johnnie Walker Walking?

One of the more famous (or infamous) Johnnie Walker Scotch advertisements placed in *The New Yorker*, *Time*, *Playboy*, etc., portrayed the bottle two-thirds empty with ice cubes immersed in a golden brown liquid. Obviously, the ice cubes have been painted on a photograph of a bottle—a common technique that most ad executives publicly deny (see Figure 36).

The label is partially hidden. But reading up along the edge of the label on the left, the word DED appears. If you consciously thought about it at all—and no one but the agency execs apparently did—you would have rationalized that the letters BON were merely on the hidden side of the label. Perhaps a million dollars was spent buying space for this layout in national and local publications. Is it conceivable some photographer could have accidentally permitted such a critical and frightening word to appear in the ad? Hardly!

The ice cubes painted in the bottle are also curious. If you turn the ad on its left side, a very distinct face—complete with moustache and goatee—appears cleverly hidden away in the ice cube. The ad was shown to several hundred people without one discovering the hidden face, even though many of them were experienced in analyzing subliminal media dimensions (see Figure 37).

Above the face is a strange-looking hat or cap—perhaps a turban, somehow reminiscent of the hats worn popularly at the time of the French Revolution. Once you have had them pointed out, the head and hat are so obvious that it is difficult to believe you repressed the embed when you first saw the ad. The face appears to be bravely smiling. Can you figure out what is so funny? Do not read further until you have figured out the humor of what is going on in the ice cube.

Just below the head, in the area where the neck should be, there is a large ax with its blade buried deeply within the neck of the turbaned head. The ad's subliminally perceived trigger mechanism is, simply, a beheading.

Beheadings are pretty much out of date today except as symbolically motivating devices. A picture of a man with his head cut off is a symbolic castration—the symbolic promise, indeed, of Johnnie Walker Scotch. Could this conceivably be a reason for the heavy Scoth drinker's self-indulgence, providing a reinforcement, justification, and rationalization for impotence fear? Having drunk too much is always a justification for avoiding sex.

A vertible mountain of data on alcoholism is available. Curiously, however, none of this data focuses upon the highly obvious relationship between mass media and drinking. It is a proven fact that *the more drinkers in a society and the more they drink, the higher the proportion of alcoholics.* Commercial media are almost singly responsible for increases both in drinkers and quantities drunk in North America over the past several decades.

If media advertising reinforcements for alcoholic consumption were suddenly stopped—in the unlikely case any political administration would brave attacks from both the liquor industry and the press (this would probably be presented to the public as interfering with freedom of the press) there would still be alcoholism. The long-term effects of subliminal programming for consumption may endure in some unconscious memory systems throughout life. The high rate of increase in consumption should almost immediately decrease. But a decade or more might pass before significant decreases in consumption and alcholism would occur.

Media advertising—like all advertising and sales promotion efforts—has two specific objectives: increase the number of consumers and increase the quantity of consumption. In alcoholic beverages, this also means an increase in alcoholics (very heavy consumers). It is quite clear and extremely simple. So simple, in fact, it is hard to believe—considering the millions in public funds spent annually on alcoholism research—that no one has put it together before this.

10

The Filter Tip Medicine Show

> *Because men are in a group,
> and therefore weakened,
> receptive, and in a state of
> psychological regression, they
> pretend all the more to be
> "strong individuals." The mass
> man is clearly sub-human, but
> pretends to be superhuman. He
> is more suggestible, but insists
> he is more forceful; he is more
> unstable, but thinks he is firm
> in his convictions . . .*
>
> *Democracy is based on the
> concept that man is rational and
> capable of seeing clearly what
> is in his own interest, but the
> study of public opinion suggests
> this is a highly doubtful proposition.*

JACQUES ELLUL
Propaganda

Puffing Their Way to Oblivion

There are an estimated 55 million smokers in the United States. In spite of intensive antismoking media campaigns over the past five years, American Cancer Society studies revealed more people are smoking more cigarettes today than ever before. The tobacco industry spends well over $250 million annually on advertising, most of which is focused upon young people under twenty.

Like the distilling industry, tobacco marketers plow about 6 percent of their total income back into advertising. But each year some smokers die off. A small percentage (very small) quit, and a few switch to pipe or cigars in the vain hope this may improve their survival chances. The smoker withdrawal rate is carefully calculated and studied by all major tobacco corporations. Should this rate suddenly begin to increase sharply, their investments would be in serious jeopardy. But they have nothing to worry about as long as they can advertise.

There are only two ways for a tobacco manufacturer to obtain new smokers for his brand. He can pirate smokers from competing brands, or he can go after new smokers, conditioning them to consumption long before they have taken their first puff.

Pirating is usually attempted by give-aways, contests, rewards, etc., but in the industry, pirating is generally looked upon as an ineffective and very expensive marketing technique. Pirated smokers are highly prone to change brands once again in response to new promotions by competing brands.

Were you to build a mathematical model of the American tobacco consumer market (which was actually done by most major tobacco manufacturers years ago), you would classify brand-changing smokers by such correlations as their time as smokers, quantities smoked daily, age smoking began, brand changing characteristics and frequencies, and include data on smoking practices, sexual and social behavior, etc.

Normal consumer brand changing usually cancels itself out over several years. One brand may lose, say, 8 percent of its consumers to one competitor, but pick up roughly the same amount from other brands. It is difficult for an individual brand to hold its own in this game of musical cigarette brands. So, new brand names constantly appear; old ones disappear.

Several years ago, a major cigarette manufacturer established in a series of research interviews that their market had distinct basic brand-changing patterns for males and females. Variations for males and females were calculated by age group, geographical location, psychological predispositions toward change, and other demographic and psychographic criteria. From the basic data, it was easy for a computer to grind out an enormous variety of correlated information. For example, they could accurately measure present brand preferences and compare them in an algebraic matrix with time smoking the present brand and brands formerly smoked. The system produced highly accurate predictions for future brand changing patterns, predictions which gave the manufacturer virtual control of his market at least until his competitors built their own system. Like cattle being herded to market, smokers behaved predictably in response to media instructions.

An enormous variety of information can be quite inexpensively developed which tells a marketing strategist just how to sell his product, much as if he was playing a highly sophisticated game of multidimensional chess. Specifically, the above survey discovered that around half the market's cigarette consumers had *never changed* brands: 41 percent of males and 50 percent of females. This dramatically demonstrated the value of forming solid brand loyalties among young smokers. Many in this market stayed with their initial brand for life, or at least for a very long time.

The Musical Chairs of Brand Changing

Of the 59 percent of males and 50 percent of females who had *changed* brands, change frequencies correlated by demographic and psychographic criteria provided a functional basis for market control and management:

TIME WITH PRESENT BRAND	MALE	FEMALE
3 years or more	58%	64%
1–2 years	18%	13%
9–12 months	19%	17%
6–9 months	2%	1%
3–6 months	3%	4%
0–3 months	1%	1%

Each of these percentages was individually correlated by forty-three separate categories such as age, education, income, and geographic location. One brand may obtain a momentary profitable advantage, but heavy and sustained market movements are relatively stable for most major companies. This is the major role of high-volume competitive advertising—to keep any one brand from gaining a quick ascendancy.

Occasionally, as happened with Winston, a brand is able through skillful market management (a euphemism for people manipulation) to capture and hold a large market segment, at least for a while. But this doesn't happen very often. Most successful cigarette marketing is a long, tedious effort. Today the game is played with high-speed computing equipment which can handle the staggering arrays of consumer variables.

In repeated studies of smoking behavior, virtually no statistically significant group of U.S. smokers has ever been able to distinguish one brand from another from the tobacco flavor. In one "flavor" study—actually an image study—nearly 20 percent of the smokers tested could not even tell if the test cigarettes were lit. These tests were made on major brands sold in U.S. markets. There would be obvious differences between "Virginia" and "Black" and menthol and plain tobaccos.

Image advertising, labeling, and peer-group conditioning toward a brand determines flavor, aroma, satisfaction, and taste. In cigarette marketing, the most important and competed for segment of the consumer market is the input—the new smoker who if managed properly will consume thousands of dollars' worth of tobacco products during his life, even though his life expectation is substantially reduced because of his addictive consumption.

The New Addicts

The tobacco industry carefully studies the new cigarette consumers who usually increase national sales between 8 and 16 percent annually.

Most of these new smokers are young, under eighteen. The average age of the new U.S. smoker is fourteen with a measurable group between ten and twelve and a decreasing proportion going down as low as five and six. Boys begin smoking younger than girls, but—as in alcohol consumption—girls are catching up fast.

Properly conditioning young smokers to cigarette consumption ideally begins several years before they purchase their first pack. To firmly establish the addiction—from first puff to inhalation—usually requires about six months.

In one specific example several years ago, the FTC began making loud noises about the industry's use in ads of young people and athletic heroes idealized by the young. The tobacco industry, dedicated as usual to the nation's welfare, immediately removed from its ads any obvious appeal to the young.

At the time, an independent market research group was contracted to study audience reactions in a test market to a series of Liggett and Myers Chesterfield radio commercials. The client was J. Walter Thompson, the world's largest advertising agency ($120 million annual billing). JWT later came to prominence during the Watergate scandal as the former employer of H. R. Haldeman and a half-dozen implicated Nixon White House aides. (Incidentally, it is remarkable how American newspapers and magazines played down the implications of so many JWT employees being involved in the Watergate scandal. If mentioned at all, the fact was deemphasized as totally insignificant.)

The Chesterfield radio ad series utilized a very bouncy melody and lyric accompanied by finger snapping. Researchers were assigned to penetrate very low income public housing (so-called ghetto areas) with an in-depth questionnaire.

The Chesterfield questionnaire was a complex and devious device that collected information from interviews with entire families. After initiating field interviews, the staff slowly began—as the completed interviews came in—to realize that the radio commericals being tested had no conscious significance whatsoever for adults. Adults could not remember the brand, the jingle made little sense to them, and most appeared completely disinterested in Chesterfields. Strangely, Chesterfield was not a widely preferred brand among the low-income workers JWT wanted interviewed. At first, it appeared as though something had gone wrong with the marketing strategy.

Then the tabulations on interviews with children between eight and fifteen began to appear. The ingenious marketing plan became apparent. Both boys and girls were memorizing the bouncy commercial. Many could recite it word for word. They frequently whistled the melody while snapping their fingers. Only about 20 percent of these youngers smoked at the time of the research, but it would have been interesting to interview them a year later.

The BRI study cited earlier defined "very heavy smokers" as using one pack or more a day. When the BRI report was published in 1969, only 16.7 percent of adult men smoked two packs or more a day. These heavy smokers, however, accounted for 57.4 percent of all cigarettes smoked by men. This figure for heavy smokers is much, much higher today.

On a cost per thousand for very heavy smokers, national publications were merchandising their tobacco addicts at the following prices:

CIGARETTES: VERY HEAVY SMOKERS (2 Packs or More Daily)

Publication	% of Total Readers	Cost per Thousand Readers (for full-page black and white)
Esquire	20.3	$ 9.87
Life	18.7	12.86
Look	17.8	12.77
Newsweek	16.8	10.65
New Yorker	19.8	12.61
Playboy	20.8	10.48
Sports Illustrated	19.1	9.74
Time	17.6	12.62
U.S. News & World Report	16.1	13.84

In addition to very heavy cigarette smokers, the BRI study also classified cigar and pipe smokers on a cost per thousand basis for the above publications. For example, 10.9 percent of adult men accounted for 97.5 percent of all cigar smoking. Further, only 11.8 percent of adult men accounted for 99.1 percent of all pipe tobacco consumed by men.

That Very Special Moment

In the February 1974 issue of *Penthouse* was published what must be one of the truly great subliminal advertisements of all time. "This . . . is the L&M moment" (see Figure 38).

Two attractive mature models appeared against a dark background, suggesting night, privacy, and isolation. The man's hand holds a gold cigarette lighter, the flame lighting her cigarette before his, his cigarette held closely and intimately near hers while the flame ignites her tip. She cups his hand gently in hers. The moment is one of great tenderness, affection, and warmth.

The female model is dressed in a metallic cocktail or dinner gown. Her earrings and hair suggest they are out on the town. Her wedding band appears on the hand holding his—a married couple sharing an evening of togetherness. Romantic?

Though numerous SEX embeds appear on the model's face, there doesn't appear to be anything really exciting in the ad that would send anyone racing down to the corner store for a carton of L&M cigarettes. Pretty dull stuff for *Penthouse* with its emphasis upon so-called mature sex—mainly the whip and boots variety.

The L&M ad appeared on page 56 of the magazine. The preceding page is somewhat more interesting—a portrait of a model's genital area (see Figure 39). The sadomasochistic suggestion in the portrait is hardly subtle. A pink rose is portrayed with its flower (the rose's reproductive organ) adjacent to the model's pubic hair. The rose stem is bound by a white (virginal?) garter, one thorn having pricked the inside of the model's thigh. The blood, of course, was merely painted on the leg to supply another fantasy for the reader's ever-frustrated sexuality. But as the page is turned, and light penetrates through both the L&M ad and the rose-with-vagina, a curious scene appears (see Figure 40).

Had the layout artist wanted the reader to perceive the illusion consciously, it would have been quite easy to arrange. But consider the rather shocking idea of connecting—at the subliminal level—darkness and light with the womb and oral gratification (cigarettes in the mouth often substitute symbolically in ads for vaginal and phallic symbols). See-through subliminal illusions have added a completely new dimension to the merchandising of addiction.

At first glance the "L&M moment" is outrageously funny. But consider the 55 million addicted cigarette smokers in the United States and the 300,000 tobacco-related deaths annually—roughly six times more casualties than were produced by the entire Korean War.

A Victory on the Ice

Hockey attracts male spectators who breathlessly watch other men display brutal masculinity. Like so many similar sports, hockey is a male struggle for dominance with clearly sexual motives and implications—homosexual rather than heterosexual, however.

Hockey was the subject for one of the Benson & Hedges advertisements. The broken, extra-large-king-size cigarette is a playoff on the theme of problems created by a large erect penis. The campaign, modestly titled "America's Favorite Cigarette Break," has included dozens of humorous insights into America's preoccupation with large penises.

A two-page four-color B&H advertisement, which appeared in the January 14, 1972, issue of *Life,* in *Look,* and a score of other national publications, portrayed spectators presumably watching a fight while two players crush a referee against the railing (see Figure 41).

This ad must have been perceived by at least 50 million individuals in numerous national and local magazines and newspapers. Most readers would have perceived the ad for only two or three seconds. Whatever was in the complex display that sold Benson & Hedges cigarettes had to get into the reader's head within seconds, or the ad was useless.

Few, if any, viewers would study the ad. Had they looked more carefully, however, they would have noticed several rather remarkable inconsistencies.

First, the eight "spectators"—models who work for $75 to

$150 per hour—do not really appear to be acting like a hockey audience watching a fight on the ice. They are kidding, funning, acting with mock concern. The spectator on the top left only pretends to be covering his eyes. The one on the top right feigns a startled, surprised expression. The man with the broken cigarette actually appears to be smiling.

The two struggling players' expressions are also curious. Their eyes appear laughing and humorous. They are grasping and hitting in jest, certainly not in anger. They could almost be celebrating a victory. The eyes of the referee, who will decide the issue, cannot be seen. We do not know what he is thinking. The meaning of shadowed or concealed eyes varies from culture to culture, but in America when eyes are hidden, so are thoughts. The referee's whistle is at arm's length. He is not yet ready to blow it.

The two players, from different teams, appear boisterously celebrating some mutual accomplishment. The ad was studied with a pupilometer—a camera machine that tracks fovea (a pinpoint-sized area in the eye's retina) saccades (rapid movements from focal point to focal point). The focal point concentration was in the central triangle formed by the top player's elbow and the coach's and bottom player's heads. The fovea did not dwell for any significant period on the spectators or on the bottom portion where the hand protrudes from the pile of bodies.

If you were uncritical and only casually perceived it, the protruding right hand would seem to belong to the referee. But look again!

The Right Hand's Left-Handed Glove

There is no possible way in which the right hand could belong to any of the three bodies, unless the referee's arm was severed and the hand pulled through the bodies. The effect was created by the artist gluing a hand on the photograph and then rephotographing after he had retouched the layout. Someone went to a lot of trouble over this hand. Why?

From evidence developed during hypnosis experiments, the unconscious brain appears very sensitive to dissonance of any sort. Conscious perception often overlooks these anxiety-producing inconsistencies, repressing the dissonance and smoothing over the perceptual rough edges. This is the process that enables us often to hide from ourselves almost anything we desire, if we desire strongly enough. However, the dissonance caused by the disembodied hand would register unconsciously. The hand would direct unconscious perception to the empty glove lying on the ice.

An empty left-hand glove or gauntlet is rich in archetypal symbolism: a right-hand glove cast down is a challenge to a superior, a left-hand glove, to an inferior. This left-hand glove apparently belongs to the hockey player in the red and blue costume on top.

Before reading further, look quickly at the name on the back of the hockey glove. Take the first idea that pops into your head. Please do not read further until you try to decipher the name.

On the top hockey player's padding appears the word COOPER, a widely known manufacturer of hockey equipment. On the glove, however, the letters have been carefully manipulated to form, quite distinctly, the word CANCER (see Figure 42). During tests on the ad, about half the test subjects who smoked either could not make out the word or saw the word COOPER on the glove. When invited to look more closely, most finally perceived CANCER. All the test subjects who did *not* smoke had no trouble perceiving CANCER. Very likely the ad was displayed in many national publications on at least half a million dollars' worth of pages, and carefully pretested before such a large investment was approved.

How it sells cigarettes or *why* can only be answered at present in terms of theory. Perhaps one reason people smoke—especially the young experiencing puberty—is involved with some kind of self-destruct mechanism each of us carries around inside our heads. On the other hand, perhaps the ad is subliminally saying that Benson & Hedges is a challenge to cancer or the B&H has conquered or defeated cancer—the idea of a victory over *something* is certainly implied.

Anyway you look at it, the manipulative potentialities in the ad are alarming. Much worse, however—if this subliminal logic is reasonable—then the Surgeon General's warning "... That Cigarette Smoking Is Dangerous to Your Health" is one of the most insidious marketing gimmicks ever developed by the tobacco industry, conning well-meaning government officials into believing they have protected the public.

Our Very Own Medicine Show

The North American "medicine show" has been part of the culture for nearly two centuries. But today, the shows are expensively produced in national media where audiences often number in the tens of millions. One thing hasn't changed, however: the manipulative patent-medicine pitch and the gullible, always hopeful audiences seeking panaceas to their aches and pains along with eternal virility, fertility, and youth. Most patent medicines are psychogenics, designed to reduce essentially self-induced symptoms. They cure nothing. On television newscasts, the worse the bad news on any given night, the more patent medicines (good news) will be sold.

What could be more reasonable—even thoughtful—than the newscast sponsor offering a cheap quick remedy for your headaches, upset stomachs, plugged-up bowels, etc.? Marshall McLuhan wrote, "It takes an awful lot of bad news to sell all that advertising good news." Indeed, but it also serves to compete for a multibillion-dollar annual market.

At least a billion dollars is spent annually in the United States on drug marketing. It is impossible to know the exact amount. Intense pressure is exerted upon every citizen to resolve his emotional (psychogenic) problems with various medicinals, pharmaceuticals, remedies, drugs, or any of the other labels used to describe these extremely profitable products. These drugs still closely compare with the magic potions of medieval magic described by what today are children's fables.

Americans are taught from infancy that any discomfort, anxiety, or systemic irregularity can be handled, for a small price, by some chemical or another. The perpetuation of the mechanical-man mythology conditions the culture for a broad series of self-perspectives. A child grows up to distrust and detest the inconsistencies in his bodily functions. Both consciously and unconsciously, he is taught to view his body as a mechanism of plumbing, wiring, valves, solenoids, gears, and cams. Irregularities cannot be tolerated from machines.

Who Sells Science?

One fascinating question North American medicine should carefully probe is whether the drug commercials were developed from our so-called science or vice versa. The endless, often destructive, search for simplistic cause-and-effect relationships in medicine makes the physician an excellent consumer and distributor of pharmaceutical products. The pharmaceutical industry gives U.S. physicians a most careful and expensive lifelong training in product consumption.

The patent-medicine mass consumer drugs, the most visible form of drug merchandising, use essentially the same subliminal media technology as the alcohol and tobacco industries.

However, the most expensive and complex merchandising in America is applied to so-called ethical drug products, which can be purchased only by prescription. The 322,228 physicians in the United States constitute a rich and exclusive market whom the drug companies tenaciously and skillfully pursue. One physician, if properly courted, may write hundreds of prescriptions weekly for a single expensive drug.

As a specialized market, physicians are so valuable that *Time* magazine has a special edition that reaches only physicians. *Time* sold its 110,000 physician readers at $2,825 for one four-color advertising page in their 1970 rate book. Ads aimed exclusively at physicians will not appear in other circulations. *Time* openly advertises their selective advertising to physicians as well as schoolteachers, students, and many other occupational groups. (It would be interesting to study these specialized editions to see if news content had been added or deleted in support of the advertisements. Much of *Time*'s news material originates in corporate public relations offices.)

It is not generally known that several large consumer research corporations offer—at a price—prescription as well as consumer drug audits. It is boring, but most profitable research. Consumer audits are also done for food and other commodities by such as the giant international A.C. Neilson Co. and Audits and Surveys, Inc. They periodically audit the sale of competitive products in samples of supermarkets and drugstores throughout America. Ad executives can then match brand and product movement against media expenditures. Many pharmaceutical houses operate their own market research and retail audit surveys despite the high cost. This type of information is vital to an efficient advertising and marketing operation.

The ethical drug products market, however, is more difficult and expensive to monitor. Specialized market research corporations audit prescriptions in drugstores. Field interviewers periodically visit drugstores and collect data from prescription forms. Almost anywhere in the United States, every prescription written by a physician is available to any pharmaceutical company able to pay the price. Virtually all are subscribers. Drugstore owners receive small fees for making the prescription forms available.

The High-Priced Pitchmen

Doctors are sold drugs directly by *detail men*: very highly paid, well-educated, and articulate salesmen who periodically visit every physician in the nation. Many detail men have had university medical training. A few physicians refuse to even see these soft-sell hucksters. But most have been educated to view their detail men as a service—a source of quick, effortless, often useful information on what is new and available. These detail men provide physicians with stacks of free samples that are usually passed out to less affluent patients. There are also occasional small gifts or gratuities made by detail men to their marketing targets at Christmas or on birthdays, but care is always taken that physicians will never feel they are being bribed. One of these detail men used to complain about how difficult it was to buy birthday presents for doctors, as the present had to be expensive yet *appear* inexpensive.

Many physicians openly admit they depend very much upon their detail men. Several described close friendly relationships with detail men of over twenty-five years' duration. These salesmen were often considered family friends.

Friendships are perhaps important between physicians and the men who service their information needs, but in the case of drug merchandising the detail men receive a periodic report on just how profitable the friendship has been for their companies. Prescription audits are a remarkably effective feedback device to assess the human relationship.

All this is usually invisible to the individual physician who—like all marketing targets—must be managed with the lilusion that he is a man who decides for himself. In addition to their management of physicians' information, drug companies bombard physicians through a whole spectrum of trade publications published under the pretense of being professional information.

Every physician throws out at least twenty-five pounds of monthly periodical literature especially designed to manipulate his decisions about drug preparations. These include medical association magazines (county, state, and national versions), elaborate graphic art productions, and a deluge of medical-related publications.

Most, including the AMA journals, are supported primarily by pharmaceutical advertising. Some medical publications obtain varying percentages of their costs from subscriptions, annual fees, etc., but for their survival, most depend largely upon drug advertising. Once again, this does not necessarily mean that these publications' editors permit the drug industry to make individual decisions for them. Nevertheless, whether the editor works for the *AMA Journal* or *The New York Times*, he is likely to think most carefully before jeopardizing a profitable relationship with an advertiser and certainly would be careful about offending an industry.

The Subliminal Ethic

To sell ethical drugs to physicians via advertising in these journals, all the subliminal techniques discussed in this book are used—sex and death symbolism, embeds, and the like.

One of the more intriguing examples appeared in a Canadian Medical Association publication. Manufactured by the Wampole Pharmaceutical Company, Magnolax is not a prescription laxative even though it is marketed as an ethical drug among physicians (see Figure 43).

Physicians are invariably hard-pressed for time and deluged with far more reading material than they can possibly assimilate. Reviewing journals, they generally thumb through and perhaps check the index, but more often just casually survey the illustrations. The abundant drug advertisement pictures are, of course, the most interesting illustrations. This is another case of intentional perceptual overload.

The Magnolax advertisement was shown to fifteen physicians along with a half dozen other similar ethical-product advertisements. Each physician looked at each ad for at least thirty seconds and was afterward asked to comment upon anything he had perceived that elicited an emotional response. Most made the usual comments about a nude young girl in one ad. Several commented upon patients they were treating with some of the advertised products. But no one made any comment about the Magnolax ad.

Look carefully at this ad before reading further.

When queried specifically, no physician seemed to have any negative or particularly positive feeling about the ad. None considered it either humorous or sad. Apparently all they perceived was a happy family, older parents with a young child off on a cruise, most likely heading for the tropics during the winter. The physicians were clearly missing—at least at the conscious level—what the ad agency's artist and photographer had struggled to incorporate into the illustration.

If you had read the copy and headline, you were advised at the conscious level that the child, Paul, and his grandparents have the same problem. The precise nature of the problem might seem to be constipation, though this fact is never stated in the copy. Magnolax is a laxative. None of the physicians seemed to make a story or logic out of the ad at the conscious level. If they perceived the artist's concept at all, it had to be subliminally. The ad includes embedded SEXes lightly etched into the surface. The subliminal sexualization of a laxative has intriguing implications. But there is more.

If you observe carefully, the three models have strained postures and appearances. (It might help to block off the other figures so you can study one at a time. By taking each out of context, the message becomes more consciously apparent.) The gray-haired, rather handsome man in the sweater is bending slightly as he holds the boy. As he looks out at the horizon, even though he is smiling, he is straining hard. The smiling grandmother, as evidenced by her clenched hands, is trying even harder. She is more bent over than her husband. But their smiles are brave.

Paul's expression is perhaps the most revealing. Though he is pointing at something, no one is looking. The grandmother and grandfather are looking in opposite directions, preoccupied by their individual efforts. Perhaps Paul knows the answer, but his grandparents are not paying attention. Paul's tight fist on the railing and his sitting, hunched-over posture clearly reveal how very, very hard he is trying. Apparently, none of the three are making the grade—pathetic victims of constipation, America's most feared affliction.

The ship's light, to the woman's right, is turned on, but none of the three have as yet "seen the light." The vertical post in the railing under the light leads the reader's eye down to the solution in the bottle—Magnolax.

The brand's only advertising had been in journals and by direct mail to physicians. Virtually all the plethora of nonprescription laxatives are very similar, differing mainly in price. Magnolax was quite expensive—and according to an Ontario drug consumer survey, the laxative most often recommended by Ontario physicians at the time. The ads must have worked.

If these techniques were limited to only nonprescription laxatives, the problem could perhaps be ignored. But virtually all drugs marketed through physicians include these techniques, as is easily confirmed by even a casual glance at any of the medical periodicals.

The Ideal Consumer

Some evidence suggests that physicians could be more susceptible to subliminal manipulation than those in other occupations. Our medical people have been exhaustively trained in linear, compartmentalized, cause-and-effect types of reasoning. Individuals with highly creative, artistic, or innovative abilities have great difficulty even getting into medical schools. Defining a desirable physician in the way we do, we eliminate almost entirely from the medical profession personalities or intelligence types who do not fit the model. Typical American physicians tend to be entrepreneurial, highly competitive, verbally dependent in their reality orientations, quite similar to engineers.

This is no accident. Their rigorous training, or brainwashing, produces people for whom two plus two must *always* equal four. Psychologist George Gordon at the University of London, England, discovered there were marked individual differences in susceptibility to subliminal stimuli. Test subjects drawn from the university's Fine Arts Department appeared far more sensitive (able to consciously perceive stimuli intended to be only subliminally perceived) than subjects from the science and engineering departments.

The phenomenon has been documented by numerous researchers. At least in terms of those rigid qualities frequently labeled as "scientific" in America, physicans as a group would easily classify as "super-rigids," highly susceptible to subliminal manipulation.

Again, it is most unsettling to find that the so-called "scientific" perceptual abilities of physicians can be so easily appropriated. And many physicians—one of the most prestigious of all high-credibility information sources—unknowingly transmit their subliminally programmed views on drugs to everyone they meet.

Which cigarette brand does your doctor smoke?

11

All the News That Sells

The way back to reality is to destroy our perception of it, to do violence to our conventional habits of thinking, and, by an act of imagination and heart, reverse the ordinary workings of the intellect.

HENRI BERGSON
An Introduction to Metaphysics

The Voice of Freedom

The Eight Canons of Journalism adopted many years ago by the American Society of Newspaper Editors (see Appendix B) outline an idealistic code of professional conduct for the nation's editorial desks. The code is a noble and inspiring document, which elaborately defines the journalist's role as teacher and interpreter in the people's interest.

Social Responsibility, expressed in its most inspiring metaphor, is cited as the fundamental obligation of the press. Responsibility, Freedom of the Press, Independence, Sincerity (Truthfulness and Accuracy), Impartiality, Fair Play, and Decency—these seven canons of American journalism constitute, perhaps, the most eloquent collection of inspirational verbiage since the Sermon on the Mount. In the various ethical codes used by the press or its related entities—the American Public Relations Association. Marketing Association,

Advertising Association, and countless smaller trade and professional organizations—no mention is made about the profit-and-loss criteria upon which so many editorial and broadcast decisions are actually based.

One might well wonder why it was necessary for newspapers and other media to so strongly emphasize ethical codes of behavior. So many ethical codes in one industry might even suggest a widespread sense of guilt.

The code, nevertheless, is a superb testimony to what could be or, perhaps, once was. All the industry really need do is simply follow it.

A great to-do is made about how editors work in the public interest, making careful decisions on what goes into print or into the wastebasket. Attempts to study this "gatekeeping" function have generally failed. Editors make their decisions on highly subjective, mostly unconscious criteria. Attempts to explain the process have usually ended as pious rationalizations about how editors serve their readers, but the ways they serve their advertisers are never mentioned. American journals loudly proclaim their belief in "freedom of the press." But in the interest of advertising profit, they are quite shy about examining the actual use of that freedom.

For example, the recent shameless behavior of newspapers scrambling for fat cigarette advertising accounts—up for grabs after the Surgeon General forced tobacco off TV channels—should reasonably have brought publishers' motives into question by their writers as well as their readers. This, decidedly, was not the case. Any suggestion that the government extend its cigarette advertising ban to the press was countered with passionate denunciations via both editorial and news columns.

This rationale was presumably quite popular with the cigarette companies, who now purchase much larger quantities of newspaper advertising space, as well as with the newspaper stockholders whose dividends fattened due to heavy feeding from the tobacco industry whom they have proven themselves worthy to represent. This endorsement of cigarette advertising was advocated by an embarrassing majority of newspapers in North America. Surprisingly, few letters to the editor appeared in rebuttal to the absurdity that cigarette advertising had anything to do with press freedom. Readers apparently accepted the argument.

Perceptual Defenses in News

Many individual journalists appear to believe—and their perceptual defense may have led them to believe—that advertising really does not sell anything and is a losing proposition for advertisers, most of whom are buying ads out of habit.

Ask most any journalist about the profit structure under which his publication operates. He will attempt to convince you—often with deeply felt sincerity—that his paper barely survives from day to day through the generosity of wealthy patrons, or through the kindness of grateful readers.

Circulation income, the amount paid for a newspaper copy, is usually a loss to publishers—at best, a break-even overhead proposition. In the words of *The New York Times* marketing director, C. C. Guthrie, "circulation income barely covers the cost of paper and ink."

But mass media are one of the most profitable investments in American society. As members of the FCC have publicly observed many times, issuing a television or radio license is like giving a broadcaster his very own high-speed money machine. Newspapers or magazines can be even more profitable. Sam Newhouse, who owns a very successful newspaper chain, once said, "Anybody who loses money on a daily newspaper has to be crazy." Well-operated newspapers, especially those in monopoly situations, return well over 20 percent in profits before taxes. Few businesses reach even 18 percent, and 10 to 13 percent is considered successful.

In 1970 daily newspapers produced roughly $7 billion in business, twice the television figure. Newspapers were the tenth largest employer in the United States, with 350,000 salaried employees, and the fifth largest United States industry in gross income. Projected growth during the 1970s was 6.2 percent per year.

An average daily in a monopoly situation in a 200,000 population city, with a 55,000 circulation producing a $5 million annual income in 1968, earned a profit of 28.6 percent before taxes—nearly 14 percent after taxes. (During 1968 the average profit margin for American industry was 5.8 percent.)

When the Canadian chain publisher Roy Thompson bought twelve papers in 1967, he paid roughly $200 per reader. Readers, like viewers, are bought and sold like cattle. Local advertising expenditures are increasing more rapidly than national, and daily newspapers derive the greatest advantage from this increase. In 1970 local and classified ads produced 82 percent of average ad revenues, compared with 18 percent from national advertisers in daily newspapers.

In North America it is virtually impossible for any publication to survive without advertisers. Reader subscriptions and per-copy payments simply cannot support any substantial publishing effort. The only way a publication can survive is through advertising or by selling a sponsor's products, which results in an integration between editorial decisions and marketing strategies.

Advertising predicates its effectiveness upon the high-credibility source with which readers will associate the ad. Remember the old saying, if you want to con someone you must first gain his confidence and respect. Newspapers are the highest credibility source among all media. In a recent national survey, over three quarters of American adults believed newspapers were the most truthful of all media. Since advertising effectiveness directly relates to this credibility factor, newspapers can still claim—in spite of high costs per thousand exposures compared with television or national magazines—a very high level of sales effectiveness.

Newspapers are administratively divided into advertising and editorial departments—if possible, housed on separate floors. To maintain itself as a high-credibility source, the image any newspaper must project demands that advertising and editorial functions are separate aspects of publishing.

Every newspaper has its hallowed myths of how various editors fought to maintain integrity against advertiser attempts to influence editorial policy. Indeed, these anecdotes are often quite true. If the editor did not defend himself against advertisers' overt attempts to influence editorial material, the publication might lose its public image of integrity. As far as advertisers are concerned, this high-credibility source image is the most vital illusion within the mass communication industry.

High-Credibility Paper

Newspapers, much like television, are low-definition mediums. Illustrations are photographed through coarse engraving screens. It might appear strange why newspapers have continued to use rough newsprint when a smoother, finished paper could easily be substituted at a negligible increase in cost. Rough newsprint texture, however, communicates with the reader's unconscious every bit as much as do printed words and pictures. The coarse, heavy texture communicates an image of integrity, a rugged tactility, even an unsophisticated simplicity.

Appearances aside, newsprint is not utilized as a low-cost form of communication, though this is certainly the meaning communicated to readers. According to the image communicated, the publisher is saving the *reader* money by using cheap paper. This is, of course, unsupportable logic. If the advertisers could be better served by higher-grade paper, the publication would have to supply it.

IBM recently experimented with newsprint as a substitute for the more expensively finished paper used in computer output printing. Substantial savings could have been realized by thousands of IBM computer customers around the world if the less costly paper were substituted. IBM customers, however, simply couldn't believe what they read printed on newsprint. For computer printouts, newsprint was a low-credibility medium.

Credibility is the name of the game, not price. Ad effectiveness is substantially higher on rough newsprint than it would be if higher-quality, smoother-surfaced finishes were used. Newspapers, hoping to increase advertising lineage, continually experiment with other paper surfaces, always returning to the familiar, rough, cheap, and honest-appearing newsprint.

The modern North American newspaper is comprised of roughly 70 percent advertising and 30 percent editorial content. The ratio might vary plus or minus 10 percent, but a newspaper with less than 60 percent of its total column inches in advertising is probably losing money.

Of the 30 percent of total newspaper editorial space, roughly one third (10 percent) is usually devoted to feature material—astrology tables, advice columns, funny pages, syndicated features, cartoons, editorials, letters to the editor, cheesecake, feature photos, and the like.

Another 10 percent appears to be news, but is in reality information with highly specific motives. Usually originating in public relations or publicity offices, this information can usually be identified by careful reading, as it represents a specific point of view. Public relations or publicity material originates in government, industry, commercial organizations, book publishers, play and motion-picture producers, publicity offices of a thousand varieties—anyone who has an idea, person, or product to sell. Publicity-oriented copy has become a mainstay of American journalism. This so-called news is free to editors, publishers, or broadcasters. Written by skilled, professional journalists—often exclusively for a particular publication—this promotional copy is a boon for the publishers and editors with their constantly rising overhead, but a boondoggle for the reader.

As an example, a book publisher who can obtain a review in *Time* magazine alone—read by over 25 million individuals—will likely sell thousands of copies even if the review is negative. If it is a good review, the book could sell tens of thousands and it will probably also be reviewed by *Newsweek, The New York Times, U.S. News & World Report,* and dozens of other newspapers and magazines.

The Value of a Plant

Some years ago, a "planter" was employed by a major aircraft manufacturer to obtain national magazine publicity for an airplane then being sold to the air force. After eight months of work, a four-page story appeared in *Look* magazine featuring the airplane. The week following publication of the story, the company's common stock increased fifteen dollars per share. This type of planting is, of course, done continuously by government agencies and large corporations.

To illustrate image manipulation, some years ago Northrop

Aircraft Corporation commissioned an accomplished artist to execute an oil portrait of their Snark self-guided missile for newspaper and magazine publicity. There was even a discussion of using the portrait the following year on a company calendar that would be sent to congressmen, government officials, and stockholders.

After several dozen hours of work, the artist came up with a large, magnificent portrait of the graceful Snark speeding high above the earth at dusk. Only minutes away on the horizon, barely visible, were the faint, flickering lights of a city—apparently the missile's target.

The Snark's only *real* function, of course, was to deliver the warhead on a one-megaton H-bomb. Yet several Northrop vice-presidents were horrified by the painting. Meetings were quietly but immediately scheduled in Northrop executive offices. The public relations director was ordered to diplomatically talk the artist into painting out the city. The Snark had to be publicly perceived as *purely* a technical and engineering problem with its phallic thrust symbolically related to flight and man's pursuit of freedom. The Snark was a mythological animal described in the book *Alice In Wonderland*. Publications which printed the picture took their readers on a fantasy trip not at all unlike that taken by Alice.

Newspapers survive as advertising media through their ability to saturate a local community. They aim at a generalized audience, usually biased toward the upper-middle class who primarily support department store, supermarket, and the preponderance of retail merchandising efforts. These readers would have little patience for an overly negative local perspective. Unless their ego needs are massaged, advertisements will not have a maximal sales effectiveness. This paradox of American media, ignoring legitimate though unpleasant news information, has been well documented by writers like Robert Cirino in *Don't Blame the People*, Edith Efron in *The News Twisters*, and Mark Lane's *Citizen's Dissent* about which several major media executives commented publicly, "We will bury that book with silence." Cirino and Efron's books also received the silent treatment.

Mark Lane's first book, *Rush to Judgment*, a bestseller, received 450 reviews. His second, *Citizen's Dissent*, which strongly criticized newspapers' money-milking the assassination of President John Kennedy for all it was worth (and then some), received four reviews. Somehow, the book disappeared after publication and is difficult to find even in public libraries. Numerous other books critical of the news media have received similar treatment. These books would have caused the news media financial discomfort and dented their high-credibility-source images.

Who Reads What—and Why?

One curious aspect of newspaper readers—long known, but usually ignored with a few easy rationalizations—is who reads what in a newspaper. Tests on news content, given a short time after reading in the normal reading environment when subjects were not aware they were to be tested, revealed that only a small proportion of readers or viewers consciously recall any substantial amount of news information that had just perceived—quite often with great inaccuracy on factual details. Hundreds of people, none of whom knew they were going to be tested, viewed a newscast on TV. Over 80 percent could not recall anything of factual substance they had viewed. These individuals were regular or chronic TV news watchers, ritualistically viewing one or more newscasts at least three times each week.

Millions and millions of people view television news, read newspapers and magazines, and yet appear to know very little about what was reported. Perceptual overload is purposely designed into news media. The assumption has always been that people read in order to learn about the world. But if few readers consciously recall even the general outlines of what they have read, what, then, is the news consumer receiving from the product?

Prejudice Reinforced

Newspaper readership studies reveal that very few readers read everything in a newspaper. They may linger momentarily on a headline, story lead, picture, or advertisement. Even if readers do consciously read specific content, few are able to recall the items when they finally put the paper aside. What is most often recalled is information supporting readers' established images, predispositions, or prejudices about themselves and their world.

The distinction between editorial and advertising content made by readers is not at all clearly divided. According to popular myth, readers presumably close their minds to advertising. The industry would have us believe that editorial content, on the other hand, is true and can be believed without qualification. Studies revealed that believable or not, advertising content is the most widely and frequently read and recalled content in news publications. Advertisements, though possibly not news in the purist definition of the term, do inform us on many aspects of our lives.

Advertising's 70 percent of a newspaper's total space is all good news. Advertising, together with at least 28 percent of editorial material—or 98 percent of most North American newspapers—tells the readers at the unconscious, attitude-formation level what they want to hear. From readership studies, this information appears far more engrossing to the average American than do the complexities of the EEC, the Vietnam War, or starvation in remote places like Biafra or Bangladesh. Advertisements, say what one will about their preposterous lies, exaggerations, and flatteries, are all good news which educates us to the world about us—not, perhaps, as it actually is, but as we wish it could be.

Some years ago, a group of concerned citizens descended upon Denver's tabloid *Rocky Mountain News* to persuade the managing editor to print more information about international affairs. The editor then showed the group his latest Schwerin Report, an analysis that evaluated the percentages of readers who read each ad and each story.

At the time, the *Rocky Mountain News* was running a boxed, two-column section on an inside page called "International Roundup" where brief one-paragraph capsules of major world events were reviewed. "Look," he explained, "when we include an international affairs piece, readership drops for the entire page and the facing page—not merely for the single story."

On the average day, newspapers publish much less than 5 percent of total available information from wire services, syndicates, special writers, reporters, public relations handouts, etc. The editor's job is primarily selection, an endless sorting of copy to find items to entertain and hold advertisers' desired markets. What has been edited out or discarded in a newspaper often comprises a significant insight into what was really happening in the world.

Subliminal News in Ads

It would be a waste of time to review the endless pages of retail ads published daily in newspapers. Most of the subliminal embeds shown in this and my earlier book appeared in newspapers. For those readers who still doubt the main preoccupation of the press, one typical newspaper ad should suffice.

Towers Department Stores are a nationwide Canadian retailing operation concentrated in suburban shopping centers. Towers' advertising concentrates, as most retail stores do, in the daily papers. Ads were designed in a Montreal art department and distributed on reproduction matts to store managers throughout the nation. These particular ads appeared in the Wednesday, February 9, 1972, edition of the London, Ontario *Free Press* (see Figure 44) and in newspapers across Canada.

The artist-photographer who made up the ads posed a wholesome-appearing young model in comparatively inexpensive clothing. Not much here at first glance to become excited about. The three figures in the ad were posed by the same model and pasted together into a single layout. The subliminal illusion suggests the "Three Graces" or, possibly, three identities available to any woman who purchased the clothes.

But did you notice the genital symbolism? An erect penis was subtly drawn on the end of the purse (see Figure 45). And the seated model's right thumb and forefinger curve together symbolizing the female genitals. The retouch artist purposely permitted the model's right hand to include six fingers, creating subliminal dissonance which draws unconscious attention to the genital symbolism.

Posed before archetypal heart symbols, which for many centuries have symbolized both love and the female genitals, the model's body language is one of display, of which her erogenous zones are the main points. The standing model's hands are posed so the fingers point at her genital area. In addition, a mosaic of SEXes has been embedded throughout the display. Notice the patterns, especially on the standing model in the foreground. A brace of four subliminal SEXes covers the fly on her slacks.

Nor has the editorial content of newspapers and news magazines excluded subliminal stimuli. It is remarkable how journalists, with their claimed preoccupations over social responsibility, kept themselves from consciously perceiving what has been going on around them for years. In discussing subliminal perception with individuals from a wide range of occupations, the strongest disbelief has come from journalists —irrespective of the evidence presented.

Of course, there is no single individual to blame. Long-term use of subliminal devices is invisible to us largely because we do not want to believe our trusted institutions capable of such practices.

A. J. Liebling, an American journalist and humorist, once remarked, "*The New York Times* began as the staunch defender of the working man and ended up as the rich woman's shopping guide." Indeed, the *Times*—with its massive Sunday edition—publishes more advertising lineage per issue than any other newspaper in the nation. To the *Times* slogan of "All the News That's Fit to Print" might reasonably be added, "Which Supplies Our Advertisers With Their Primary Markets."

It Pays to Know Your Reader

Typical of most major United States publications, *The New York Times* has studied and dissected their readership in a thousand ways through large-capacity computers, comparing it with their competition—the New York *Daily News* and New York *Post*. For example, 35 percent of *Times* readers own their own homes compared with 36 percent for the *News* and only 16 percent for the *Post*; 41 percent of *Times* reader families make over $15,000 per year compared with 17 percent for the *News* and 36 percent for the *Post*; 53 percent of *Times* readers are college-educated compared with 16 percent for the *News* and 38 percent for the *Post*; 45 percent of *Times* readers are professionally or managerially employed compared with 23 percent for the *News* and 36 percent for the *Post*.

Like the magazines, *The New York Times* knows precisely the cost per thousand for heavy gin drinkers, mutual fund purchasers, and the hundreds of other merchandising categories upon which any mass media must base its existence if it intends to compete for advertising lineage.

The *Times'* research department can provide detailed information on their own and their competitors' audiences in terms of geographic areas, children's ages, household size, family member occupations and employment, income, home ownership, membership in company boards of directors (a surprising 7.7 percent of employed readers), amounts spent weekly on food and groceries, car year, purchased new or used, air conditioning data, car rental experience, credit cards, life insurance, personal and household product purchases, securities owned, TV sets, vacations, and travel.

The Marketing of Information

The front page of the Sunday, April 30, 1972, *New York Times* can be viewed as an advertisement for the newspaper. A number of elements contribute to the publication's image and what it promises the prospective reader as a rationalization for selling the advertisements (see Figure 46). If the top half of this page were selling cigarettes, fashions, or automobiles, it is doubtful if it could have been more effectively designed.

The classic type face on the masthead is small and simple, nothing ostentatious—as is the entire group of headline types used by the *Times*. With an image established over many years, the *Times* could not sustain this image if the type faces appeared lush or sensational. A comparison with the *Daily News*—a very noisy tabloid designed for advertisers attempting to reach the lower socioeconomic reader—quickly reveals these two publications are essentially noncompetitive. There is a small overlap of circulation who read both, but the majority of readers are exclusive to each paper.

The *Times* is read by upper-middle-class, generally well-educated families. Of a total 1.6 million Sunday *Times* circulation, roughly one third is distributed within New York City, one third outside the city but within one hundred miles, and one third throughout the nation. According to their own

191

marketing data, the *Times* was read in 11,333 cities and towns in the United States—the closest thing to a national newspaper in America. In California the *Times* sold 12,600 copies each Sunday. Weekday circulation averaged slightly over 1 million copies.

This front page offered a mosaic of verbally symbolic excitement to readers. The excitement, however, was respectable and restrained, a proper upper-middle-class view of the world.

The page's focal point was, of course, the United Press International photo of a helicopter leaving a battle area in Vietnam. The helicopter was American, suggesting dominance (possibly phallic) over the pathetic Vietnamese soldiers clinging desperately to the landing skids. The ARVN soldiers appeared frantic and terrified as they tried to escape the combat zone.

Strangely, this combat photo also appeared during the same week in the Soviet Union's *Pravda*, telling the Soviet reader how cruelly the American imperialists treated their hapless Vietnamese allies who were often left to die while the Americans fled. Either meaning could be true—entirely depending upon which frame of reference readers were predisposed to follow. The photo told the *Times* reader, at least at the unconscious level, what he wanted to hear about himself. His self-image as an American would have been reinforced whether he favored or opposed the Vietnamese conflict.

To make certain the photo's sales value was increased to maximum, a mosaic of subliminal SEXes had been either double-exposed into the negative or drawn into the engraving plates (see Figure 47). The technique does, indeed, sell the news—which sells the advertising which sells the products.

The *Times* merchandising of news is successful. Net income during 1971 was $9.5 million, even though down from $13.7 million the preceding year. This was from a total 1971 revenue of $291 million, up from $283 million during 1970. This is very big business by any standard, involving twenty-five corporate subsidiaries and affiliates including book and magazine publishing, newspapers in Florida and Paris, broadcasting stations—AM, FM, and TV—paper companies, microfilm, news services, and educational materials publishing.

The time has certainly arrived, however, when someone should ask the *Times* what all this merchandising does to the quality of information, facts, and descriptions of reality. Even though these pages and the pictures are viewed for only seconds, they will be perceived and registered in the readers' unconsciouses, forming an attitudinal frame through which they perceive both themselves and the world about them. The sexualization of war is hardly a worthy activity, even if the end result is increased ad lineage.

American society has always been taught to assume through its educational system that a proliferation of media also means freedom of the press. Anyone is free to publish any kind of periodical they wish—if they can afford the financial costs of publishing, that is. But unless what is published *sells*, publication overhead does a job of censorship far more effective than any totalitarian government could impose.

It once appeared possible that many diverse views could coexist and compete for attention. But as greater numbers of publications appeared, there was actually a decrease in varied perspectives.

There exist today thousands of periodicals, but all they compete for are their readers' money, advertising, and agency-preferred reader demographic strata. Magazines sell first themselves, second their advertised products. And most are not at all inhibited about how they go about it. Slanting of news is simply a patronizing technique of reader massage that makes for effortless reading. Editors keep it sexy, brief, and chatty. They leave the bigger issues alone or handle them with gentle caution.

The reality is that United States commercial media are rarely utilized by anyone whose prejudices are likely to be mistreated or bruised. Individuals trained in self-indulgence, as Americans have been, will simply not attend to a medium that fails to tell them what they want to hear. "Mirror, mirror on the wall, who is the fairest . . ." *Fortune* magazine, for example, is rarely looked at by readers of *Ramparts*—and vice versa. *Berkeley Barb* subscribers would find themselves most uncomfortable even in the company of someone who reads the *Wall Street Journal*.

The Real Sonny and Cher

Television's Sonny and Cher were modestly talented entertainers propped up by ingenious television production, direction, and publicity machinery to represent the "ideal" American couple—if only they had not blown the whole fantasy with a messy divorce.

In late 1972 and early 1973 it was difficult to pick up a magazine anywhere in America without confronting Sonny and Cher. If all those pages had been sold as advertising, it would have cost the television networks who sponsored the promotion easily $10 million. In a nation of 220 million people—some of them quite remarkable, some even newsworthy—what could explain the coincidence whereby dozens of highly paid editors suddenly decided to feature Sonny and Cher in lead articles?

This is known as the *treatment*. Pushed by a small army of network and sponsor publicity specialists, the couple were carefully engineered into the top United States print media. Publicity work today rarely involves direct payoffs to writers, editors, and publishers, but it does involve expensive planning and strategies, lavish luncheons, and invariably a long list of personal favors done by whoever has a product to publicize—in this case, Sonny and Cher—and the media who are buying for resale to their readers.

Over a five-month period (December 1972 through April 1973), three of the many publications who took part in the Sonny and Cher promotion were *Vogue* (December 1972), *Redbook* (February 1973), and *TV Star Parade* (April 1973). Each treated their Sonny and Cher feature as a cover story.

Find Your Very Own Fantasy

Vogue readers are married (80 percent), average thirty to forty years old, rich (average annual income over $25,000), and mostly college-educated. *Vogue* features advertised products with expensive price tags, jet set amusements, and a fantasy world of wealthy, indulged, pseudo-sophisticated pretty people who wear sexy clothes from exclusive stores such as Bonwit Teller and Peck & Peck.

194

Redbook, on the other hand, is slated toward the young married homemakers with young children and modest middle-class incomes, some college or vocational school, and great insecurity over their identities, sexuality, and future. Ads feature prepared foods, book clubs, household appliances, furnishings, and children's merchandise.

TV Star Parade is designed for the grass-roots young American woman, both married and single, with up to high school education, a lower-middle income, and erotic fantasies about life among the celebrated. This reader thrives on celebrity romances with a touch of scandal, such as "The Night Elvis Waited for Ann-Margret." Ads involve self-improvement and bust development schemes, weight reducing, inexpensive wigs, and provocative attire from Fredericks of Hollywood. It is difficult to imagine readers of any one of these magazines encroaching upon the illusions of the other two.

This commercial fantasy manipulation of reality is clearly demonstrated in a comparison of the three treatments of what the respective readerships wanted to believe about Sonny and Cher.

Vogue's five-page picture series was titled "The Sexy Beat of Sonny and Cher." Photography was by Richard Avedon, one of the most celebrated and expensive fashion photographers in America. The brief article was written by Phyllis Lee Levin.

Tailoring to *Vogue* readers' emotional need to believe in upper-class fantasies, the first paragraph is worth repeating:

This year's love story is upbeat all the way. Its leads are two recruits from rockdom to establishment television. They compose ringing folk-rock songs, sing them and every other variety of song to the rafters, toss insults more often than bouquets at one another, and succeed in looking buoyant and loving every moment they are together. Sonny and Cher Bono—elegant clowns with appetites for the better extravagances of life such as a private plane with a French-speaking and cooking steward, such as a forty-room mansion piled onto five acres in Holmby Hills, California —have a philosophy about their work and a theory about their success. "There's an awful lot of cynicism everywhere about marriage, so much that's negative. Well, we like to think we make being married a positive thing. There's this myth in America about romance ending the minute marriage begins. I think we're showing people something different. We're married, we're in love, we kid each other a lot, but we're still in love."

The young middle-class *Redbook* housewife's fantasies of Sonny and Cher were much different. The entertainers' images were changed and adapted to the publication's readers. In an article by Claire Safran titled "Sonny and Cher: Even When We Fight We Love," staunch middle-class values and sentimentalities prevailed:

The lady of the antique-filled, chandelier-festooned, 45-room house runs around it in blue jeans. When she wants to talk to her husband she bypasses the 17-century French drawing room, and they flop together in a string hammock stretched between two trees on the vast expanse of back lawn. When they dine with friends at Hollywood's chic Bistro restaurant she neither smokes nor drinks, but she beckons the maitre d' again and again for extra helpings of dessert—strawberries dipped in brown sugar. Her host explodes in laughter, "For heaven's sake," he says, "what we've saved on booze with you, we've spent on strawberries."

The piece is reader-oriented down to the last sentence. The lush description of "strawberries dipped in brown sugar" is fascinating when you consider the nine pages of food and dessert advertising in this issue of *Redbook*, also including an article and many ads on weight reducing.

And, Finally . . .

TV Star Parade deeply probed the successful entertainers' marriage in a cover story titled "Cher Tells Sonny About the Baby That Can Never Be His!" The story begins:

Sonny and Cher had been married five years when their daughter, Chastity, was born. They had almost given up hope of having children when Cher discovered she was

196

pregnant, and they were both delirious with joy over the prospect of becoming parents.

Throughout the entire nine months Sonny went out of his way to pamper and protect Cher. He even lied to her about their financial situation. Sonny had invested more than a million dollars of their money in a film starring Cher entitled Chastity, *and the results had been a disaster. They were broke. Cher was riding around in a Rolls-Royce while Sonny was borrowing money anywhere he could get a loan.*

"I was really frightened," he admits now. "We were wiped out. I didn't know what we were going to do. But I couldn't tell Cher. It was Christmas. She was pregnant. I couldn't bear to worry her."

In the best tradition of TVSP and similar publications, anyone who makes it big must first have been a loser with whom the reader can identify. Notice how even the sentence length, syntax, and vocabulary of each article has been adapted to the reader's educational level. The sad and possibly tragic part of all this trite, reader-patronizing nonsense is that readers have been trained to uncritically seek out identification with their group's respective illusions and cling desperately to them. Knowledge of these hidden publishing motives and manipulative adaptations are either unknown or repressed by readers. These publications thus constitute a subliminal background to the value systems and culture of their readers.

Who, then, is the *real* Sonny and Cher?

Psychological Inventions in Print

Time magazine is a complicated psychological invention difficult to analyze by itself, but by comparison with its major competitor, *Newsweek,* at least some of the intracacies of *Time*'s emotional appeal become apparent.

Time presents a dominant, aggressive view of the world. It is action-oriented, and its readers like to believe they are too. Upward mobility, as rapidly as possible, is one underlying, constantly repeated basic theme.

Newsweek, on the other hand, is far more passive.

Newsweek readers have much less emotional need to see themselves in a dominant-aggressive role. They have other hang-ups—avoidance of conflict, passivity toward power in the belief that man's rational nature will always prevail and that there are answers (if we could only discover them) to all our problems. Both *Time* and *Newsweek* must reflect a strong national point of view, but *Newsweek* tends to present a more reflective version of world events.

Demographically—age, sex, income, education, etc.—it is extremely difficult to differentiate between the two magazines' readerships. In terms of psychographics, or psychological predispositions or attitudes, however, each publication has staked out an almost exclusive circulation, each of which perceives itself in a distinctive way.

Saving "Time"

In a media study some years ago, it was discovered that *Time* readers saved the publication—behavior that could be described as highly anal. Throughout North America, *Time* readers' basements and closets are stacked to the ceiling with old issues. If you have subscribed for three years, very likely you will have over 150 copies stored about the house.

When asked why they kept these old issues, *Time* readers almost unanimously responded that they wanted to be able to look up events, people, and situations. But almost no one had ever actually located a reference in the old copies.

Many, nevertheless, had tried. You can spend an absorbing afternoon, day, week, or even month going through old issues of *Time*—ostensibly looking for an item you believe you have read. One hardly ever finds his specific item. But many readers, in the study, found deep satisfaction in a nostalgic *Time* review as they went over a lot of other things.

Of course, should readers really want to look up an event in *Time*, a periodical index, available in any library, would direct them to the specific issue. None of these *Time* readers, however, had a periodical index in their homes. Few had used such an index, even in libraries.

Curiously, *Newsweek* readers did not accumulate such large quantities of back issues. Could *Time* readers have a special need to save *time?* Could the publication preserve, in verbal formaldehyde, the events of yesterday as *Time* readers need to remember them, in a ritual affirmation of their dominant, nationalistic, aggressive view of the world?

Time's editorial style and techniques assure advertisers of a premium audience both able and willing to purchase advertised products. The *Time* presentation is highly readable, dramatic, and oversimplified to the point of absurdity, presenting a unique American view of the world.

Time language presents a rigid authoritarian identification between news personalities and their functions. This technique is not unusual in American journalism, but is carried to an extreme in *Time*. By using what philosopher Herbert Marcuse described as the inflectional genitive or possessive, people are made to appear as integral properties of their place, occupation, company, or activity. *Time* introduces the reader to "Minnesota's Hubert Humphrey," "Jordan's Hussein," "Apollo 16's Command Module Pilot Ken Mattingly."

A person thus becomes owned, possessed, or identified with a thing, rather than the other way around. The hyphenated attributive construction also contributes to rigidity of meaning and classification: "Literature's heavy-handed, light-haired, problem-child Norman Mailer announced last week . . ." The author, his field of work, his emotional and physical features, as well as a critical—strongly negative—reference to his age, were homogenized into a single verbal structure emphasizing compound adjectives which imprint and harden Mailer's simplified-negative image upon the reader's mind.

The *Time* syntactical structure poses little room for reader qualification or thoughtful evaluation. There is no invitation to reflect upon the fairness, accuracy, and honesty of the sentence's meaning.

Another type of abridgement or condensation used heavily by *Time*, though also by other publications, is the alphabet soup of collective initials—SEATO, WHO, AFL-CIO, NATO, AEC, DAR, even USSR. The abbreviations can be useful time and space savers in print, but often expand subliminally from mere abbreviations into a superb technique of inclusion-exclusion manipulation. UN, for example, nicely evades meaningful emphasis upon the concept *united*. NATO, North Atlantic Treaty Organization, silently avoids any reference to Greece and Turkey. SEATO, Southeast Asia Treaty

Organization, gently excludes reference to those countries that are not members or who oppose the organization. AEC dissolves the Atomic Energy Commission inconspicuously into the anonymity of hundreds of alphabetically abbreviated government agencies. These abbreviated meanings are, of course, static, fixed concepts and very often inaccurate and simplistic.

The language of images forms a barrier to the development of concepts by identifying things and people with functions, rather than distinguishing things and people from conceptualizations. In the image simplifications used by *Time* and other news publications, thinking is unnecessary—critical thinking circumvented entirely by stereotyped stimuli, stereotyped thought and stereotyped reaction. Knowledge and an understanding of dynamic conceptual transition in realities and meanings have been sabotaged, transforming falsehood into truth.

The hyphenated compounding of images is another aspect of the famed *Time* style—"brush-browed" Edward Teller, the "father of the H-bomb," "bull-shouldered missileman von Braun," "science-military dinner," and the "nuclear-powered, ballistic-missile-firing" submarine.

These integrated images project a complete absence of contradiction, disharmony, or alternate point of view. It's no accident that this syntax frequently appears in metaphors uniting technology, politics, and the military into an impregnable holy trinity.

The technique is also strengthened through the use of personalized familiarity. The reader's kitchen table, living room, friends, jobs, etc., are intimately related to the reader as is "your president," "your schools," "your favorite restaurant," "your rights," etc. The world is presented patronizingly especially for you.

Worth a Thousand Words?

Time has learned much from its sister publications which more heavily depend upon picture stories to sustain their massive circulations. Aside from the linguistic techniques of verbal style and typography affecting the unconscious, the photographic essays utilize every possible subliminal trick.

The Vietnam battle montage is typical (see Figure 48). The five pictures included were selected from several hundred possibilities, possibly several thousand, considering the extensive resources of *Time-Life*. *Life* photographers are famous for shooting hundreds of pictures in order to obtain a half dozen for actual publication. The caption reads:

> *(Clockwise) Gear-laden young ARVN soldier smokes on rubble-strewn street; tank rolls up for defense of Dong Ha; bodies of Viet Cong soldiers lie on roadside; worried civilians head south for safety in jam-packed bus; ARVN artillerymen fire 155-mm howitzer at advancing units of North Vietnamese army.*

Other minor interpretation variations were possible, of course, but—at the consciously perceived level, in logical, reasonable terms—this would seem to be what the photo page was overtly all about.

The *Time* caption pointed out the obvious. Reader tests on the pages containing the caption and photograph suggested that fewer than one reader in ten would scan the caption. But *Time* editors certainly understand how a picture page is read. Experiments with the McNaughten and pupilometer cameras have shown that the fovea moves in a saccade from point to point in response to symbolic content. Symbols involving the two polarities of love and death will pull the eye irresistibly toward a specific point in a scene or picture. Design elements—lines of movement or attention within a photograph—also play a part in directing the fovea.

The first object on the Vietnam montage to attract the eye is the picture of death in the upper right-hand corner. If you close your eyes for a moment, then open them suddenly, as they momentarily focus you will probably find yourself looking at the dead body. Roughly 60 percent of a test audience perceived the body as a primary focal point. About 40 percent began with the mother's face, then moved upward to the body. A photograph of a nude *Playboy* bunny might strongly compete for primary focal point with the dead North Vietnamese, but it is doubtful that sex could win. Death appears to have a much stronger symbolic hold on the human psyche.

Focal point saccade paths—though unconsciously motivated—are highly predictable within a culture.

From the body, the eye saccades along the bloodstained earth to the second focal point—the tank and pigs. The pig facing right will saccade the fovea into the photograph of mother and child.

From the mother and child, the test subjects divided. About half followed the line of the mothers' eyes diagonally down into the soldier's photo at the bottom left, then to the right from the breech of the howitzer to the second man with his fingers in his ears, then back up to the dead body again, and the sequence was repeated.

The other half of the test subjects moved from the mother's hand on the panel down into the howitzer picture, then to the soldier at the bottom left, and then upward at an angle set by the slung carbine—again reaching the body, where the sequence was repeated.

The picture editor's objective was to keep the reader's eye moving about the montage as long as possible so a mosaic of picture concepts would be unconsciously perceived. Instead of the linear meaning in the caption sequence provided by *Time*, consider what the actual meaning of this montage involves.

Meaning is derived from the sequence of microsecond stops compulsively made by the fovea in its saccades—the totality has been described as a "mosaic" or "montage" or "aggregate of visual stimuli." The *sequence* of the mosaic is all important. Change the sequence of fovea saccades, and the meaning changes, even though the individual picture content remains the same.

The Good Guys or the Bad?

The primary focal point on the *Time* montage is the upper right photograph of two dead soldiers, presumably North Vietnamese, though it is impossible to tell from the uniforms. However, the bodies have been on the ground for some time—the blood has soaked into the earth. If the dead soldiers were South Vietnamese (our side), the bodies would have been removed and the mess cleaned up as soon as possible. The torn paper and debris suggest the bodies have been searched or looted—certainly not a pleasant set of alternatives for the secure *Time* reader.

The box behind the body in the foreground has archetypal symbolic significance. A box has traditionally symbolized a maternal influence, possibly establishing a relationship between the bodies and the mother in the picture below. The box also symbolizes unexpected destructive potentialities, as in Pandora's box.

The tank, the second picture perceived by most readers, shows the tank commander giving orders as he perches atop the powerful machine—the turret cannon appearing as a phallic extension of his genital area. From the subliminal fantasy projected by the layout, it is entirely possible the deaths to the right were a direct result of the tank's destructive power.

The editor's inclusion of the two pigs is intriguing, as they could easily have been cropped from the photograph. The pig is an ancient symbol of impure desires and of the amoral plunge into corruption. (Recall the discussion of pig symbology in *The Exorcist* chapter.)

At the time of this issue's publication, *Time* was undergoing an antiwar swing in its editorial policy—one that changed frequently, but remained consistently parallel to the fluctuating currents of reader opinion.

The third focal point in the montage is the mother and child—possibly a modern-day Vietnamese version of the Madonna. Specifically, the reader's fovea will move from the mother's nose to her right ear, then across to the child's face before taking one of two different paths.

The mother's facial expression would have many levels of meaning in both the reader's conscious and unconscious. Her face is old, more than just merely old as calculated by years. Her expression includes fear, but not as a dominant emotion.

One detail likely to remain repressed in the reader's unconscious is the discrepancy between the lines in her face, the very young child, and the absence of gray in her hair. She is, apparently, a young woman—prematurely aged by war, clinging in silent desperation to her bewildered child. Both she and her child are attempting to comfort and support one another, but the mother's face expresses the ageless plight of the refugee.

Few of the 25 million readers made conscious interpretations of these five photographs as their eyes quickly scanned the montage. Nevertheless, considering the delicate sensitivity to even the smallest detail in human perceptual equipment, these interpretations, or something reasonably close to them, did occur within the unconscious of almost everyone who perceived this page for even an instant.

Conscious meanings appear to only reinforce and confirm underlying subliminal predispositions. Whether or not you were opposed to the Vietnam War, most probably you would interpret the page of photographs in support of your predispositions. If you were neutral, however, the display might move you into opposition. Conscious perceptions are often merely accommodations to the unconscious basic program.

The Vietnamese soldier, standing with his phallic carbine pointing at the ground, symbolizes defeat. The soldier appears to be a very young boy. The open-mouthed expression, as he carries his heavy load through the garbage-strewn roadway, suggests someone not terribly bright—certainly not a strong, shrewd, battle-hardened combat soldier. Several dozen test subjects, reviewing the montage, were asked whether the soldier was going toward or *away from* battle. Almost unanimously they responded "away," many adding, "and in a hurry."

The two artillerymen tending their howitzer, the final picture in the fovea saccade, portrays the soldiers as relaxed, casual, and almost indifferent as they observe an explosion, presumably caused by their weapon, which has been retouched into the photograph's horizon. The Vietnamese soldiers do not appear threatened or even involved in the war—in spite of their helmets (whose chin straps are not in place) and flack jackets. The gun placement, exposed on a hilltop, with its inept camouflage and casual gun crew, subliminally communicates incompetence or indifference.

Test subjects were given three alternatives as to what was going on in the howitzer photograph—attack, retreat, or sustaining position. Again, unanimously, they responded with *sustaining position.* In other words, the war is going nowhere. The soldier with fingers in his ears is certainly symbolic of uninvolvement—or as the archetypal concept is often expressed, "He hears no evil!"

At the time of publication this view was consistent with the opinion of large segments of United States public opinion. The media, especially the big, national, ad-full media, *follow* public opinion. They rarely, if ever, *lead*, nor could they without jeopardizing their high-credibility positions. To make certain the five pictures have maximum impact upon the 25 million readers (especially at the unconscious level, where *Time* would establish itself as the ultimate authority on the war), their retouch artists have covered the Vietnam photo montage with embedded subliminal SEX triggers to deeply relate the content into the reader's psyche (see Figure 49). Some of the SEXes have been left unmarked so the reader can experiment with discovering *Time*'s real opinion of "The Big Test—Vietnamization: A Policy Under the Gun," as the cover story was called.

These visual representations of war unquestionably sell *Time*, which sells ads, which sell merchandise. But, what is the effect of this symbolic subliminal enrichment? What are the effects of sexualizing war and death? Were reader perspectives toward the entire Vietnam affair conditioned, manipulated, and managed by these techniques as a side effect of merchandising the news?

Various autocratic governments have schemed relentlessly to control the power of the press. Hitler's Nazi party succeeded in total · thought control in less than a decade through careful direction of mass media. It has taken American advertising agencies a little longer. American society may, indeed, be approaching a point where freedom *from* the press will become as vital an issue as freedom *of* the press.

Free access to information may be central to the survival of democratic institutions. An unrestrained, responsive, and responsible information media is an absolute necessity for this type of society—media which, incidentally, appear to be rapidly vanishing. Information media must serve—as forthrightly as possible—the citizen's interests, not merely those of advertisers and corporate investors. As recent events have eloquently demonstrated, what is good for investors is not necessarily good for the nation.

12

Even the Killings Are Funny

> It is just as important to the
> capitalist mass producer as to
> the Soviet functionary to
> condition people into uniform,
> unresisting subjects. . . . We
> ostensibly free, Western,
> civilized people are no longer
> conscious of the extent to
> which we are being
> manipulated by the commercial
> decisions of the mass
> producers.
>
> KONRAD LORENZ
> *Civilized Man's Eight Deadly Sins*

Culture Is Not Accidental

One of the most significant discoveries in the studies that led
to this book was that culture—especially the dynamic American culture—is today a manufactured product. And, media
are the factories. By creating a vast materialistic technology,
humans created the illusion they could control their environments. This illusion made them even more vulnerable to
forces and influences involving the unconscious.

Knowledge of man's ability to deceive himself through perceptual illusions would, to say the least, be highly embarrassing when focused upon treasured concepts of free will,

omniscience, national or cultural superiority, God-given prerogatives, etc.—all those fantasies that reinforce Western civilization's ego needs. Perhaps the reason why no culture in history has ever been continuous lies in our ego-driven inability to believe that we cannot be influenced by what we cannot consciously perceive. It is not difficult to conclude that man has done a superb job of conspiring unconsciously against finding out about himself.

It would be quite simple if the *good* and *bad* guys were clearly defined in this issue of mass manipulation. Our solution would be simple if we could legislate the advertising agencies out of business or, perhaps, execute or imprison their executives as societies have often done to those who embarrass their own systems. Sacrificial scapegoats would be a simple answer. But the problem is just not that simple.

Skilled media technicians, including those in advertising, are doing precisely what they have been trained to do by their society, according to the society's own rules of business and commerce. Further, they are doing it extremely well. All of us have benefitted from incredible levels of self-indulgence in comparison with most of the world's peoples. Many of these "benefits" are directly attributable to mass merchandising. We have, in a very real sense, sold out our individualism and freedom in return for a handful of baubles while we play-acted at being free individuals.

There is one basic and very unsettling aspect to the perceptual illusions presented in this book. The artists, writers, and composers really hid nothing from us. The obscene and taboo embeds were always clearly there for us to consciously perceive had we wanted to. Indeed, we *did* perceive all of them unconsciously. Whenever I have shown these apparently hidden details to lecture or reading audiences, most (over 95 percent) have consciously perceived them instantly. We had hidden the obscene details from ourselves.

Many labels attempt to describe the phenomena of hiding perceptions from oneself—repression, denial, or some of the other perceptual defenses. But the fact remains that all of us prevent ourselves from consciously dealing with what is going on around us. We are, simply, party to the manipulation—and a willing party. We benefit, of course, from the deceptions. This is the hardest pill of all to swallow.

One simple fact about human behavior—known for many centuries—is that no one can possibly con, manipulate, or lie to anyone unless that person is willing to go along with the game. As a nation and culture, America is every bit as responsible for these deceits as are the advertising and media executives who deceive us.

The Media-Dependent Society

The British Broadcasting Corporation recently made a study of television viewers' ability to live without television for an entire year. One hundred eighty-four families were paid roughly thirteen dollars weekly not to use their sets. This was a fairly good sum of money at the time in England—certainly a worthwhile bonus for any working-class family.

Families began dropping out of the study almost immediately. No one lasted beyond five months. The researchers unanimously agreed their volunteers had "suffered withdrawal symptoms similar to those of drug addicts and alcoholics." There was total agreement among a professional panel selected to evaluate the study that in the future there would be "increased dependence upon television among the general population, and that television minimized self-reliance, social contacts, and creative pursuits among its audiences."

The BBC study was a replication of similar research performed a year earlier in Germany. In the German study the first volunteer dropped out after three weeks. Similarly, no one lasted beyond the fifth month.

We can now discuss *media dependence* as a valid psychoneurotic syndrome, perhaps even a meaningful personality characteristic. Americans, not to mention other technologically advanced peoples, should no longer ignore and take for granted their media-managed environment if they hope to survive as human beings.

Obesity, for one example, is dramatically apparent in America. Visitors from less well fed areas of the world are often astonished at the large numbers of fat individuals within the United States. The National Council on Health recently announced that 60 percent of the United States population was overweight. North America has more per capita obesity than any nation in the world. Obesity, of course, leads to a great many serious systemic diseases and disorders, but the relationship between media and obesity has never been publicly examined. Advertisers discovered long ago that TV sports programs, for example, were superb platforms upon which to merchandise food and beverages. The oral gratification compulsion within each human is quite easy to stimulate in a context of action, suspense, and uncertainty. TV sports provides an illusion of participation by the viewer that, of course, is only a fantasy. A well-trained TV sports addict will consume several thousand calories during an afternoon or evening of baseball, football, and hockey. Even the reruns, and the reruns of the reruns, appear to sell nearly as well as the originals though audiences become progressively smaller. Consider also the game shows, soap operas, and dramatic programs where food and beverage sponsorship is heavy, and how the program content integrates with the commercials.

The roughly two hundred hours average viewing endured monthly by the some 50 million American families is permeated with strong subliminal stimuli which hypnotically program individuals for compulsive acts. Virtually no one is exempt, though some are more responsive to the stimuli than others. TV ads are reinforced by radio, newspapers, magazines, and billboards—the so-called media mix or integration now worked out for large advertisers by highly sophisticated computers which can assemble a strategy for the most efficient expenditure of marketing money.

Earlier in history, national and regional cultures were the painful evolutionary product of centuries. Changes were slow and uncertain until advanced media technology entered the picture. Now consumers in one culture are pretty much the same as those in others, though illusions of uniqueness may persist. Brand names may be different, but the programmed response and value system are identical. Changes in self-image, hero myth, death orientation, etc., occur most rapidly in the service of commercial objectives. When a newly introduced cultural entity no longer serves as an objective, it is quickly scrapped or modified into another form.

All this, of course, may be doing great and shattering destruction to individual psyches whose basic value systems are remanipulated every few years and sometimes every few months. One fourteen-year-old boy hung himself in Calgary,

Canada, during 1974 while attempting to imitate a mock hanging performed on television by rock music star Alice Cooper. A coroner's jury investigating the death called once again for "definite and immediate steps to ban these programs of violence." Predictably, however, nothing changed.

Strangely, Americans appear consciously convinced they are the world's most peaceful, nonviolent society. This is a superb example of the repression mechanism operating on a societal level. Dr. McLuhan would call it *narcissus narcosis*. No one has, as yet, done anything to reduce violence—except, perhaps, to hire more police, which often has the effect of creating more violence. Further, no one is likely to do anything about violence except to sponsor more of the endless investigations or studies that only serve either to appease the public conscience or confuse the issue.

The answer to violence in America is really quite simple: Americans have developed violence into one of the world's most profitable enterprises—from war (defense) to athletics (spectator sports). Violence is a merchandising staple for every mass communication media in America—every bit as virulent as sex, perhaps even more so. Sex and violence, in fact, go well together in movies, television, music, etc.

Big Money in Death

Attitudes toward death and killing in America are intriguing, and over the past decade or so have changed substantially. The fantasy of death portrayed in movies and television is now often described as "humorous" or "funny," especially by young people. The bloody, sadistic slaughter, without which few movie or TV producers could obtain financing, is a formidable fantasy which keeps audiences buying tickets and tuning in. The next time you witness a movie death, execution, or massacre, listen carefully. You will hear portions of the audience laugh and giggle as the blood spurts, heads roll, or bodies contort.

Hero myths, very important as part of the maturation process, have changed drastically over the past few decades. Traditional hero figures from Beowulf to El Cid to Galahad to the Lone Ranger to Davy Crockett to John Wayne—the archetypal heroes who challenged and inspired the young with noble and ideal values—would be perceived by today's young as camp, fake, unreal, and ridiculous. Contemporary hero myths among the young feature such characters as Alice Cooper and David Bowie—perverse, degenerate caricatures of the ancient heros, who profitably glory in their contempt for traditional values.

Through their media, societies perpetuate the mythologies that serve their basic goals. Nietzsche once described history as the lie through which nations survive. He may have been correct, in that certain kinds of lies or illusions are necessary to individual and national survival. It is doubtful that anyone ever really believed John Wayne was as brave as his endless succession of roles portrayed him. In any respect, the hero-image projected for the young in search of an ideal—even though pure fantasy—reflected individuality, honor, integrity, and manhood.

It may be important to remember that media does not ever present reality. The fantasy-entertainment death or violence on film has no relationship at all to real-life death or violence. Real death is very complicated. It even has its own very distinctive odor. Where the realities of death are carefully concealed, deodorized, romanticized, and hygienized, media's fantasy of death becomes the symbolic reality at the unconscious level.

In a recent NBC-TV news program about juvenile crime, John Chancellor interviewed several teen-aged murderers. One, about to be released from a New York City juvenile detention center, casually admitted to fifteen or sixteen murders—most of which occurred during muggings.

The boy was asked, "What did you feel during and after the killings?"

"Nothing," he replied in a matter-of-fact tone.

"Nothing? Even when they lay on the ground bleeding and gasping," the interviewer questioned.

"No, nothing. Nothing, really! It was like watching a TV play or a movie. It wasn't real."

At present North Americans want to deal only with the superficial symptoms of their social cancer, not with the actual disease and the sources of infection. Probing too deeply into the commercially motivated and controlled madnesses of our time might be a devastating experience for the national ego.

It would be folly to suggest that government control and operation of media could ever be a simple, practical answer. Noncommercial information systems operated by dictatorships appear quite as capable of transporting the world's peoples into the *Brave New World* or *1984* as effectively as commercially motivated systems.

Laws Can Tranquilize

The Canadian Radio Television Commission, similar to the FCC in the United States, recently amended their regulations to forbid the use of "any advertising material that makes use of any subliminal device." Like the FCC, the CRTC is pathetically ineffectual in its attempts to manage the broadcasting industry in the public interest. North American media are controlled by a handful of powerful advertising agencies whose single dedication, preoccupation, and obsession is selling. Executives courageous enough to advocate changes that interfere with short-term profit goals are few and far between.

Similar attempts to ban subliminal stimuli were made by the British in their Broadcast Code, by Belgium in a 1972 law, and by the United Nations Commission on Human Rights in a report to their Secretary-General on October 7, 1974. A United Nations task force discovered it was technically possible to broadcast subliminal content internationally via satellite. It is even technically feasible for anyone with the equipment to infiltrate a satellite broadcast signal with subliminal stimuli. Their report stated it was possible to modify or even eliminate *cultures* through subliminal reprogramming of the unconscious, and strongly recommended that all member nations pass rigorous laws prohibiting such techniques, especially when the media crossed national or cultural frontiers.

Attempts to legislate the unconscious perceptual system could serve a good purpose by bringing the issue into public awareness. However, North American news media ignored the significance of the CRTC regulation, the various laws, and the United Nations study. If the subject was discussed at all, it was done superficially with tongue in cheek, or twisted into a nonsense story usually quoting some behaviorist psychologist that there was no such thing as the "unconscious."

212

The UN study failed to mention that subliminal techniques are already in wide international use by American advertising agencies.

Print and broadcast media, of course, have a vital interest in pretending the subliminal issue is a farce. Business institutions in general have a similar investment to protect. Should North American audiences begin to carefully examine advertising and news manipulation, it would be like opening Pandora's box.

If there is an answer, it will not be in a simplistic attempt at legislation, though drug, alcohol, and tobacco merchandising might be legislatively banned from public communication media due to the epidemic proportions of the problem they create and sustain. The control of public information by commercial interests must cease. But this is much easier said than done. If changes in media are to occur, they will probably emanate from far more basic changes in the society. A corrupt media merely reflects a corrupt society.

Education for Consumption

Analytical media studies in both universities and high schools are currently considered subversive by many school administrators who patronize business and media. Business and advertising groups have successfully pressured educational institutions into offering only an endless succession of vocational media courses that only describe the obvious and sustain what society wishes to believe is going on. Moral and intellectual cowardice is difficult to rationlize when encountered among University officials. Much like The Who's *Tommy*, students are told not to perceive consciously meanings that might upset their parents and the society.

Perceptual education has never been attempted on a large scale in America. Most educational efforts appear to have a primary objective in conformity, uniformity, and intellectual predictability. So much of the incredible potential in life that should be available to young Americans remains hidden from view, ignored, suppressed or, more damagingly, repressed. The manipulative culture teaches Americans to pretend or play at nonconformity while they conform like mass-produced robots—most of whom find their places in consumer demographic or psychographic categorization, moving from work to stores to television to bed with occasional interruptions for food and beverage consumption, infrequently interrupted by sex.

The Con Man and the Conned

So much of the social and political nightmare that has continued in America this past decade had its roots deep in the widespread acceptance of lying, manipulating, and misrepresenting reality as a preferred and rewarded mode of behavior. For many decades, American media have venerated the con man and his endless games—games that all require the sucker to trust before he is taken.

Jonathan Schell, in his chilling book, *The Time of Illusion*, documented the tragic record of lies, misrepresentations, image manipulations, and covert strategies which continued throughout the Nixon and earlier presidential administrations. With exhaustive factual documentation, Schell probed the near destruction of democratic government by the now disgraced President's small army of advertising-public relations experts who—with the help of media—flim-flammed America with self-flattering illusions of reality.

Nixon and his staff simply used communication technology that is a normal everyday tool of both business and government in the United States. The technology of deceit has been developed more highly in America than ever before in Western civilization.

The con man is one of the most cherished of our cultural stereotypes—*Sergeant Bilko, Man in the Gray Flannel Suit, Man at the Top, The Hucksters, The Flim Flam Man,* O'Henry heroes, W. C. Fields characterizations, etc. American literature is loaded with sly heroes who trick the unsuspecting mark, usually someone of power and wealth. The tradition goes back even to Herman Melville's *The Confidence Man*. But modern Robin Hoods, when examined carefully, usually turn out to be stealing from the poor and giving to the rich—instead of the other way around.

At this point in history, however, it appears useless to blame any individual for what has occurred in American media. Driven by relentless pressures for continually increasing profits, media and its advertisers have simply maximized the returns on their capital investments. Most would not have anticipated the casualty rate or would not have permitted themselves to even consider such a possibility.

After six years of media study, resulting in two books on subliminal perception, this author searched his data exhaustively for some redeeming quality, some constructive potential, some hope for human betterment and survival within North America's system of commercial mass media. Nothing surfaced that appeared even vaguely optimistic.

North America appears, at the moment, trapped in a rapidly accelerating spiral toward self-annihilation. Out of control, motivated by avaricious self-indulgence and sustained by repressed blindness toward reality, human survival probabilities decrease each day. There is strong evidence that news information involves a similar repression to that of the advertisements. Even educational data appears repressed—if it does not serve our ego needs or self-flattering illusions.

It is simply not, at present, in the interest of media to sponsor significant social-economic-behavioral change. And as long as profit or economic survival is the major preoccupation of public information sources, meaningful change will be most unlikely.

In Closing

From the research for this and my earlier book, *Subliminal Seduction*, developed two highly disturbing insights.

First, that such subliminal technology—certainly neither new nor unknown in Western civilization—had been so cleverly and exhaustively adapted to mass merchandising.

Second, and vastly more significant, was the slow realization that Americans—as a nation—apparently do not wish to deal with the issue of their manipulation by their media. Much like the proverbial ostrich, both heads and intellects appear deeply buried in the sands of self-indulgence. This is a sad commentary on a nation which has sacrificed so much on the altar of human freedom.

Even though these explorations in communication have suggested a different perspective toward the human condition than that currently in vogue within American educational and governmental institutions, the promise of utilizing subliminal techniques in the public interest is substantial. For example, both theory and experimental evidence suggest that some forms of addictive behavior may yield to subliminal therapies. If subs can channel some individuals into addiction—as appears to be the case—they should also work in the opposite direction. We will never know until someone tries.

The educational potential in utilizing subliminal stimuli are enormous, even though students would have to be clearly informed of the techniques before they were applied. If entire populations can be subliminally taught the complex behavior, decision making, and value systems which support high-level consumption, they can unquestionably be subliminally educated in other areas of life.

Indeed, it would appear the techniques of production and communication now in use (even though perhaps often for the wrong ends) could make of our world virtually anything we desire—a place of happiness, fulfillment, and meaningful relationships. On the other hand, we can just as easily turn our world into an island of despair, which we may have already done, where fear, alienation, distrust, avarice, and senseless indulgences dominate our existence and waste our life spans.

Both these alternatives are clear and immediately available.

Epilogue

The vital question today is not whether there will be life after death, but whether there was life before death.

MARSHALL MCLUHAN
Understanding Media

Appendix A

BRIDGE OVER TROUBLED WATER*

When you're weary, feeling small,
When tears are in your eyes, I will dry them all;
I'm on your side. When times get rough
And friends just can't be found,
Like a bridge over troubled water
I will lay me down.
Like a bridge over troubled water
I will lay me down.

When you're down and out,
When you're on the street,
When evening falls so hard
I will comfort you.
I'll take your part.
When darkness comes
And pain is all around,
Like a bridge over troubled water
I will lay me down.
Like a bridge over troubled water
I will lay me down.

Sail on silvergirl,
Sail on by.
Your time has come to shine.
All your dreams are on their way.
See how they shine.
If you need a friend
I'm sailing right behind.
Like a bridge over troubled water
I will ease your mind.
Like a bridge over troubled water
I will ease your mind.

Appendix B

THE CANONS
OF JOURNALISM

This widely known and important code, the Canons of Journalism, was adopted by the American Society of Newspaper Editors.

The primary function of newspapers is to communicate to the human race what its members do, feel, and think. Journalism, therefore, demands of its practitioners the widest range of intelligence, of knowledge, and of experience, as well as natural and trained powers of observation and reasoning. To its opportunities as a chronicle are indissolubly linked its obligations as teacher and interpreter.

To the end of finding some means of codifying sound practice and just aspirations of American journalism, these canons are set forth:

I

Responsibility. The right of a newspaper to attract and hold readers is restricted by nothing but consideration of public welfare. The use a newspaper makes of the share of public attention it gains serves to determine its sense of responsibility, which it shares with every member of its staff. A journalist who uses his power for any selfish or otherwise unworthy purpose is faithless to a high trust.

II

Freedom of the Press. Freedom of the press is to be guarded as a vital right of mankind. It is the unquestionable right to discuss whatever is not explicitly forbidden by law, including the wisdom of any restrictive statute.

III

Independence. Freedom from all obligations except that of fidelity to the public interest is vital.

1. Promotion of any private interest contrary to the general welfare, for whatever reason, is not compatible with honest journalism. So-called news communications from private sources should not be published without public notice of their source or else substantiation of their claims to value as news, both in form and substance.

2. Partisanship in editorial comment which knowingly departs from the truth does violence to the best spirit of American journalism; in the news columns it is subversive of a fundamental principle of the profession.

IV

Sincerity, Truthfulness, Accuracy. Good faith with the reader is the foundation of all journalism worthy of the name.

1. By every consideration of good faith a newspaper is constrained to be truthful. It is not to be excused for lack of thoroughness or accuracy within its control or failure to obtain command of these essential qualities.

2. Headlines should be fully warranted by the contents of the articles which they surmount.

V

Impartiality. Sound practice makes clear distinction between news reports and expressions or opinions. News reports should be free from opinion or bias of any kind.

1. This rule does not apply to so-called special articles unmis-

takably devoted to advocacy or characterized by a signature authorizing the writer's own conclusions and interpretation.

VI

Fair Play. A newspaper should not publish unofficial charges contesting reputation or moral character without opportunity given to the accused to be heard: right practice demands the giving of such opportunity in such cases of serious accusation outside judicial proceedings.

1. A newspaper should not invade private rights or feelings without sure warrant of public right as distinguished from public curiosity.

2. It is the privilege, as it is the duty, of a newspaper to make prompt and complete correction of its own serious mistakes of fact or opinion, whatever their origin.

VII

Decency. A newspaper cannot escape conviction of insincerity if, while professing high moral purposes, it supplies incentives to base conduct such as are to be found in details of crime and vice, publication of which is not demonstrably for the general good. Lacking authority to enforce its canons, the journalism here represented can but express the hope that deliberate pandering to vicious instincts will encounter effective public disapproval or yield to the influence of a preponderant professional condemnation.

Bibliography

Attneave, Fred. *Scientific American,* July 1974, "Sources of Ambiguity in the Prints of Maurits C. Escher"; December 1971, "Multistability in Perception."

Bayley, Harold. *The Lost Language of Symbolism.* London: Ernest Benn, Ltd., 1957.

Becker, Hal C. U.S. Patents 3,060,795, Oct. 30, 1962, and 3,278,676, Oct. 11, 1966 — Apparatus For Producing Visual and Auditory Stimulation.

Bedini, Silvio A. *Scent of Time.* American Philosophical Society, New Series, Vol. 53, Pt. 5. Philadelphia: August 1963.

Bergson, Henri. *Introduction to Metaphysics.* New York: Bobbs-Merrill, 1955.

Castañeda, Carlos. *A Separate Reality.* New York: Pocket Books, 1973.

Cirino, Robert. *Don't Blame the People.* New York: Vintage, 1972.

Dixon, Norman F. *Subliminal Perception: The Nature of a Controversy.* London: McGraw-Hill, 1971.

Efron, Edith. *The News Twisters.* New York: Manor Books, 1972.

Ehrenzweig, Anton. *The Hidden Order of Art.* London: Paladin, 1967.

————. *Psycho-analysis of Artistic Vision & Hearing.* New York: Braziller, 1965.

Ellenberger, Henri F. *Discovery of the Unconscious.* New York: Basic Books, 1970.

Ellul, Jacques. *Propaganda.* New York: Vintage, 1973.

Ferkiss, Victor C. *Technological Man: The Myth and the Reality.* New York: New American Library, 1970.

Fiedler, Leslie A. *Love and Death in the American Novel.* New York: Criterion, 1960.

Freud, Sigmund. *Letters.* New York: Basic, 1960.

Friedman, P. "Some Observations On the Sense of Smell." *Psychoanalytic Quarterly,* Vol. 28, (1959), p. 307.

Fromm, Erich. *The Anatomy of Human Destructiveness.* New York: Holt, Rinehart & Winston, 1973.

Gordon, G. "Semantic Determination by Subliminal Verbal Stimuli: A Quantitative Approach." PH.D. Thesis, University of London, 1967.

Gorman, Warren. *Flavor, Taste and the Psychology of Smell.* Springfield, Mass.: Charles C. Thomas, 1964.

Haber, Ralph N. *Scientific American,* May 1970, "How We Remember What We See."

Held, Richard. *Perception: Mechanisms and Models* (Readings from *Scientific American*). San Francisco: W. H. Freeman, 1972.

Johnson, Nicholas. *How to Talk Back to Your Television Set.* New York: Bantam, 1970.

Jung, Carl G. *Psyche & Symbol.* Garden City: Doubleday, 1958.

Karsch, Yousuf. *Faces of Our Time.* Toronto: University of Toronto Press, 1971.

Key, Wilson Bryan. *Subliminal Seduction: Ad Media's Manipulation of a Not So Innocent America.* Englewood Cliffs, N.J.: Prentice-Hall, 1973.

Kinsey, Alfred C. *Sexual Behavior in the Human Male.* Philadelphia: W. B. Saunders, 1948.

Kinsey, Pomeroy, Martin, and Gebhard. *Sexual Behavior in the Human Female.* Philadelphia: W. B. Saunders Co., 1953.

Klapp, Orrin E. *Collective Search for Identity.* New York: Holt, Rinehart & Winston, 1969.

——. *Currents of Unrest.* New York: Holt, Rinehart & Winston, 1972.

——. *Social Types: Process, Structure and Ethos.* San Diego: Aegis Publishing Co., 1971.

Krugman, Herbert E. "Electroencephalographic Aspects of Low Involvement." New York: General Electric Co., 1970. Paper delivered at American Association for Public Opinion Research Conference.

Laing, Ronald D. *Politics of the Family.* Toronto: CBC Learning Systems, 1969.

Levi-Strauss, Claude. *Tristes Tropiques.* New York: Criterion, 1971.

Lewis, Wyndham. *The Art of Being Ruled.* New York: Haskell, 1972.

Lidz, Theodore. *The Person.* New York: Basic Books, 1968.

Lilly, John C. *The Center of the Cyclone.* New York: Bantam, 1972.

Lint, J. *The Epidemiology of Alcoholism.* Substudy No. 556. Toronto: Addiction Research Foundation, 1973.

Lorenz, Konrad. *Civilized Man's Eight Deadly Sins.* London: Methuen & Co., Ltd., 1974.

Lusseyran, Jacques. *And There Was Light.* Boston: Little, Brown and Co., 1963.

Malinowski, Bronislaw. *Myth in Primitive Psychology.* Westport, Conn.: Negro University Press, 1971.

Marcuse, Herbert. *One Dimensional Man.* Boston: Beacon Press, 1970.

Masters, William H. and Johnson, Virginia E. *Human Sexual Inadequacy.* Boston: Little, Brown and Co., 1970.

———. *Human Sexual Response.* Boston: Little, Brown and Co., 1966.

McCartney, William. *Olfaction and Odours.* New York: Springer-Verlag, 1968.

McLuhan, Marshall, and Burrington, Nevitt. *Take Today: The Executive as Dropout.* Toronto: Longman, 1972.

Montagu, Ashley. *Touching: The Human Significance of Skin.* New York: Columbia University Press, 1971.

Nietzsche. *Thus Spoke Zarathustra.* Baltimore: Penguin Books, Ltd., 1971.

Nin, Anaïs. *D. H. Lawrence: An Unprofessional Study.* Chicago: The Swallow Press, 1964.

Piaget, Jean. *The Origins of Intelligence in Children.* New York: W. W. Norton, 1963.

———. *Structuralism.* New York: Harper & Row, 1971.

Poetzle, Otto. "The Relationship Between Experimentally Induced Dream Images and Indirect Vision." (1917. Monogr. No. 7, *Psychol. Issues,* Vol. 2 (1960), pp. 41-120.

Popham, Robert E., Schmidt, Wolfgang and De Lint, Jan. *The Effects of Legal Restraint on Drinking.* Toronto: Addiction Research Foundation, 1973.

Putney, Snell and Putney, Gail J. *The Adjusted American: Normal Neurosis in the Individual and Society.* New York: Harper & Row, 1964.

Reich, Wilhelm. *Listen Little Man.* Farrar, Strauss & Giroux, 1974.

Rudofsky, Bernard. *The Unfashionable Human Body.* New York: Anchor Press, 1974.

Schell, Jonathan. *The Time of Illusion.* New York: Alfred A. Knopf, 1976.

Thompson, William Irwin. *At the Edge of History.* New York: Harper Colophon, 1972.

Wilentz, Joan Steen. *Senses of Man.* New York: Thomas Y. Crowell, 1968.

Zakia, Richard D. *Perception and Photography.* Englewood Cliffs, N.J.: Prentice-Hall, 1975.

Index

225

About the Author

Wilson Bryan Key received his Ph.D. at the University of Denver and has since served as Professor of Journalism at four different universities. The author of the widely-hailed *Subliminal Seduction,* Dr. Key is currently president of Media-probe: Center for the Study of Media, Inc. He lives in Southern California.

Other MENTOR Books of Related Interest

☐ **THE TRUTH ABOUT SELLING by Samuel S. Susser.** A straight-to-the-point book about the most essential part of the business game: the salesman and the art of selling. (#MW1360—$1.50)

☐ **BIG MAC: The Unauthorized Story of McDonald's by Max Boas and Steve Chain.** The widely publicized behind-the-scenes expose of an American empire . . . "Their slogan ought to be, 'At McDonald's we do it all to you'!"—Washington Post (#ME1561—$1.75)

☐ **THE BROTHERHOOD OF OIL: Energy Policy and the Public Interest.** How the great oil companies continue to profit at our peril. . . . "A devastatingly thorough study that will be used for years to come."—Publishers Weekly (#ME1670—$2.50)

☐ **OIL POWER: The Rise and Imminent Fall of an American Empire by Carl Solberg.** The great American oil companies and their influence on the country's social, political, economic and military structures . . . "A gripping narrative . . . fact filled . . . persuasive."—Publishers Weekly (#MJ1531—$1.95)

☐ **CONCEPT OF THE CORPORATION by Peter F. Drucker.** An up-dated edition of the classic study of the organization and management policies of General Motors—the company that has become the model for modern large-scale corporations across the world. (#ME1637—$2.25)